Miracles for Breakfast

How Faith Helped Me Kick My Addictions

by Danny Brooks

WILEY

John Wiley & Sons Canada, Ltd.

Scripture quotations are taken from the *New King James Version* (Thomas Nelson, 1975).

I owe a great deal of my thanks to Michelle Sim and her Northern Praise Ministries. You can discover more about this incredible woman and her ministry through her web site http://www.awocanada.com, which is her Authentic Women of Canada ministry. Thanks also to Richard L. Wright, and Octavio and Gena.

Library and Archives Canada Cataloguing in Publication Data

Brooks, Danny
    Miracles for breakfast : how faith helped me kick my addictions / Danny Brooks.

ISBN 978-0-470-15413-7

    1. Brooks, Danny. 2. Musicians—Canada—Biography. 3. Recovering addicts—Canada—Biography. I. Title.

ML420.B863B87 2008   782.42164′092   C2007-907609-2

Production Credits
Cover design: Ian Koo
Interior design and typesetting: Tegan Wallace
Interior photos: provided by Danny Brooks
Cover photography: Debra Middlebrook
Printer: Printcrafters

John Wiley & Sons Canada, Ltd.
6045 Freemont Blvd.
Mississauga, Ontario
L5R 4J3

This book is printed with biodegradable vegetable-based inks. Text pages are printed on 55 lb. 100% post-consumer waste recycled cream paper.

Printed in Canada
1 2 3 4 5 PC 12 11 10 09 08

HAPPY BIRTHDAY ANITA
+ MANY MANY MORE.
ENJOY !!

Monique

To my parents, Bill and Julie, for their instruction on
living a life grounded on the Truth
and to
my beautiful wife, Debra,
who rescued me from the gutter

~ 2009 ~

Miracles for Breakfast

Once there was a man, workin' on a chain gang
Layin' blacktop on a highway, in the Southland
Many years later, on that same old road
Drivin' with his family, in a brand new automobile

I believe that dreams come alive
And miracles for breakfast, happen all the time
Oh I believe, I believe, I believe in Miracles

Once there was a lady, had to say goodbye to her kids
Check into a re-hab, and try and find herself
Now she's showin' others, there's a way back home
You gotta believe, you gotta keep holdin' on

I believe that dreams come alive
And miracles for breakfast happen all the time
Oh I believe in miracles every morning

Sometimes we all hold on, cuz it's all that we know
Only to learn we can fly once we let go.......I believe

There are Angels that walk among us
Who want to help and show us the path
But we gotta take that tiny first step
And believe there's something bigger than ourselves

I believe that dreams come alive
And miracles for breakfast happen all the time
Oh I believe in miracles every morning

Contents

PART III – CHANGE IS GOING TO COME

PART IV – THE BEST IS YET TO COME

Foreword

IT WAS SEPTEMBER OF 2002 and I had contracted an airborne virus while traveling through the southern United States. It wasn't just some old virus that goes away in a couple of weeks. I still remember the day the doctor told me (after I had been reluctant to take "the cure") that if I did not take a strong dose of prednisone right away, this virus could attack major organs in my body, resulting in a very unhappy ending. Key word here was ending. No one had ever said this to me before, or since. I took the pills.

Shortly after that I was sent a copy of a CD by The Northern Blues Gospel Allstars called Saved. I got stuck on a track called "Still Standing Tall" by a guy named Danny Brooks. I had never heard of him at the time. I found out quickly that he had been so down and out that "everything looked like up to him," but he had been revived spiritually by the Holy Spirit and his devoted wife, Debi.

I listened to Danny's "Still Standing Tall" over and over and over again. It was a song about being down, frightened, in pain—and coming out the other side. I would say that I'm a fairly religious man, but when you are very ill your childlike spiritual feelings from youth reappear. The innocence of blind faith. I was raised a Catholic and up until the 9th grade was set for the priesthood.

Suddenly, as I was listening to this track for about the twentieth time, something happened. I suddenly just lifted my hands up and I prayed. Tears welled up in my eyes. I asked God, if he wasn't too busy, to heal me. I told him that I would put it all in his hands.

Believe me, in hindsight I remember hearing of people doing this, but I did it at the time so naturally. Without thinking. Then, within moments, I felt like a load had been lifted from my body. I had for the first time in my entire life felt the power of prayer. It was absolutely overwhelming. I knew then that everything was going to be okay. I still play that song over and over; through tough times.

I sometimes wonder what would have developed had I not heard Danny Brooks and "Still Standing Tall" that day. It was the healing music of Danny that has made us good friends today. What a voice. A raspy growl that will make you stand up and take notice!

Thank you, Danny, and may your music … take you Higher.

John Donabie
Broadcaster, musicologist

Introduction

THIS BOOK IS ABOUT pointing people to a lifestyle of happiness, joy, peace and hope for today and tomorrow. It tells of a journey involving terrible loss and an expectation of the miraculous. No matter where you have been, what you have done, how hopeless you may even feel at this moment, *you* can make it, because there is nothing that God and you together can't accomplish. The size of the miracle you need doesn't matter; God wants to blow your spiritual socks off! Why? So you will tell people about it and thereby spread the good news of what He can do!

I am a former substance abuser—but the story I am about to tell you is not about how bad I was or how tough I thought I was. (I really became tough when I decided to do right. It takes courage and strength to do what is right). Rather, this book is about turning failure into success and sorrow into joy. JOY beyond words!

"Miracles for breakfast" has more than one meaning, and it is my deepest desire and reason for writing this book that you find those reasons out and start having *your* miracles for breakfast.

part one

in the beginning

chapter one

Peering into Madness

Lightbulb dangles from the ceiling, wall cracked like a road map
Flashing lights from the Lincoln Hotel, neon shadows dancing on the wall
Young man came down to Beale Street, wanna shake hands with the blues
Met 'em head on like a freight train, young man never going to be the same
There ain't no, ain't no easy way out

| From "No Easy Way Out" by Danny Brooks

I HAD BEEN UP for over three or four days on this particular "speed run" with a few other addicts in my basement apartment, where I dealt speed. It was a long, low and drab tenement building with no shrubbery or flowers or lawn for that matter, in a bit of a rough blue-collar neighborhood.

We were starting to come down pretty hard, as we had run out of our supply. Actually, it was *my* supply of speed; I was the dealer and holding court with my loyal following. It is true that misery needs company, and when you've got the stuff you will never lack the company if you're willing to share it for free or next to nothing. But as soon as you run out, so does your company. You start to get very agitated in this state of coming down and your mind plays tricks on you, like mine was currently doing. Just being up with no sleep for over twenty-four hours without drugs, you can achieve this state and start complicating your life with all kinds of misjudgments; but when you throw in a few more sleepless days, the methedrine, and a body and mind already ravaged by drugs, you have a wider view through the window of insanity you are about to peer through.

It is difficult now, with the passage of time, to remember exactly every detail of this particular night, but I do recall seeing a tiny piece of something that was white on the floor and dove at it, thinking it was a piece of meth—short for methamphetamine, speed or crystal.

"Midds—what the #$#@ are you doing?" someone said. "Midds" was my nickname, short for Middlebrook. I excitedly said, "I'm finding pieces of crystal!" I wasn't, but it got me to thinking that somewhere down on the floor and carpet there was some speed and I was going to find it. I spent the next hour or so, on my hands and knees searching and I had rubbed them raw in places. Everyone else in the room started to look as well, caught up by the fleeting thought of a possible find and another hit.

We were all scurrying around in a mad dash to be the first to discover the mother lode, occasionally bumping heads in our spaced out zeal. My friends soon realized it was madness and left my apartment to search for more speed. They also probably left as they figured I had gone offside and would soon be doing crazier things, like possibly accusing them of stealing from me or holding out, and we paranoids know where something like that can lead. One of the side effects of prolonged use of speed is acute paranoia leading to completely erratic behavior.

As they left in the early morning darkness, I mumbled "see ya later" and, like a mad scientist, continued to scrutinize every piece of lint, dirt and any substance I found that looked white or off-white. I had found some stuff that dissolved in the water in the spoon, pulling out fragments of hair and other non-dissolvables as I drew up the murky substance in the syringe and injected it into my vein, believing it to be speed. As I said, the mind plays tricks on you. Seeing the flag (the blood trickling through the syringe) only heightened my belief that I had scored big, injecting the filth from my floor directly into my vein. I pushed slowly, savoring the moment after my crazed search, and then I pulled back again to get another flag, in part to prolong the ritual while getting off on the sick process.

Needless to say I didn't get the desired rush, but this only spurred me on to continue my frenzied quest for the lost treasure of speed that was still somewhere on the floor or imbedded in my carpet just waiting to be found. In truth, a fair amount of speed and other drugs had been spilt all over my apartment while I was dealing there and, that night, I may have found some real traces of narcotic, but most of what I found wasn't that—it was just garbage of some sort.

At some point I passed out from exhaustion and crashed for about twelve hours (sometimes for twenty hours in a soiled bed), waking up alone in a delirium of disjointed thoughts and acute hunger. I knew I needed to eat as I had not eaten anything over the speed run and this became my dominant thought. I had to eat and could feel my body screaming to me with shooting hunger pangs while shaking like a leaf. If you have ever seen the haunted hollow looks of Holocaust survivors, then you know how I looked at that moment. I had no money but I had one thing of value from my childhood—an old coin collection of pennies in those neat little three-way folding blue holders. It was a wonder that I still had this collection considering my lifestyle and the company I was keeping, but I guess I had hid it well enough that no one could find it. I picked up my phone and called Stephie's Restaurant, a local eatery that stayed open late, catering to the late-night set that would often use the washrooms for more than the intended purpose.

But I'm jumping the gun a little here. I feel I should start at the beginning, let you know who I was before I descended into this madness, how I managed to cheat death many times, survive, and arrive at where I am today.

I tell you this: no matter what your views are philosophically, your faith or lack thereof, or station in life, you will get something of value out of this book. Any time a loser becomes a winner it attests to the possibility of overcoming the odds. We all need to be encouraged in this manner, constantly. We are all born on an uneven playing field and any time we can discover new ideas that can help us even up those odds, it's a worthy pursuit.

SEEDS

Dream your dreams, give 'em wings and watch them fly.

| From "Hold Your Head Up" by Danny Brooks

When I was a kid, my family lived in a small three-bedroom house in Mt. Dennis, a suburb of Toronto. It was a blue-collar community sandwiched between Weston, a more affluent neighborhood, and the Junction, a tough place but not without its charm. The street ran north off Weston Road a short way, ending at the train tracks. Those trains ran through my dreams every night, shaking the house ever so gently, and sometimes they took me to a far-off place to perform to an adoring crowd just waiting to hear the great, the one and only...

At that time there was Bill, the oldest, then Greg, then me and Shannon, and Michael had just entered this world. It wasn't long before sisters Kristin and Karla came along and then brother Peter, rounding the family out to a nice even number of eight. It was a little crowded and with one washroom and an ornery toilet that kept acting up, things sometimes got very interesting in the morning with everybody in a rush and, as you can imagine, a little vocal. I can smile now, but I know that, at the time, tempers rose and so did the decibels, by which some of the neighbors could, like clockwork, mark the time of the day.

I remember going to bed at night with my little transistor radio and listening to the excited DJs of the day raving about the latest hit song. I had to be careful not to have the radio too loud or I would wake up Greg in the bottom bunk and be yelled at. I was so captivated by these high-energy DJs and their colorful names such as "Howlin' Wolf Man Jack" that in my seven-year-old mind I imagined that one day it would be my name they were announcing, and I tried to figure out how I could get that to happen. Already, I was adhering to the biblical principle, "As a man thinketh, so he is." Years later I was able to see this principle work its wonders.

I had a great musical heritage. There were Mom's Hank Williams and Rev. Jumpin' Jim Jericho records; my older brother Greg's records that he purchased in Buffalo, by Solomon Burke, Joe Tex, and Bobby "Blue" Bland; I discovered Taj Mahal, and the artists who came prior to that, the old blues greats—but it was Taj who really did it for me on the blues front. He bridged the old with the new and he was and is today probably the most soulful man in music. He can do it all: blues, gospel, soul, country, bluegrass, rock, R&B, Cajun, and mountain, being strong in all genres. Only a few can do this and do it all with authority. Looking back I am so thankful for the musical upbringing I received, and I was in complete awe of these entertainers who knew how to write songs and play a musical instrument.

One day, I told my parents that I was going to be a whistler on the radio. Caught up in this thought I whistled constantly, even in my school classroom, and the teacher give me detentions to stay after school and sit in the cloakroom, where I'd have to whistle for twenty minutes. This was my first crack at showbiz as I always had an audience of at least five to ten kids staying in for their detention and catching up on homework. After several times, the teacher caught on that I was enjoying this and in fact getting the detention on purpose. She was a nice (and wise) teacher and told me I had a beautiful whistling technique and probably had a future in the music industry. I was thrilled to hear her say this, and when she asked that I please not disrupt the class anymore but practice for my undoubted future success elsewhere, I readily complied.

Our school had Tuesday nights for games and fun, which we nicknamed "Boys' Night," and one evening I walked into one of the rooms and heard three of the older boys playing acoustic guitars. I was in grade three then, and I'll never forget that night. I was transported to a very special place. I knew right then and there what I was going to do with my life: I was going to be a guitar player and a singer, and I was going to travel the world. I felt a tingling all over my body and wasn't conscious of anything except the thoughts running through my head. For a moment there was no one else in the room. When I came back to my surroundings, I knew something had changed within me. Looking back now, I believe the hand of God touched me, I really do. What happened to me at that moment filled me with a sense and power that would later on save my life, as you will discover in this story.

That year, my mom and I and friends from the neighborhood marched to the corner music store—the only music store I knew existed—and watched as my mom purchased a nine-dollar ukulele. Proudly walking home I had thoughts of grandeur: "Ladies and gentleman, direct from Mt. Dennis, Canada, let's have a big round of applause for the one and only Danny Middlebrook!" I heard that same announcement in my head for years, especially as I lay in my bed at night dreaming before I fell asleep.

I picked up the ukulele quickly, and that Christmas I got a new acoustic six-string guitar. When I saw the guitar, I had a smile wider than a sumo wrestler's waistline, and from that day on it was solidified in my mind what I was going to do in this world. I was going to tour the world and play at the Grand Ole Opry. Yes indeed, folks, the next Hank Williams would look you in the eye and tell you it was so.

Just like that, lickety-split!

DAD

> *He was a man of means, he didn't mess around,*
> *A bundle of trouble that got turned around...*
> *...from a hard drinkin' gamblin' man who hit the skids,*
> *he worked his fingers to the bone to raise eight hungry kids.*

| From "Rough Raw & Simple" by Danny Brooks

When Dad came back from World War II, Mom said he was a different man. He had picked up habits in the war and brought them home with him, such as smoking, drinking, and gambling, and I can't say I blame him. Dad didn't do anything halfway; it was all or nothing, and this applied to his newly acquired habits. While Dad was very industrious, he liked to play hard as well.

My dad's story explains mine in many ways, so I must share a bit about him and the power of God to affect change in anyone. Before I was born and until I was four, Dad ran a restaurant that became successful. He opened up two more: one was called Bill's Lunch; one was named Danny's Place, after me, and the third was Switzer's Delicatessen. He was always nattily attired and drove nice cars; the last was a 1953 fire-engine-red Chevy coupe convertible. Dad also gambled quite a bit—cards, the ponies, anything. He was involved in things outside the law, and brought illegal items across the border. Mom once recounted being chased by the police until they had an accident bad enough that they had to be pried out of the wreckage with the Jaws of Life.

The drinking, gambling, and rough life caught up with Dad and he eventually lost everything, including his family when my parents separated. Even while they were together he would sometimes be gone days on end. One day, during their last period of separation, Dad was running errands for some big-time gamblers. He was walking past Varsity Stadium at which a traveling evangelist, A.A. Allen, was having a service. Hearing the music and seeing many people walking in Dad was curious to see what was going on. He went in. He was drunk at the time and soon passed out, but for some "strange" reason he still heard the music and the preaching, and upon regaining his senses, he felt different, as though he was a changed man. When an altar call was given for people to go to the front and accept Jesus in their lives, Dad went up. Dad later told Mom that A.A. Allen pointed his finger directly at him and said, "You need to get saved, get up here!" A.A. Allen was a colorful character who was no stranger to the bottle or the women, but he could preach a good sermon. I guess this proves the verse in Isaiah 55:11 that His word won't return void, but will accomplish what He pleases. What happened to Dad that night certainly was miraculous!

Dad came home that night and knocked on the door. When Mom answered he showed her the tracts about getting saved and where you can spend eternity. He told her she had to read them, to which Mom replied, "Bill, you need to read them more than me." Dad told Mom that he had given his heart to Jesus and wanted to do right by her and come back home. Prior to that night, on top of his gambling and illegal activity, Dad was a heavy drinker and smoker, often drinking a two-four of beer and a bottle of whiskey and smoking two packs of cigarettes—a day!

Mom let him back in the house, but not without a healthy dose of skepticism. After a two-day respite from drinking, swearing, smoking, and when he came home when expected, Mom started to have hope, and after a week of this un-Dad like behavior, she knew something had happened. Happened, indeed! I have heard of miraculous conversions, but as a former drug addict/alcoholic going through rehab, the comedown, the medications, the years of struggling mentally and emotionally, I can say that what happened to my dad so instantaneously was as miraculous as any biblical miracle. My doctor said that I would probably die from convulsions, quitting cold turkey (but more on this later).

After Dad's conversion, he went from one extreme to another. I don't fault him, as it was his means of surviving and coping, and he was true to his convictions. Dad was a good provider and he and Mom raised us eight kids in a house full of love, albeit tough love. He worked two jobs to stave off bankruptcy from his previous lifestyle and provide for us as well, which was no small feat. He was a hard worker and said to us, "You want to get ahead in this world, you work for it, and you work harder than the next guy." He had a plaque with an inscription that I would one day put into the words of a song I wrote in honor of him: "When the going gets tough, that's when the tough get going." He would know; his first job had been as a street-corner newsboy at the age of twelve. Dad went to Toronto when he was twelve, leaving the family farm in Malton, Ontario. (There is a picture of the farm in the offices of the Toronto International Airport where it was before the airport was built.) He quickly learned that he had to be tough and on his toes on the mean streets of Cabbagetown, a tough neighborhood.

You had to fight for your corner and the toughest guy had the best corners. My dad had one of the best, at Yonge and Dundas Streets, hollering, "Extra, extra, read all about it." He always had to be ready when other kids challenged him for his corner.

Often, with his two jobs, Dad put in eighteen-hour days and in his spare time—and he always somehow found the time—he handed out gospel tracts in downtown Toronto, visited hospitals and tended to the needs of the sick (three times a week) by reading the Bible to them, feeding them, bringing fruit, helping to change soiled clothes, and so on. He took me with him every Sunday. Dad also started going door to door and, in later years, he went into the Projects to take people tinned goods and to drive a dozen people to church every Sunday. People called him "the bread man" because of all the various Dimflmeier breads he brought to them.

The basement of our house was full of Bible tracts and we thought Dad was overdoing it. But he was on fire for God! He wanted to do all he possibly could, and what a legacy he left behind for us! Every night after supper we had family altar, for which my dad would read the Bible and give his interpretation of the scriptures. After the reading we got down on our knees while he prayed.

When my friends called on me to go out and horse around in the neighborhood, it was usually during family altar time, and I used to cringe because Dad would say, "Come on in, Rick, Gary," and whoever was there, "you're just in time for family altar." When it came time to pray they got on their knees, too. You know, it was years later when I realized that my friends knew what would happen, coming to my house at that time. They must have felt something good and wanted more. Dad didn't waste time and would get right to the heart of the matter with all my friends regarding salvation, heaven, and hell, and being right with God. My friends knew my dad was right but were like the rich young ruler in the Bible who didn't want to give up certain things. As a matter of fact, years later—and by now some of my friends had become gangsters—they all remarked how much they had loved and respected Dad.

We went to church every Sunday, which was a short walk up to the top of the street and across Weston Road to the Mt. Dennis Pentecostal Holiness Church. We all followed Mom and Dad dressed up in our Sunday finest, we boys with a bit of a scowl, having to wear white shirts, a tie, and a suit jacket, which sometimes we purposely got dirty before leaving the house in the hope of changing into something else. We couldn't fool Mom, though, who was always able to somehow clean us up again.

Years later, our neighbor Mrs. Brundage recounted to me that we had looked like a wonderful family, and that she had respected my parents for their beliefs and faithfulness in going to church every Sunday whether rain, sleet, or snow. As a matter of fact, we had to be very ill to get out of going to church, and none of us at that time were skilled enough in our acting abilities to fool Mom or Dad.

Mrs. Brundage also reminded me of what a rascal I had been as a kid, and got a twinkle in her eye when she said years later, "Danny, you looked like a little angel, there, scurrying up the street with your family in your little suit and tie, and I would forget about all the pranks you pulled on me—but I think it was that Montgomery boy who was mostly at fault." I smiled at her and apologized that I was as much to blame for all the things we put her through. We used to throw mud balls at her clean laundry on the clothesline and leave dead fish on her back porch (suckers a foot and half long). Once, after shooting peas through her open side window, we left to play in the Montgomery boy's backyard. (The "Gomery Boy," as he was sometimes called, lived right beside Mrs. Brundage.) We were on a ladder trying to catch squirrels when suddenly we were jolted and almost fell about ten feet off the ladder. Mrs. Brundage yelled at us in her nasal, authoritative, and theatrically trained voice. She was at the foot of the ladder and we decided it was probably safer to stay where we were, as it was unlikely she was coming up after us. However, we did concur later that we both felt she was capable of shaking us off the ladder as she yelled, "I ought to wring your little necks, you little whippersnappers! You were shooting peas in my window and hitting us while Aunt Clara and I were trying to eat a beefsteak!" Her jowls shook, her eyes were aflame, and we wouldn't have been surprised to see steam coming out of her ears and nostrils. Then she abruptly turned and walked away, yelling, "It's all your fault, Montgomery!" I felt bad enlightening her those many years later, but I could see she still thought it was the Gomery Boy's fault.

Dad was so busy working and "hustling for the Lord" that we didn't do a lot of things together, although I do remember him taking me swimming a lot, but as I got older and he was working such long hours I found I had a lot of time to start planning my own way in the world. My mom noticed this and she did everything in her power to keep the reins on me, but with all she had on her plate it was next to impossible.

Also, at this time my love for music was becoming a source of worry for my parents. They thought the music too worldly and, according to Dad, "of the devil." He and I were becoming worlds apart. The thing that I loved most, music, was separating me from him. Dad had worked clubs as a bartender and waiter and had seen the entertainer Joe King (and the Zaniacs) who used to expose himself onstage. Joe King lived an outrageous lifestyle. Dad saw a lot of unsavory goings-on in the clubs with the gangsters, gamblers, ladies of the evening, boozing, and drugs, and he must have feared his son getting involved in the music world. At that time, though, he didn't know how to communicate his feelings about it other than to be flat-out against my musical endeavors, and I had trouble explaining how important it was to me. I was a kid, and I didn't know how to explain that music was as important as the air I breathed (not to mention the girls I hoped to meet!). I guess this was the crux of our drifting apart. It was not so much my dad; he loved and cared for me even though I didn't understand it at that time, but I grew rebellious and resentful toward him because I took it personally, thinking he wasn't *for* me but *against* me. It was very cool many years later when I was a Christian and Dad heard my lyrics and the power of the songs and fully understood where my place was in this world. Having his blessing meant so much to me.

Still, as much as Mom and Dad tried to discourage me, little did they or I realize just how much they were preparing me for a life in the music industry. For starters, before I could leave the house after supper, I had to have a Bible verse committed to memory. I memorized a lot of verses. Dad was bringing my younger sister Shannon and me to churches where we both got up behind the pulpit (we were eight and five when we started this) and took turns reciting from memory a verse for each letter of the alphabet. Then we would recite all the books in the Old and New Testaments for a total of sixty-six books in all. After that we recited the Beatitudes, the blessings of Jesus from the Sermon on the Mount found in Matthew 5:3–12 and Luke 6:20–23: "Blessed are the poor in Spirit for theirs is the kingdom of heaven," "Blessed are those who mourn..." Today I am able to commit to memory hundreds of songs—and don't think that necessarily goes with the territory. I know many club entertainers who read lyrics on stage, and as well when appearing on TV!

Dad went to be with Jesus fifteen years ago. I am so thankful I had seven fabulous years of mentoring from him before he went. So badly did I hurt him and Mom that it took a little over six months of my being a Christian before we had a really close relationship. That may sound harsh to some people who believe we should be like God who can forgive immediately and forget our sins. It did hurt me at first, but it also taught me humility and a lesson in patience, and, to be honest, I didn't blame him. When we finally became close it was exciting for both of us. I would call on him often day and night, wanting his take on various scriptures—especially his and my favorite ones, those concerning the last-day prophesies and the entrance of the Antichrist—and on current world events and how everything measured up to what Jesus and the prophets of old foretold. I believe this time was all the more exciting during these discussions because Dad, for some reason, used to talk to me about these things when I was around seven or eight years old. Some people don't like to dwell on the end times as they find the subject frightening; I just see it as our Heavenly Father warning us and preparing us, much the same way my loving dad warned me about things.

BALA AVENUE PUBLIC SCHOOL, 1964: FIRST PROFESSIONAL GIG

Dreams are like guardrails to hold you up.

| Danny Brooks

In grade eight, in 1964, I started up a band with Rick Hicks and we called ourselves The Soul Possessed (the name reflected our love for soul music). The sixties were heady times for young musicians like me who were in their own bands. We were the only band in Mt. Dennis in our age group. There was only one other band in our neighborhood, made up of older guys. They called themselves King Blues, and were fronted by Terry Tipple, who sounded like Bill Medley of the Righteous Brothers. He could really sing, and watching them rehearse outside in his backyard used to give me goose bumps and fill my head with dreams of making it one day.

We were "somebodies" though—we were special—and the kids treated us as such. We all need to feel wanted and needed and at that time it felt great to all of us in the band: Rick Hicks (also known as "Hicks" or "Hicksey") on bass, Gary Jefferson on drums, Eddie Jacob on guitar, and me on guitar and the lead vocals. Our music made a way for us and gave us status.

Also at this time Beatlemania was hitting North America, fueling our dreams of riches and fame and traveling the world. We were going to be the next Beatles! All of us were serious and committed to this dream, rehearsing at least three times a week.

Near the end of the year the principal of Bala Avenue Public School, Mr. Paul, asked us if we could perform at our graduation. We were elated by the thought of our first real gig. There was an excitement around the school and our status grew to almost Beatles proportions. We were permitted to rehearse in the school and the kids used to come and watch and get as keyed up as we were. It was good fun all around and we reveled in our popularity. On the night of our performance, we were ecstatic and nearly floating off the ground and nervous and scared at the same time, and I think most of the kids in the school were feeling the same, too. This was a first for them and the school; even the teachers were excited.

When we went onstage we had to wait almost five minutes for the screaming and cheering to die down after the announcement of "Ladies and gentleman, tonight we have The Soul Possessed." I can still see us looking out at the adoring, wild crowd, and then at each other with wonder in our eyes. I went over to Rick and said, "What do you think we should do? We can't hear ourselves!" Smiling, he said, "Let's wait and soak it up till it dies down a bit," so we kept conferring with one another: "Isn't this just great… were you expectin' this…I didn't think it would be this good…" and on we went until the applause finally died down. Then we started to play and the place went wild. After our first song—we played four in total—we had to wait another few minutes before we could play again. I knew then what I wanted to do for the rest of my life. This touched the deepest part of my being, and even though I didn't have an understanding of it all, deep inside I saw and realized the power music could have on people. Music is a gift from God, and when you attach meaningful lyrics that edify, you are not only encouraging but infusing a powerful life force into people. Proverbs (18:21) says the power of life and death is in the tongue. Today I fully realize this truth and am in awe of the responsibility that comes with it!

chapter two

The Sixties

The times they are a-changing.

| Bob Dylan

THERE WAS A BUZZ of excitement around my neighborhood and in neighborhoods all over the country—the world, even. It was in the songs on the radio—"Puff the Magic Dragon," "Satisfaction," "Eight Miles High," and so on—which had kids talking about this "new way of walkin'" and saying, "Daddy, let your mind go round," from "Walk Right In" by The Rooftop Singers. Songs talked about free love and a new kind of brotherhood, and the whole phenomenon was like a new religion. It was catching on and spreading like a wild brush fire, and I bought into all of it hook, line, and sinker. Yes, the times they were a-changing.

By now, I had already started sniffing large quantities of glue, buying boxes of it with friends at Fuhrman's Drug Store. Mr. Fuhrman once asked us what we needed all the glue for, and we told him that we were building lots of model cars and airplanes. We did buy the odd model from him, but he must have wondered a bit about the quantities we were buying.

Sniffing glue is extremely dangerous and I'm lucky I didn't die like a few others in Mt. Dennis. Glue sniffing can be highly toxic and mind-bending, and it's easy to sink into a euphoric fog and suffocate in the bag you use to cover your head, as the glue is poured out in the bottom of it. Many times we would finish inhaling, taking our heads out of the bag, and stare at one another, fixed in a maniacal, paranoid state. We'd often think we were going to get killed by one another.

We were in my room sniffing once and my sister Karla, the youngest of the girls, said in a very loud voice, "I smell glue." My dad, who must have had suspicions already, raced upstairs and came into my room. It was the second (and last) time that my dad ever gave me a beating. I couldn't feel a thing, although I remember being scared. He held me against the wall, punching me and yelling, "What do you think you're *doing?*" I don't think he knew what else to do. I don't say this to make my dad out to be a bad guy. Lord knows I had it coming. I had certainly developed an attitude, and he probably should've knocked the chip off long before this.

Dad left the room and my buddy looked at me and said, "What just happened?" That's how screwed up you get from glue. "My dad just beat me up," I told him.

That night, I suddenly remembered, I was supposed to be downtown for a guest spot at the old Club Bluenote. I had hustled this spot and the owner of the club had said he would let me perform a couple of tunes with the house band. I was fifteen at the time and this meant a great deal—it was one very hot room, where a lot of heavyweights from both the United States and Canada performed. Our band was making good money in those days; we had low overhead, a small PA system, we could all fit in one car, and away we went. We were making $225 to $350 each a weekend in 1965.

I got to the club just in time, and went up and did my first song. During a guitar solo, I did a spin and went into the splits and one of my slip-on shoes went flying through the air. I would laugh about it later, but at the time I was more than a little embarrassed. I sat on the edge of the stage and lifted my arms up as if to say "what can I do?" Someone threw my shoe back to me and I put it on and finished the song, to the delight of the crowd, and then I ran out of the club. Never did go back there!

It wasn't long before I stopped sniffing glue, but I started smoking pot, and let my hair grow long. Folks thought I was weird. My poor parents, they didn't know what to do with me. I had dropped out of school, thinking I was going to be a millionaire by twenty-one (still working on it more then thirty years later, and making little headway!).

I had also quit my job (I had been a *Globe and Mail* paperboy from the time I was seven). So no school and no job, and this night I came to the dinner table with the munchies, as I was high. Dad grabbed the plate of food in front of me, and said, "You don't work, you don't eat." I got up from the table, went upstairs, packed some things, and left the house. Mom was upset with Dad and I remember her calling out to me as I left.

Dad had been right to do that though, and not only did the Bible support it (2 Thessalonians 3:10: "If anyone will not work, neither shall he eat"), but had he not taken the food away, I would have continued to take advantage. It set an example for my younger brothers and sisters, and it really taught me to dig in and hustle. I now had to do something in order to eat.[1]

That night I stayed with a friend, and the next day I rented a room down in the Cabbagetown/Regent Park area in downtown Toronto. These were big, old houses that had seen better days. The folks who lived in them usually started the day off with a few cold beers.

REGENT PARK: MY FIRST HUMBLE ABODE

Billy was born in Regent Park, angels took his mama broke his daddy's heart.
Grandma tried to rarise him right, after Daddy took to drumming
And the bottles won the fight.

| From "Running with the Best of Them" by Danny Brooks

Perhaps I shouldn't have painted the neighborhood as being mostly populated with morning beer drinkers, but there were quite a few. There were plenty of hard-working folks, too, with their backs to the wall, doing what they could do to improve their lot in life and provide for their families. I saw them leave for work in the mornings and could read their tired faces and see the weight they carried on their shoulders. I didn't know it, but I was still at a kind of school; I was being prepared to be a voice for them one day. I would have to experience their pain, and more, to earn the right to be that voice.

I awakened in the morning to the clang of empty beer bottles being clunked into cases, just as punctual as my siblings fighting over getting into the washroom every morning. Like the Junction, Regent Park was a tough neighborhood, and I quickly learned to be alert and on guard, to be aware of my surroundings. My early morning paper route had taught me to be careful, and dealing with irate and sometimes dishonest customers prepared me somewhat for this new phase in my life.

I felt free, though; I had my own place, could do whatever I wanted, and I was excited by this prospect. Still, it didn't take long to feel a certain loneliness creep in. I missed Mom's cooking and I missed *home*.

It didn't take me long to develop a taste for beer, although I was not a morning beer person yet and wouldn't graduate to this status until a few more years had passed. I ate a lot of pork and beans with bread and butter, and the colorful gentleman who had the room next door sometimes complained about it. He was actually not a bad sort and at the time was road managing Jackie Shane, who was a soul singer in Frank Motley & The Crew. They were quite popular and controversial as Jackie was the only open cross-dresser/transvestite in Toronto in the sixties. It was quite daring at that time and, because he was so talented, he got away with it.

Up the street and around the corner from my place on Ontario Street was a famous or, rather, infamous restaurant called Norm's Open Kitchen, which was open all night. It was just a skip and a jump from the Warwick Hotel, a notorious strip joint that never seemed to lack for business day or night. I tell you this to give you an idea who you might see dining at Norm's in the wee hours of the morning, or anytime, for that matter. Norm's had many names other than its illustrious owner's, but Cockroach Inn seemed to be the favorite, as the insects could be seen scurrying all over the place, darting from between salt shakers and ketchup bottles, racing up the walls and sometimes up your pant leg. It was not the place to impress a date, that's for sure. Had someone complained to the waiter or counterman that there was a bug in their coffee, they would've been told "don't sweat it, we ain't chargin' extra."

I went to Norm's sometimes when I felt lonely and needed to be around people, and ordered coffee and a plate of fries and just watched the different types of people coming and going. There were musicians, strippers, pimps, late-night partygoers, drug addicts using the washroom to shoot up, and dealers selling their wares. It was like watching TV. I was getting a bird's-eye view of the fast lane in the big city, down-in-the-alley style.

I did move back home a few months later, only to move out again and back downtown to the same area, this time on Shuter Street, right across from the old Forbes Tavern. I guess a taste of being on my own and the growing rebellion against my dad and the rules of the house made it difficult for things to work out at home. I was constantly hiding from my dad because he always seemed to know when I was high and I wanted to avoid the hassle.

I MET A GIRL whom I will call Shelly on Yonge Street while I was living downtown. It turned out we had met before at a party back in my old neighborhood. We hung out for the day and we both had an enjoyable time talking and taking in the downtown sights. It was a beautiful sunny summer day and I could feel myself being drawn toward this vision of loveliness. I felt as though I was one of the luckiest guys around. She too had left home and at the time didn't have a place to live, so I gallantly let her know she was more than welcome to stay with me until she found a place which, at that moment, I hoped was never.

She came back to my place. We talked some more, got a little high, and then, like two young, free-spirited hippies, got into bed. Afterwards, I noticed a change in her that was chilling. She even looked like a different person as she accused me of taking advantage of her and screwing around with her mind. Her voice was strange. She whacked me across my face and screamed some more insults. I was completely taken aback, and not a little afraid of her.

Frantically trying to figure out what to do next, I realized that Shelly really believed I was out to harm her, so I did my best to tell her that I did care for her and would do what I could to be her friend. Gently, I grasped her arms and spoke words of comfort to her as she tried to pull away. My hands slid down her arms, and that's when I happened to notice the scars on both wrists. Suddenly, the light came on that she had tried to commit suicide. Now I was really scared.

She broke free and yelled that I was like all the rest of the people in the world who didn't care for her. I said, "Shelly, please, let's sit down and try to talk. Can we do that? Let's just talk and work this out." She looked at me sweetly, like the girl I had met earlier, and said, "Sure, Danny, let's talk," as if nothing at all had just happened.

I looked across the table at her and then out the window at the darkened street illuminated by a nearby lamppost, while the song "Crimson and Clover" played on the little radio on the table. Looking back now, it was an eerily appropriate musical backdrop: "Ah, now I don't hardly know her, but I think I could love her, crimson and clover." The hauntingly repetitive tremolo guitar added to the surreal feeling in the little room. I believe I aged just a little that night, right then and there. I asked Shelly about the scars on her wrists. She was evasive, just saying she had some problems. We seesawed through the night, she sometimes drifting into this other personality, while all the time I tried to let her know I was her friend. She started to believe me because I meant it.

I think God has given me a unique gift that comes with good songwriting (I do not say this out of vanity). At times I can get inside a matter, an emotion, the experience that another is going through. Sometimes it makes me cry and I can feel pain. "Remember the prisoners as if chained with them ..." (Hebrews 13:3). I felt for this girl, I really did, and I'll admit I was torn between having her stay with me and the benefits of cohabitation, and trying to get her help. The best way seemed for her to be back with her family. We were only sixteen.

We spent the next few days together and she would now and then slip into her unpredictable moods, and although I was getting a bit of a handle on how to cope, I was feeling guilty. After giving it much thought and with trepidation, I found her number and phoned her dad. I nervously introduced myself to him and told him how I had met his daughter and that she was staying with me, and that I realized she needed some kind of medical help. He was so thankful that I had called. He asked for my address and that I not tell her he was coming down to speak with me.

The next day, I gave Shelly an excuse about leaving to go to the store for some things we needed, so I could meet her dad at the top of the street. He was a nice man and I was surprised by how decent he was with me, which made me feel guilty because I had slept with his daughter. He just wanted to know how she was doing and that she was all right. He was a concerned dad and obviously loved his daughter. After all she was still his little angel.

Shelly's dad made me take some money and also gave me the medicine she needed. I had to tell Shelly of our meeting and I would try to convince her that we both should go and visit her folks soon, just to let them know everything was okay. I realized he had already been to hell and back with her, and my being with his daughter was the least of his worries.

When I told Shelly I had been speaking with her dad, she hit the roof and thought I had betrayed her. Between the insults she was screaming at me, it took everything I had to convince her I was still her friend. I cried, and she was taken aback by this and calmed down. I finally convinced her that we should both go to visit her family. I still had mixed feelings about this, but knew it was the right thing to do.

The day I brought her to her parents' house in an upscale neighborhood all hell broke loose. It was one of the most difficult moments I have ever experienced. We exchanged polite introductions and then sat down in the spacious, beautifully furnished living room. All of a sudden, Shelly started screaming because I wasn't sitting next to her, and then it seemed as though we were all screaming. I tried telling her not to treat her folks this way, which only made things worse, of course, and she started punching me.

Shelly ran upstairs. Her parents began to apologize to me. Then, we heard a loud scream and ran to the stairs. Shelly was on the landing, blood spurting everywhere. She had slit her wrists again and was holding onto a broken beer bottle, slashing herself more with it and screaming as she did so. Struggling, we managed to take the bottle from her and tried to calm her down. An ambulance was called and on its way, and her mom and sister tried to keep Shelly quiet.

When the ambulance came for her, Shelly wanted me to come and I told her it was best to have her family with her. She looked at me with knowing eyes that she was not going to see me again, and I was unnerved by the unspoken perception and pain. I said goodbye to her and her dad and I walked outside. He shook my hand, thanked me yet again and said if I ever needed anything to just call.

I felt pretty good but sad at the same time as I took the bus and subway back home. I had an hour and a half to reflect on my experience of the past week, and part of me was already missing Shelly, problems and all, as she had filled the void of loneliness.

When I got back to my apartment and into my kitchenette, I grabbed a beer and rolled a joint and sat down at the little table by the window. I had never felt so lonely as then, and I cried like a baby. Loneliness can make us do strange things at times. My heart aches now as I think about all the lonely people out there. Back then I had my first real-life introduction to the blues, but still didn't fully understand how long and winding and painful the road ahead would be.

chapter three

On the Road ⟍

Left my home in '67, heard the wild wind call my name…

| From "What Dreams Are Made Of" by Danny Brooks

I WAS STARTING TO develop as an artist by this time, and although I was underage, I was able to sneak in (or was let in) to the Forbes Tavern and the Colonial Tavern to see big name blues artists. I think they took a liking to me at the Colonial; probably got a kick out of seeing this wide-eyed kid going overboard watching the acts that came in. At the Colonial there was a table on the upper level right by the railing, and I would peer over and watch spellbound, seeing up close and personal the bands that were performing in town. It was electrifying. I saw Muddy Waters, Willie Dixon, John Lee Hooker, James Cotton, Otis Spann, Buddy Guy, and Junior Wells, to mention but a few. A year or so later I would see my biggest blues influence, Taj Mahal, at the Electric Circus, one of the new psychedelic rooms that were springing up all over North America after the huge success of Monterey Pop in '67. These were artists who shaped the music world. The Rolling Stones, Led Zeppelin, Cream/Eric Clapton, even the Beatles were shaped by these artists and covered some of their songs. I was watching history, poetry in motion, and being schooled and taught the rudiments of live performing and working a crowd.

Muddy was a real gentleman, nattily dressed, humorous, very natural and smooth. I hung off every word he said. In some ways, the manner in which I conduct myself on stage today is influenced by what I saw in Muddy Waters. Still, every song you perform has to be an extension of your natural self or it won't go nearly as far in reaching the spot you want to find in people's hearts.

The most memorable blues performer at the Forbes Tavern was Richard "King Biscuit Boy" Newell. His first record, *Official Music*, was the most exciting record I had heard after Taj Mahal's *Statesboro Blues*. Richard Bell (who passed on June 15, 2007) played keyboards with me and produced both of my *Soulsville* records. He performed and recorded with Richard Newell back then. I ended up doing gigs at the Forbes a few years later after a little travel and my penchant for getting high had started shaping my music a little differently.

NINETEEN SIXTY-SEVEN, early summer. I was sixteen and performing with Soul Possessed at R&B rooms around Toronto, Brampton, and Hamilton. We were being booked by an agency called Top Ten Agency, run by a Fieldsian (after W.C. Fields) character named Sammy "Joe" Romanof, who was as colorful as they came. My brother Greg worked for Romanof as a booking agent and that helped us to get gigs as well. When I answered an ad for a soul singer who could dance, I met Dominic Augustino, who managed an R&B band called The Stroke Revue. I met him at an Italian espresso bar across from Christie Pits on Bloor Street in Toronto, and after speaking for five minutes we discovered we were on the same page. I also found out that the band was in Boston at the time and that it needed a new front man. Dominic took me downstairs to a room with a turntable and some records and asked if I could show him some moves. I demonstrated a few spins, splits, and some mic techniques. He asked me if I could do two fast spins, throw the mic stand outward (tipping it forward, the base staying in front of me), then snap it back and catch it while I went down into the splits. He must have been to a recent James Brown concert.

Well, I was game to try; I didn't quite have it down, but Dominic said, "You got the gig, Danny. We leave in two days. I gotta go do a few things right now. I'll come back in three hours and I want you to have perfected that move." He left and I went to put on the music to practice the move, but I thought I heard him locking the door. I went to check and sure enough, the doors were locked. "Hey! Whattaya doin', lockin' the door on me?" I yelled, and he yelled back down from the top of the stairs, "Don't worry kid, I'm comin' back. And ya better be good!"

For a moment I was scared. I looked around the dingy basement with the restaurant supplies, a record player in the middle of the room on the floor (it was a floor model, those little square suitcase types) and I thought, "I'm kidnapped, he's kidnapped me. I've been kidnapped by some *wop* I don't even know." (I do not speak this way today, but back then that is the way we all spoke on the street.) I started to calm myself by saying, "He says he's coming back, he seems to really need a singer." I also reminded myself that he had said I'd better "be good" with this new move.

With nervous energy I started to tackle his double-spin-mic-trick-splits thing and after an hour or so I got it. Finally, I heard a click at the door: true to his word Dominic had come back, and with food, too. But first he said, "Okay, kid, let's see it." I did the move for him and, impressed, he gave me some food. "What'd you have to lock the door for?" I asked. "Ya learned it, din't ya, so what's the problem?" he answered, and I figured it best to let it go.

I actually grew to like the guy. The next day I met the trombone player in the band, the three of us went to Rocco's mom and dad's house for dinner. Rocco had come back from Boston with Dominic. Me being all of 120 pounds soaking wet, I'm sure they seemed even bigger than they really were. Still, Rocco's dad was in the construction business and he had to be six-foot-four and 300 pounds. Rocco was only a shade smaller.

There were about ten of us at the table (I was the only non-Italian) and we had a feast I will always remember; the food was incredible and there was a ton of it. We started off with a blessing and thanks to God, then instantaneous loud laughter and banter shouted across the table—"Hey, Pasquale, you get any bigger you gotta make a new doorway!" It was friendly and upbeat and a lot of fun. I'll never forget that after eating a huge plate of pasta and being as full as I have ever been in my life, Mama Rosa put another heaping pile of food on my plate. "Mama [that's what I was told to call her and I wasn't going to argue with anybody in that room], I'm full," I groaned, and she, not having any of that, slapped me on the back, almost putting me in the next room, and said, "*Mangia, mangia,* look at you, you is thin as a rake, you needa all the srengtha you can get. Pasquale, tell him I'ma right." "Mama, you right, you alwaysa right. Danny, you gotta listen to Mama. *Mangia!* Here, take some more wine, it'sa gonna help you eat." I decided to listen to Mama, and Pasquale was right—the wine did help. After somehow eating most of the second helping, I couldn't force in anymore. Thankfully, Mama was satisfied because now she knew I was really full as I had left some food on the plate. I could have done that the first time around, but my upbringing had been, "You eat what's on your plate; there's starving kids in China."

The next day we drove into Boston and the first club I was to perform in was the Downtown Lounge. (Later the Intermission Club, in the heart of downtown Boston). The first day I walked into the Downtown Lounge and met the band, who were all from Calabria, Italy. They were a decent bunch but a little guarded and I found out why later. They had a little fun with me and told me to walk up to the guitarist, who had just come in the front door, and say, "Hello, Cavalla," which almost got me strangled. Then he realized they had put me up to it and said, "That's not my name. Don't call me that ever again. My name's Vince." In my innocence I asked why they called him that and, to his credit, he said, "Because of my snozzola."

"Cavalla," as it turned out, was akin to calling him "horse face." Nevertheless, we became good friends and before long I was calling him "Cavalla" and he referred to me as "the little shit."

I noticed that the club owners and bouncers for the most part looked like characters in mobster movies, and noses that weren't too sure of what direction they should be going in were a common sight. It was then that I figured I was in a Mafia band, but I knew I would be okay. My dad had once said, "Son, when you're a straight shooter everybody respects you, even the gangsters because they know they can trust you." They were hard but they were decent, and this was my first taste of being on the road. We would go to some of the espresso bars in Little Italy and that was a real eye-opener. You could feel it in the air that you had to be careful, although I was in good hands with seven Calabrians and they had relatives there. At one of the first clubs

I performed in with the band, there had been a gangland-style shooting a year or two earlier during which several mobsters and patrons were killed. That explained why at another club, when I was going to a noon rehearsal, I was greeted by three very large Dobermans as I came in the back door. I got about ten feet in before I saw three snarling hounds from hell coming at me. I barely made it back out the screen door. They would have probably gone right through it, but one of the club owners screamed at them to halt. He was as scary as the Dobermans were.

I quickly earned a reputation as a wild man; I was known to run across tables, knocking over people's drinks. At one club (The Bowery) that was on Revere Beach where they sometimes had circus acts, I would soar upside down on an acrobatic swing, traveling through the air above people and causing them to duck.

I found out that the band already had a singer named Billy, who was from the north of Italy, and he was still in town. Billy was a good singer, but he was glued to the floor and Dominic and the band wanted a front man who was a showman. There were a few uncomfortable moments between Billy and me, and I wasn't sure how to handle that. I felt bad for him and a little scared regarding where the situation would lead and how it might end. They ended up paying Billy for a month's work and sending him home.

During this time I was drinking but there was no pot; these musicians and Dominic were dead set against drugs. That was all right by me since I wasn't a regular pothead, but had it been just a little farther up the road, about six months, that wouldn't have worked at all.

When the band broke up in Boston three months after I had joined, I decided to hitchhike home. It hadn't been the most amicable split and, though I'd learned a lot, I had been through a fair bit and decided to take off on my own. The next morning, after our last gig, I headed out onto the highway. I had about $30 in my pocket. Dominic saw me, picked me up, told me I was going the wrong way, and we drove back to Toronto. He said my share of the gas was $20. It was a little while later that I figured "my share" had covered the whole trip, but I was happy for the ride.

chapter four

The Needle

Like a bird in a hurricane wind, I lost my way back home again.

| From "What Dreams Are Made Of" by Danny Brooks

AFTER COMING BACK TO Toronto from Boston, I got the old band going again and we had a great little gig in the Yorkville Village at a spot called Chez Monique's, just down a bit from the Myna Bird, where Neil Young was in the house band. It was a funky little R&B/soul room and the only club of its type in the Village at that time.

One night I accidentally learned a valuable stage trick that I would later use to get a crowd worked up and on my side. It was a hot night and with all the jumping around I did I fainted from heat exhaustion. When I came to, there were people all around yelling, "Undo his belt, let him breathe," and "Get back, get back, give him room!" Rick and another bandmate carried me to the dressing room. When I went back on stage, people went wild. In the future I made it a point to faint every now and then, and it worked every time. Give them something unusual and, especially if they think you might be hurt, you got a winner. (I don't faint anymore, of course; I just give it all I got and then some. Besides, when you're singing about the Power that moves the universe, you don't need cheap tricks.)

We were now Brandy, Scotch and the Kingdom Showband. Brandy was a beautiful black girl who could sing like Gladys Knight and she sure made me look good. I was Scotch, which I came by just because her name was Brandy.

We were developing quite an act and soon had a third singer/front man in Virgil Scott. Virgil was a real spark plug and we fed off each other's energy. During a part of our show he and I would run toward each other from opposite sides of the stage, meet in the middle, clasp hands, and go into the splits, sliding in the direction we had been running and bouncing back up into some dance moves. It looked great when we pulled it off, but timing had to be right on as you could pull the other person off balance and rip a tendon or a muscle. I learned that the hard way.

By now my bass player and best friend Rick and I were starting to get really turned on. We were smoking pot all the time and swallowing acid and MDA, which was considered the love drug because it made people feel so good. There's a saying that goes, "There is pleasure with the devil, but he hides the price tag," and that is certainly the case with MDA. I have seen tough guys like my friend Rick, who was as tough as they come, sitting down, holding their heads in their hands and sobbing because the comedown was so bad. "Head Help," a talk show on Toronto's Chum FM that helped people calling in with drug-related problems, called MDA "total destruction." It had the elements of speed and downers (like a speedball—heroin mixed with speed), so it pulled on your nervous system. The drug marked a dark valley in my life, one I am very fortunate to have escaped, although it left some scars and I did end up in the psych ward in prison, as you will read later in the story. Institutions and graveyards are full of people who abused themselves in this manner.

Rick and I started performing while high on MDA, acid, pot, or booze, and needless to say we created some real interesting musical moments. When a band goes completely off the rails, it's called a "train wreck" in musical vernacular, and we caused a few of them. You can have a band that has drinkers and non-drinkers, but you can't keep a band together very long when there are both straights and heads (stoners). They just don't mix. The stoners are considered screwups by the straights, and the straights are considered dull and backward by the stoners. The end of the Kingdom Showband came due to such a situation, although it was more than just differences of opinions. It didn't help matters when Rick and I started to knock equipment and microphones over and mess up on the acrobatic moves. It was a nightmare. When we created such havoc, to the rest of the band's shock, we would laugh uncontrollably as if we were having the times of our lives and couldn't understand what everybody else's problem was.

1968–1969

You try to hold on 'cuz that's all you know, one more fix in exchange for your soul, payback time oh I didn't know, payback time you reap what you sow.

| From "Payback Time" by Danny Brooks

Just as the band broke up, I got a call from Sammy Joe from Top Ten Agency asking me to become a front man for a band in Ottawa. The name of the band was The Timothy Eaton Showband, which before long I had renamed the Eaton Brown Band. I lived with the bass player in downtown Ottawa on Metcalfe Avenue in a small flat. His name was Brian Frennette (his older bother Matt played with Kim Mitchell) and he and I hit it off well. We were staying pretty much stoned all the time on good weed and hash, and that was as important as playing in the band. We had some lean times, though, and Brian and I sometimes would go to a church and eat lunches they provided for the destitute in the city.

Once I had been worked into the show and they learned the new material I had brought to the table, we started performing more often. We were becoming a pretty hot local band and getting some good gigs. Our agent was Vern Craig, who used to perform with the Staccatos, who later became the Five Man Electrical Band. Rod Phillips, the band's keyboardist, would take us to the gigs in his parents' Buick Electra 225. It was a big boat of a car and we would enjoy the ride getting high smoking pot and feeling quite important by the time we got to the gig. Rod performed in the Toronto area for most of his career and was known and will be remembered as a great player and soul singer. He unfortunately passed on in April 2007.

One night I met some people who had come to our gig and I went back to their pad to party and get high. At parties where drugs were involved, it seemed the serious stuff always took place in the kitchen. I was in the living room toking up and getting into the music when I noticed people coming and going into the kitchen, and that the ones who came into the living room from the kitchen were definitely on a different planet than I was. I went into the kitchen where there was a guy shoving a needle into somebody's arm. He pulled back on the plunger and a little bit of blood came into the plastic tube of the syringe. This was called a "flag," and when that happened, you knew you had the needle in a vein and could gently push the plunger down, emptying the contents into the bloodstream. I watched, mesmerized, especially when the guy who had just taken the shot opened his mouth, sucked in some air, eyes as big as saucers, said, "Wow, man, that's heavy shit, man." He sat there for a moment with his buzz while people around the table started talking and asking the guy who seemed in charge for a hit. He was holding court and collecting money and preparing hits for the next buyers. As the guy who had just gotten the hit went into the living room to sit down, and blank out, I followed him, sat down beside him, and asked, "Hey, man, what's it like, what you just did?" He looked at me wide-eyed. "Wow," was all he said. He went back into his own little world, and I had just made a decision in mine.

I remember now I was once sitting around a table shooting up and a very charismatic old friend (dead now from overdose), while flicking his syringe with his finger to get rid of air bubbles, said, "Who says pot don't lead to this?" It was a profound statement, and although not everybody who smoked pot became a needle freak, every needle freak I knew had started off smoking pot.

BLAST OFF

…many years ago out on the road and life didn't mean that much to me, easy come and easy go, I'll pay for it later, just let me be.

| From "Payback Time" by Danny Brooks

I walked back into the kitchen and about four or five people were sitting around the table buzzed out and speaking with the guy who had the drugs and syringes. I asked him how much for a shot and he said ten bucks a cap. I said, "All right, I'd like some." He asked if I was going to drop it or hit it and I said I wanted to take a hit. He asked if I'd ever done it before and I said no, so he asked if I wanted him to shoot me up. I told him yes. He asked for the money and I gave it to him, breathing faster out of fear and anticipation. Prior to this I had heard stories of things going wrong with needle freaks and I was starting to wonder if something bad was going to happen to me.

He pulled out a capsule from the bag and said, "Because this is your first time I'm only going to shoot you up with a third of the cap." I didn't even ask till later what the drug was. He poured the powder from the capsule onto a spoon and put the capsule back together again for later. He sucked up some water from a glass and squirted about 10 cc's onto the spoon, mixing it with the powder, then ripped a bit off a filter from a cigarette and put the piece onto the spoon. He checked the end of the needle to see if it was sharp and barbless (a barb works like a fish hook when you pull the needle out of your arm and can tear your vein; I learned this the hard way later). After inspecting it, he lightly dragged the needle over the back of his hand just to make sure. He sucked up the fluid, getting it all into the needle, pointed it upward, and flicked his finger against the side to force out any air bubbles. He told me that if any air bubbles got shot into your bloodstream and up your arm you could die. The gravity of what I was about to do really started to sink in and a part of me wanted nothing more to do with this—just run and get out of there—but the other part of me won… and would keep winning for years to come.

"Let's see your arms to see where you have a good vein," he said, then picked my left arm. I held it out and he handed me a long, thin rubber tube about two feet long and said, "Tie yourself off," and I wrapped it high around my arm, pulling it tight and cutting off the circulation. The vein popped out nice and big and, like a mad scientist with a gleam in his eye, the guy said, "Nice vein, this is going to be easy. Keep holding the tie until I get the flag and then relax your grip and try and stay still."

I was hyped and staring at every move. I felt the prick in my arm and tensed. "Relax," he said, "I know what I'm doing." I was completely tense and scared. He pulled back the plunger, and a trickle of blood showed. "Let go of the tie," he said. I did. I held my breath and he slowly pushed the plunger in until there was no more fluid left in the syringe, then pulled the needle out of my arm.

He wiped the little bit of blood from my arm with a Kleenex and told me to bend my arm a few times, which would help pump the drug through my bloodstream. I had felt a little sensation before all of the drug was injected, but when he pulled out the needle and a few seconds went by, I experienced an incredible rush. I felt both exhilaration and fear and I gasped for air. My head felt as though it might explode and my body was doing things it had never done before. I was looking straight ahead but I was aware of everybody's eyes on me. They looked worried and I was starting to wonder if I was going to make it.

All of a sudden I leveled off, stoned out of my mind but no longer worried if I was going to die or not—in fact I couldn't have cared less. Everyone seemed relieved. I was more stoned and relaxed than I had ever been. I tried talking to the guy who had hit me up but words couldn't come out at first, my mouth and face feeling like floppy rubber and out of control. Finally, I was able to mumble a "Thanks, man, t-t-too much."

"Just sit tight for a while," he said. "Relax."

Everything around me looked different: colors, the wall clock, the people around me, the air, my mind; it seemed as though everything in an instant had changed—nothing was the same. It was like waking up in a strange place you'd never been before and being caught up in wonder about everything. Little things became huge, matters of profound complexity, proportion, and import. Lyrics in songs took on prophetic meaning with incredible depths. After I regained my senses somewhat I asked him what it was he'd shot me up with. "T, man," he said, "THC. It's synthetic pot. Powerful stuff, eh?" I agreed and did my next hit about an hour later and rethought the meaning of everything in life before crashing for the night.

I became addicted right then and there, but especially to "the ritual," which is very intoxicating, since you build to incredible anticipation. It's a very integral part of the process, and every drug addict I knew got as much out of the ritual as the hit itself—well, almost.

The next day, with the zeal of an evangelist, I introduced Brian to THC. When I got turned onto something that wowed me I wanted to share it with everybody. When I changed my life many years later, this was a source of pain as I realized what I had done to so many people. If not for the power of God's forgiveness, I wouldn't be able to handle a lot of things today.

Brian and I got so stoned we had trouble making it home and Brian almost got run over by a truck. He said he got off on the rush, as the truck blew by him. I felt I could have lain down anywhere and not cared what happened one way or another, whether getting run over by a car or being trampled by a crowd. Scary.

Some of my Toronto friends came up to Ottawa and partied with Brian and me, and my friend Louie was making me homesick telling me about what was happening back home. New clubs were popping up, the music scene was exploding, and some of my old friends were starting up super groups and were interested in having me sing with them. It was too much. I had to get back, even if it was just for a few days.

I left on a Monday morning after our weekend gigs and told Brian that I would be back for our next Thursday gig. He seemed to know otherwise. I can still see Brian leaning over the upper balcony of our pad and waving with a look as if to say, "So long, Danny, it was nice knowing you and I'm going to miss you. We had some good times together…." I knew I had hurt him and I felt bad about it, but back then you just followed what you were after.

TORONTO: GETTING CRAZY

> *…living high and mighty on borrowed time, when I got the bill,*
> *I said it couldn't be mine.*
>
> | From "Payback Time" by Danny Brooks

It was the fall of '68 and the beginning of one of the craziest times in my life. Rick and I got another band going and we had Frank Federico on guitar, who was a cut above the rest and was similar in style to Robbie Robertson or Dominic Troiano. But Frank got so messed up on heroin his family sent him back to Italy to dry out and get his life in order. We teamed up with another singer, Steve Romolo, who was a great singer and showman, and we had a cooking little rock/blues band. We played mostly parties and small clubs in the Toronto area.

I was getting high every day now and living just to stay stoned. We would go to the Rock Pile, the old Club 888, which featured bands coming over from England just before they exploded on the international level. Led Zeppelin, John Mayall, and Cream had performed there, and at the Electric Circus you could catch Bad Company, Canned Heat, Taj Mahal, Tony Joe White, the Allman Brothers and so on. My long-time bassist, Dennis Pinhorn, used to perform there as well in a band called Manchild. The Electric Circus was designed for stoners, and in addition to the lighting schematics, which featured lots of strobe and black lights designed to cause a purple haze and affect the high of the club patrons, it had various rooms for tripping out. One room had these body-shaped chairs on which you would lie back facing a ceiling of changing psychedelic lights. There was also a maze and a room with pictures designed to mess with your head. But the best feature of the club was its big concert ballroom, where people could stand and watch the band. Apart from the odd "festival dancer" who would glide around flailing arms and legs in a reckless freestyle form of dance, heavily induced by a narcotic fog/frenzy, dancing was considered uncool.

I was doing what I wanted as a free-spirited hippie but getting restless and needed a change, and in the early part of '69 I went to meet my brother Greg in Los Angeles. Greg had joined the navy in '66 and around the tail end of '68, got an honorable discharge, came back home briefly, and then went down to L.A. with some guys from our neighborhood. I missed him and wanted to see him.

chapter five

Los Angeles, 1969

I've known a lot of people, some good some bad. Took a wrong turn and
never made it back. Who's worried about tomorrow when today I feel fine,
till the devil smiled at me and said you're all mine.

| From "Payback Time" by Danny Brooks

I WAS QUITE THE fashion statement back then: I had bell bottom blue jeans streaked with bleached stripes I'd done with a toothbrush, hand-painted running shoes, a black tee-shirt with a peace sign and a joint on it, and a red jean vest with buckskin fringes, festooned with macaroni shells as beads. I had a black felt hat with a little bird that swayed on a wire sticking out the top and handmade buckskin arm bracelets with fringes hanging from them. People must have thought that at any moment a circus would be coming behind me as they saw me approach.

Greg came to meet me at the airport in Los Angeles. Even though he was smoking pot and was considered a head, he appeared a little taken aback by his "freaked out" younger brother. Greg picked me up with a biker friend and we drove to their apartment in Anaheim, Orange County. We got high and caught up on old times.

Greg and his buddies had jobs, and during the day for the next week or so I spent a lot of time at a swimming pool in an apartment complex nearby. At night they took me around and showed me the sights and then we went to Hollywood and hung out in Sunset Strip. It was pretty wild; people looked as crazy as I did, and the smell of pot in the carnival-type atmosphere was everywhere. I should also add there was a very visible police presence, and their cruisers were mounted with loudspeakers. It wasn't uncommon to hear "Get back on the curb, get off the road," if you had started to walk across the road, anticipating a green light. Also visible were the riot shotguns they carried in the cruisers.

We were living a pretty good lifestyle, went to the beach quite a bit, checked out the head shops, and just hung around in the California sun. Again, though, my restless spirit was saying, "Move, Danny, do something." One day I asked Greg if he would drive me down to Sunset Strip on his way to work; it's about thirty-five miles from Anaheim. He asked why, a little concerned and protective. I told him I wanted to try and hustle some gigs at clubs and check out the music scene. He reluctantly agreed.

It didn't take me long to discover the 9000 Building, just up the road on Sunset Strip, a little ways from the Whiskey-A-Go-Go. I walked in not knowing it was the nerve center of the music world! I looked on the index and saw every big name in the entertainment world: Frank Sinatra, Dean Martin, Andy Williams, Johnny Rivers, Sammy Davis Jr., and so on. This building had all the major players in the industry from music lawyers, management firms, PR companies, record label offices, you name it. I started knocking on doors and introducing myself. Now remember, I'm quite the man of fashion and in some offices after saying good-naturedly, "Hi, I'm Danny Middlebrook, a blues singer and harp player from Toronto, Canada, and—" before I could finish I was told, "Not interested, please leave." Some places weren't so polite and it was just a simple, "Get out!" I was undeterred, however, and felt it was my calling to knock on every door in the place. I have always been a hustler. If you want something, you go after it—simple as that. The catch isn't the hard part; it's getting started that is. That old Field Holler gospel song "You've Got to Move" sends out the same powerful statement.

After about an hour of door knocking, I gave my spiel to Paul Taney in the last agency I visited. After my pitch, and to my surprise, he said, "Come on in my office here, and sit down." He introduced himself, and asked, "Do you have a harp on you?" and I said yes and he told me to play. I broke into a harp rhythm and start singing Sonny Boy Williamson's "Don't Start Me Talking."

"Play me another," Taney said, "I like what I'm hearing." I played him another song and after this I happened to look up at one of the walls in his office just as he said, "You remind me a bit of one of our artists." I was blown away and excited, for up on his wall was a picture with their company name on the bottom showing none other than one of my heroes, Taj Mahal. They also handled Strawberry Alarm Clock, a huge band at the time. I couldn't believe it! You can imagine how I felt when Paul said he wanted to take me into the studio to do some recording demos and then told me they also handled the Beatles' North American interests.

Paul talked plans of putting a band together, shopping the demo, and introducing me to the owner, who was going to love me. I was feeding off this guy's energy and take-charge style. "You hungry?" he asked, and I said yes. "Let's go," he said.

I was more excited than I'd ever been as we left the 9000 Building's underground garage in Paul's '67 bright yellow convertible Shelby Mustang. With the warm breeze blowing through my hair, I looked everywhere at once at the incredible sights. "Wait till I tell Greg," I thought, "and call the band back in Toronto and Mom and Dad."

As we drove along Sunset Boulevard, Paul pointed out places of interest and told me we were heading to a cool restaurant that had a great lunch and patio and we could talk more about what we were going to be doing in the next little while. Believe me, I understand now how the music biz can turn a young kid's head around; it was doing just that to me.

During our lunch Paul introduced me to people he knew passing by and told them he'd just discovered a new talent from Toronto, Canada. He seemed to know everybody. He asked where I was staying and I told him, and he said I could stay at his place on Mt. Olympus, where there was lots of room. I readily went along with Paul's offer, and he told me to call my brother. My head was spinning as I called Greg. Greg came down and met with Paul and me and made sure that I was all right, and, seeing that I was fulfilling a dream, he agreed to meet me in two days' time.

Over the next two days, I met the owner of the agency and hung out with Paul. I attended a couple of Hollywood parties—one at his incredible house on Mt. Olympus and another at a place called the Factory, a primo night spot in L.A. that had once been a chocolate factory but was now an industry hangout and showcase room for "the next big thing."

At the Factory party I met and shook hands with the presidents of RCA, Columbia, Capitol Records, and many others. It's hard to put into words so many years later, but the experience was overwhelming and kind of surreal. The Factory was a huge restaurant with large lush plants, trees, and flowers everywhere, rustic old brick, rugged wooden furnishings, and everything designed to make anyone comfortable from any walk in life.

Paul and the owner talked about bringing me into the studio and using local musicians to do the demos. Later I could use my guys for the road gigs. I didn't put up any argument on this issue and they told me who they had in mind: musicians from Max Frost's band who had just done the movie *Wild in the Streets*. The musicians were actually from Davie Allen and the Arrows, who did the soundtrack.

I had taken some acid earlier and was starting to feel its effects, and trips to the washroom to toke up were starting to show on me. Paul smoked but I still sort of considered him to be straight.

"Danny, are you all right?" he asked me at one point. "You seem pretty high on something."

I was but I downplayed it and said I had smoked a little grass and was just really excited to be there. Truth was if I had peaked any higher I would have been in trouble. Paternally, Paul told me, "We can't have you getting too stoned, Danny. We've got some big plans for you up ahead and we've got to stay cool." It is difficult to put into words the elation of a young artist getting this attention and feeling that you are wanted, valued, and even loved by a major player in the industry, and I'm sure a big reason why many make a deal with the devil.

We left the Factory with plans to meet soon to get the demos started. Off we went to Paul's to call it an early night, if you can call two a.m. early.

The next day, plans changed and Paul had to do some business. "Do what you want," he said, "You can even take out my Shelby Mustang; I'm taking the Mercedes." He said there were going to be some people coming over that night for a party. I went swimming in his pool and later checked out things down at the Strip. Man, I was on top of the world!

Later that night I crashed out early, being a little too high. The next morning Paul was out and, while he was gone, I received weird phone calls with sexual implications, which had me wondering about whether I was being checked out for some reason or another. When Paul came back, he took me to see my brother. I filled Greg in on what had happened and what was about to take place. He was proud and was as excited as I was. Paul and I were to touch base in a few days and make plans for going into the studio. Greg and I went back to Anaheim and talked of moving to Sunset Boulevard.

I called some of my musician friends back home and told them it was a possibility that they would be coming down to L.A. to start recording with me. They were flabbergasted and couldn't believe their ears but they were eventually convinced that I was not just a little high.

Things happened so fast and we moved to the Sunset Doheny Motel, right across the road from the Whiskey. We ended up staying there for two weeks. One day, taking a walk down the Strip, we were tripping on Orange Barrel Sunshine, a popular acid that was very hallucinogenic. It was the first time I had ever experienced a bad trip. Up until this night, everything I had experienced on drugs had been fun and enlightening.

I remember seeing buildings and signs and everything else along the Strip starting to melt in front of me like a Hollywood Doomsday film. People's faces were melting and becoming anything but friendly looking; they were contorted, dark, strange, and evil. All of a sudden I'd started to exist in a Salvador Dali painting that had become a living reality. I had to sit down. The drug was too overpowering. My equilibrium was completely off and I was experiencing a fear I had never had before—something that got right into my bones, the very core of my being. It was similar in some ways to the paranoid feelings I got sniffing glue with the Gomery Boy, but this was a whole lot worse and much more intense. Back then I had been scared but sensed it would pass, while on this drug I was petrified to the point of paralysis, and thinking, "This is it: I'm done, it's finished, it's all over." Greg was worried and tried to tell me that the buildings were not melting, that I was only hallucinating. I tried to convince Greg that he was in danger because he couldn't see what I was seeing. I felt I had to warn him.

We met two girls who were walking down the Strip. I guess they saw the worried expression on Greg's face and the terror of the end of the world in my eyes and were drawn to helping us. They approached us and got the gist of what was happening from Greg. Both spoke to me with sincere, reassuring voices. They had a calming effect on me and helped me come around. I was very fortunate that my bad trip did not end badly as I could have easily run, freaked out, into oncoming traffic or done something equally drastic. The Guess Who's hit song "She's Come Undone" tells of famed TV personality Art Linkletter's daughter, who jumped out of an apartment window to her death because she thought she could fly. Also, many people never come out of a bad trip and end up the rest of their lives in a psyche ward, or in a harmless semi-vegetative state. I can sadly recall many people I have met that never fully came back after too many acid trips that bent their minds.

We ended up going to this club called the Last Chance Saloon and became quite friendly with the girls. They were looking to rent an apartment somewhere close by, just as we were planning. Several days later, after going out a few times, we all agreed to get a place together and save some money.

THE LAST CHANCE SALOON

Come with me, my little kumquat, for a little libation…

| Fieldsian verbiage

During our stay in Los Angeles, the Last Chance Saloon became our constant hangout. It was decked out like an old-style saloon from the Wild West. It sported a long bar that was sprinkled with sawdust so the bartender could shove a mug of beer from one end to the other to the waiting customer. Rarely was any spilled. The telephone booths all had the separate ear and mouth sections of the first telephones. An elderly ragtime pianist played tunes and customers could sing along with the lyrics, as on each table was a booklet of the songs. Humazoos were available, too, for those who wanted to accompany the piano player. On top of all this, the saloon daily featured all the W.C. Fields films and other old-time comedies of the Marx Brothers, Jimmy Durante, and Charlie Chaplin, but the most popular were the Fields films. Everybody in the place imitated Fields when speaking to one another or calling out an order, which was hilarious most times. Even the heavyset waitress took it in stride when we said upon receiving our beer, "Thank you, my little trinket, my little pachyderm." I still have the odd Fieldsian time-warp experience.

We were dropping acid now on an almost daily basis. When you take acid, certain things can stick in your head and influence your attitudes and actions and the Last Chance Saloon's Fieldsian fare and influence had a long-lasting effect on both Greg and me, and it got us into trouble more than a few times, not to mention the fact that it annoyed a lot of people from Los Angeles to Vancouver to Toronto.

On the Strip we met all kinds, and there were dealers everywhere you walked, selling Orange Barrel, purple microdots, hash, weed, uppers or downers. It was a Harper's Bazaar of drugs. I recall one fast-talking weed dealer who tried selling us a bag of tea leaves and when I said "This is tea leaves, man," he quickly replied "No man, this stuff is Chicago Green." I told him he was probably run out of Chicago for selling it there. There were fans and followers of Johnny Rivers ("Secret Agent Man" and "Mountain of Love," two big hits of his at the time), who wore bells and smelled like an entire bottle of patchouli oil. They were well meaning and harmless and easy to be around, much like the Jesus Freaks, whom to me were like hippies but without the drugs—they were high on Jesus.

We also checked out a club in Topanga Canyon, I believe, where Charlie Manson and his followers hung out. It was a strange place and we had heard of it on the Strip and had also met people who had partied with Manson and his followers. They would refer to Manson as this strange but cool "far-out dude." We would soon discover just how "far out" he was. One night—the last night we ever went to this club—around midnight, a hush fell on the place. On the stage a trap door opened and a man dressed like a Dickensian character came up holding an oil lamp, wearing spectacles and a night hat with a long tail, a pompom on the end. He wore a long night shirt with strange-looking slippers curled at the toe, and was bare-legged from just below the knees. He started reading passages from a book on a lectern— "What is and what shall be and we shall shortly see…"—gibberish as far as we could tell—and then he got into this weird and very strange thing about the "strangers amongst us." I was with Greg and his biker friend Dave. We were high on peyote but we weren't out of it by any means. We looked at each other as this strange character went on about the strangers amongst us and felt he was referring to us, and we noticed people staring at us, too. Our suspicions were confirmed when people started reaching out and touching us, grabbing us from in front and behind. Dave shouted, "Get your *@#$&^*% hands off us!" and we backed out of there, covering our backsides and telling people to back off, just trying to make it to the front door and out.

Once outside and in the car speeding out of there, we went over the chain of events and we all concurred we weren't just trippin'; something weird had been happening and it was good we got out of there.[2]

THE DEMOS

We're going to be a household name, driving Rolly Royces, living insane, having parties lasting two weeks long, makin' money out of crappy songs…

| From "Household Name" by Danny Middlebrook

I got hold of Paul a few days later, as we'd agreed, and we met for lunch. Paul said they had lined up the studio and we were going to start getting down some demos in two days' time. As well they had the musicians ready and Paul wanted me to stay with him at Mt. Olympus for the next two nights to get ready, stay focused, and write. I agreed, and things were cool at first but then my dream turned into a nightmare.

The next day, while alone in the house I received calls like the ones I'd taken earlier at Paul's house that made me feel as though I was being tested to see what kind of moral fiber I was made of. After I told the man on the other end that Paul was out, he asked who I was. I told him and said why I was there and he asked if I would be interested in doing some film work. I said yes. He went on to say that there was a little nudity, at which my alarm bells went off. He sensed something and asked if I was all right with that and I said that it depended on how much nudity. For the most part, just a little, he said, but there would be some scenes that would involve intercourse, and with several couples all together. I told him that I wasn't interested. Another call a bit later I was asked about swinging, and swinging both ways. I politely told him no, that it was not my scene.

That night Paul started to make gentle but obvious passes at me and it came out that this was the way things were in town. You wanted to make it, you had to swing both ways. I was very disturbed and not a little disillusioned; I was also a little fearful but I felt that Paul was not going to try anything forceful, and, to his credit, he didn't.

The next day I went into the studio and things went well and we laid down five songs. One of the members of the Max Frost Band was dressed in drag and hanging out at the studio, bringing to mind the events of the night before. I asked Paul for a tape of the recording so I could play it for my brother, and he complied.

That night Greg and I played it back in our apartment, getting high listening to it and feeling good about the future. We started spending all kinds of money we didn't have but thought was just around the corner. I also started thinking again about what Paul had said and I was uneasy. I countered these thoughts by reassuring myself that I did have talent and songs and they needed this to help keep the wheel going around. Soon I had convinced myself that I was in the driver's seat. Drugs, at times, have a way of making you feel much more important than you think you are.

I could not have been more wrong.

The next day Paul and I got together and he let me know that things weren't looking so good and I asked why. "You know why, Danny." I asked how the owner felt about all this and Paul told me to go ask him, so I did. He said the same things Paul had told me the night before. They were doing so much for me and why was it such a big deal to have a little harmless fun on the side? Everybody down there did it, so what was my problem? They got to enjoy themselves a bit and I got what I have always wanted: backing by a major management company with a record deal in place. He was smooth. I began to wonder if I was the problem, maybe just too uptight; after all it was a free-spirited time.

Right then in my mind I heard a voice quoting a scripture Dad had taught me. "Danny, what should a man gain if he inherit the world but forfeit his own soul?" This rattled me to my core and I sadly looked out the window from the ninth floor at the Hollywood Hills and saw my dreams float away with the soft-moving, billowy, distant clouds. I looked at the owner and said in a barely audible voice, "I can't do it that way."

"Well, I'm sorry to hear that, Danny," he simply replied.

I walked out of his office in a subdued, zombie-like state. I was seventeen years old and what I had been dreaming about since I could remember turned out to be something I was not ready for. I was in a state of disbelief. I wondered why I had the gift of music if that was the way the business was. I started thinking about my dad and his opposition to my being in the music biz, and I thought that maybe he had been right. Then the scariest of thoughts: if this was what it was all about, where did that leave me?

I believe this is where Satan tricked me big time and I started a downward spiral that lasted from 1969 right through to 1987. August 1969 pushed me into high gear in seeking out a type of a death wish. I started to think I had nothing to really live for—that the thing I loved most, my music, was going nowhere if you wouldn't sacrifice your soul. Part of me died right then and there, but it was my childhood experience of knowing for certain what I was to be that would keep me from certain death. I guess it could be said the downward spiral started the night I first stuck the needle into my arm back in '68 in Ottawa, but this moment in '69, my dreams, hope and even faith in humanity came crashing down.

When I told Greg about the experience, he was very disappointed for me, especially because he knew it was my childhood dream and that it meant everything to me. All this put a real cloud over everything and soon we were getting high and more broke by the day. When we were busy spending all kinds of money we didn't have and imagining our new digs, Greg had quit his job. The girls were getting tired of our goings-on and soon we had a falling out and they decided to leave. In about two weeks' time we would have no place to live. We were going down, just like Freddy King sings, "I'm going down, down, down, down, down, down."

We were also getting ready to leave L.A. and making plans to hitchhike up the coast to Vancouver in a couple of days. Now, however, we had no money and I told Greg I would hustle a few tricks on the Strip because we were so desperate. This would bring in maybe fifty to a hundred bucks. But I was thinking, "Here I am, ready to sell my body for a measly few bucks when I turned my back on a career because of the same thing." I reasoned this was different as it was money for food, not for something I coveted.

I met someone and we agreed to a fee of $40 and I went back to his place, which was dimly lit. A man came out of another room and looked at me. "Make yourself comfortable," said the guy I'd met on the street, and I said, "Forget that, this is not what I agreed to." They tried to coax me but I was angry and defiant, and I got out of there fast. I tell you for this reason: to show God's provision! I look back now and shake my head and breathe a sigh of relief for God's provision; many youngsters don't make it out of situations like these.

Later when I met Greg he was beside himself with fear. He said he had had a bad feeling about the whole thing and had gone looking everywhere for me. We were both so relieved, and we decided we had to leave the madness into which we were starting to descend. We started our journey back home, somewhat defeated, beat up, and emotionally drained.

chapter six

Heading Home

You only go so far in this world on your own;
you're going to need somebody someday on your bond.

| From "Payback Time" by Danny Brooks

GREG AND I PANHANDLED enough for pancakes and coffee and headed out into the morning as the sun was starting to rise. It was going to be a beautiful day and I was reminded of the euphoric feeling I had had coming into L.A. about five months earlier, only now I was leaving, and under very different circumstances. The beautiful day was oblivious to my feelings of failure and rejection. My soul silently wept.

We managed a few short rides that eventually took us to the coastal highway and we realized we had a long journey on our hands. There's a book in itself on our trip into Vancouver, but I will only re-count two or three situations.

We got a ride with a happy-go-lucky black gentleman and it didn't take too long for us to realize why he was so happy. He was filled with the spirit, and not the Holy One but that of Mr. Jack Daniels! We weaved along the highway and Greg and I were more than a little concerned. We tried telling the gent, named Sam, to watch the road, but he told us not to worry, that we were in good hands. So we shared a few things together and before too long, I was playing my harmonica and he was singing and Greg and I shared his bottle of Jack. How we made it into San Jose is a miracle.

Sam had an older brother he was visiting who was having a party and we were welcome to go with him. We got to his brother's place, deep in one of the Projects in San Jose, and Greg and I had a feeling that we were in for trouble. For one, we seemed to be the only white people in the neighborhood. We got out of the car and knocked on Sam's brother's door, which was answered by a stern, stately-looking woman who said, "Sam, what are you up to, now?" She was Sam's sister-in-law, who informed us that there was no party going on and that she was getting the children ready for school. She was gracious, though, and invited us in and we met Sam's brother, Bill. Bill and his wife were very decent people who made us feel at home and offered us coffee and some sandwiches.

Sam said he was going to call on his girlfriend and bring her over and he asked Greg to go with him, saying that it was just around the corner, and Greg reluctantly went. While they were gone Bill explained that his brother meant well but was a real character.

Sam had mentioned upon arriving that I was a good harmonica player and singer, so Bill invited me into the basement where he had some equipment he rehearsed on. Turns out he was a local blues man who performed up and down the coast. I'll never forget this impromptu jam. At one time, cigarette dangling out of his mouth, he was playing a cool guitar lick, and he said, "My pappy showed me that," smooth as can be.

Sam came back but without his girlfriend. Greg told me later that she was a hooker who had screamed at Sam for his nerve inviting her out when he owed her money.

We had supper with these kind folks but Greg and I were a little restless to carry on. They gave us some food to take on our journey and ten bucks as well. We were blown away by their kindness and generosity. I wondered later what might have happened had I taken Bill up on his offer to have me sit in with his band that night at a club they were playing in San Jose. Every time I hear Burt Bacharach's "Do You Know the Way to San Jose" so beautifully sung by Dionne Warwick after this, I fondly think, "Man, do I ever!"

One day we were hitchhiking and a pickup truck stopped to give us a ride. As we ran to the truck, a car came up speedily behind us and stopped. A man jumped out and yelled at us to stop. We did, wondering who it was. The driver of the truck got out and said he was giving us a lift and the guy with the car said, "No, you're not. These boys are coming with me." He flashed a government truancy badge and the driver of the truck took off, shooting a wake of dust and stones. Greg and I were a little confused by what had just happened and seeing it on our faces, the official told us we were lucky. He said that people who looked like us (long-haired freaks!) were getting picked up in these parts and were never heard of again. Makes me think now that perhaps the guy in the truck was suspected for earlier disappearances and this truant officer was keeping an eye on him.

The officer gave us a ride all the way to Seattle, telling us tales of wayward kids and saying how one ought to just bear down, work hard, find a good girl and raise a family, go to church, and enjoy life (not a bad plan at all—ah, hindsight). He warned us not to hitchhike in Seattle or anywhere in Washington as we could wind up in trouble. He didn't have to convince us.

Greg and I panhandled and we had eventually begged enough money to purchase two tickets to Vancouver. I don't know what it was but in getting cleared and passing customs into Canada, some sort of weight was lifted off our shoulders and we felt pretty good about it. Looking back, I think we had gone through a gauntlet but had come out the other end with our heads still on our shoulders, and that was something to feel good about.

CHEMICAL ROW

People, people listen to me; the things you let go of will set you free.

| From "Payback Time" by Danny Brooks

Why do we hold on so long to things that destroy our health? I guess we like the familiar as much as our comfort zones even if the familiar hurts us and the comfort zones aren't that comfortable. I am so thankful that bad habits can be broken; destructive paths can be left behind. We can make it and with God's help we can do anything we set our minds to, we just have to learn to believe we can. As a man thinketh …

I wish I had let go of my drug habit ways then, and for a brief moment Greg and I talked about it and it felt like a good plan, kind of like a new beginning, a fresh start. It did have its appeal but that was very short-lived. We found a place that gave aid to transients and we ended up being able to find temporary lodging on 8th Avenue or, as it was affectionately known, "Chemical Row."

That night Greg and I got high on acid and a bunch of other people started shooting up speed and we ended up taking a few hits as well. We spoke with some extremely troubled youth. I knew I had problems but some of these kids made me feel like a social worker.

Speed is highly addictive and can be lethal, often made in filthy homemade laboratories using ingredients such as drain cleaner and battery acid. I know people who would spray Quick Start on it, the ingredient used to spray on carburetors in the winter to get your car going. It can give the user hallucinations and the feeling of bugs crawling under your skin. I have seen people scratch themselves till they bleed. Speed also can induce strokes, out-of-control rages, severe depression, and incredible paranoia. It has sent many around the bend. Many people today have hepatitis and HIV from using it.

When you do drugs like speed you open yourself up to all kinds of situations that can turn nasty depending on how you deal with the people, and how they react to the drug. For example, we met one guy at the 8th Avenue travel aid house and he was hopped on speed. According to his rant, his uncle was "Jo Jo" in the Beatles' song "Get Back," which his uncle had actually written, and he wasn't a loner, he was the life of the party and he was also in the Mafia, and the Beatles had better be careful as he was going to come after them and get his song back. He continued that he was a better writer than his uncle but he wasn't going to jam with anyone as there were thieves everywhere. The whole thing can get pretty crazy and you can either let a guy keep spouting and let him fizzle out or you can tell him to shut up; sometimes they will and other times you will have created a violent situation.

The next morning Greg phoned home and spoke to Dad, who agreed to wire enough money for train tickets home and food. Dad was there when we needed him most: there was no way we could have hitchhiked from Vancouver to Toronto. We were too worn down from the drugs. I also believe that, had we started to hitchhike home from Vancouver, we probably would not have made it back home.

It felt good to board the train and I was looking forward to seeing Toronto and old friends and starting a band back home again. The train ride was one long party of jammers and tokers and we congregated in the back coach car that had a skylight and swapped stories and songs all the way to Toronto. We bade farewell to some of our new "best friends" and swore to keep in touch. To this day not one of us held to that sacred, solemn oath.

Greg and I stayed with Mom and Dad for a short time and then moved out again. We started helping Dad do his *Globe and Mail* run; he dropped off bundles for the paperboys and filled the paper boxes in which he sold the newspapers that he purchased. Dad sensed that we had been through some things but he didn't press. He was happy to have us around and wanted to try and rekindle a relationship. I think Dad realized that he had been a bit hard on us and wanted another chance to make things better. He tried, he really did. Dad was a good man.

chapter seven

Toronto: Late September, 1969–1971

Helpless, helpless, helpless, helpless…

| Neil Young

I STARTED SEEING old friends, doing gigs on weekends and helping Dad and Greg and Bill, who also had routes and boxes for the *Globe and Mail.* Bill had started his own moving company, A. Bill's Express, which we also helped with.

In some ways I was getting it together but in other ways I was setting up for a bigger fall. Instead of saving the money I was earning, I was spending it on drugs such as speed and MDA, booze, hashish, and pot. I was starting to go on three-day runs (a run is the time period spent doing all the drugs you have in front of you; we sometimes bought more to make the run last longer) during which I hardly ever slept and then crashed hard when sleep was badly needed. Whereas before I had been using the needle only semi-regularly, I got into it on a regular basis. Once, a few of us did a run of MDA in a friend's basement apartment for three days. My friend got worried and said, "Look, if anything happens to one of you guys, this is the way it's going to be. I'm going to drag you out into the alleyway, dump your body, stick the hype in your arm, and leave you there." He meant it and you couldn't blame him. I got really messed up during and after that run, seeing hallucinations for some time of multiple-colored little birds and other animals flitting by me. It was strange and I was frightened. I remember thinking about the line in a Beatles song: "Once there was a way to get back home …" I thought that now there wasn't a way to get back home and my eyes welled up. I was lost.

At one point we got a little crazy, doing "stereo hits," where you get two people to inject you in both arms at the same time. This can get hairy when someone has trouble finding a vein and keeps missing, causing bruising and swelling. You need to press down on the swelling to disperse the drug in your system. Looking back, I think the ugliest memories are those of the shared needles and the sharpening of the needle on a match book. I was jaundiced from dirty needles, diagnosed at least three times between 1969 and 1971. I was down to eighty-five pounds, sickly, and yellow-skinned and so were a lot of other people who were shooting up with me. Had the AIDS virus been rampant then, I guess I would have died some time ago from it.

On this particular MDA run we shivered and felt cold and then got so hot we took off our shirts and leaned against the basement wall to cool down. I can remember staring at Salvador Dali prints and discovering all sorts of secret hidden meanings the universe hinged on. At times of such discoveries I felt important, privileged to be given such knowledge. It's amazing how deceived you can get frying your brains with drugs and having everything twisted to the point at which you actually consider yourself enlightened and given special knowledge and status. (I believe this is how a person can be overcome by deceiving "spirits," which can lead to being controlled and eventually possessed by demonic spirits.)

What we think we can attribute to the use of drugs is often something we just don't realize we already possess. That particular night, the acid only intensified what my mind was already working on. Today I accomplish the same thing through my faith and prayer. I pray for something, believing it will happen, and I carry on with the expectation of it happening, even thanking God in advance. It's working together with God on a matter. I have seen this work so many times in my life yet it still amazes me and each miracle feels like the first one!

On the morning of our last hit during that MDA run, my friend Terry hung his head and cried. I said, "Hey, Terry, what's wrong, man?" and he asked if I had ever done an MDA run like this before and I said no. He said he had and it was murder on the comedown and he was already starting to feel its effects even then. We only had a bit left and not enough to lift him from the hell he was starting to feel. My last hit just made me feel normal. I was like an alcoholic waking up and having a shot with a beer chaser; all it does is clear the head a little.

During this MDA binge I met a cute girl whom I will call Katy and we got along well as far as talking and enjoying each other's company, although I don't know why. I was a nut bar and was certainly considered "offside," a term used back then for people who had gone over the edge. I guess she sensed I was running from something and was hurting deep down, and she was gripped with the Florence Nightingale syndrome. She was right: I was hurting. I still couldn't get over the loss of not having something to live for in my music. I wasn't in it to be a part-timer; I wanted it all, only I couldn't abide with the reality I had learned in L.A. I felt cursed.

Katy got pregnant and I was the father, and as far as my twisted mind allowed me, I wanted to do what was right. I went with her and told her heartbroken, aghast parents that their daughter was pregnant. Her mom wailed and her dad grabbed his heart (they had had Katy late in life and he was around sixty) and said, "I need a shot of brandy." I feel sick recounting this and can feel their pain somewhat, imagining them looking upon this long-haired freak telling them of the defiling of their precious daughter. I was every parent's nightmare. I know it takes two to tango but to them I was the bad influence. Their daughter didn't have the appearance of a rebellious hippie and I did, so to them it was me who ruined everything, and they were right to a large extent.

Katy ended up going away to a home, having the baby, and giving it up for adoption. In spite of being a drugged-out hippie, there was a part of me that wanted it all to work out and I went and rented a cheap basement apartment on Clearwater Heights in Toronto near Keele and Eglinton (not a great area). I was supposed to have a meeting with Katy's dad at their house one night and I tried instead to get him to meet with my parents but he wouldn't. I was counseled by Greg and some of my friends not to go alone to meet with her dad so I didn't go. In hindsight I think I should have gone, and my not going certainly ended any kind of chance for us. Somewhere out there, I have a thirty-six-year-old son named Shaun, and maybe he wants to meet me one day, maybe he doesn't. I can't blame him if he doesn't but I would be happy to see him.

Greg moved in with me for a while and he met a girl in the neighborhood. I met another girl, too. Everything in Greg's life and in mine was drug centered. We were working, doing the *Globe and Mail* run, doing speed on a regular basis, and getting more and more mentally screwed up.

One night I was messed up from speed and I was taking a downer called mandrix, which is one of the ketamine-animal-tranquilizer drugs. This is also considered the "psychedelic heroin," and it distorts your sense of time, causes you to forget your identity, makes you delirious, and physically impairs you. It can also cause convulsions, heart failure, vomiting, and temporary paralysis. I was in my bedroom and I suddenly lost all sense of time and place. I found myself sitting in front of an old water pipe heater believing I was driving a truck and the tap on the bottom right of the heating pipes was my clutch. I didn't know where I was, and I guess I was making truck noises, because my brother came in the room and demanded to know what I was doing. I looked at him, bewildered, and told him that I was driving a truck, but I was lost and I needed his help. Realizing I was messed up, Greg gently tried to explain where I really was and I started coming to.

That's when I realized I had gone around a pretty big bend. This happened to me again while driving in an old VW and it was one of the scariest moments in my life because it seemed that not only was I lost but I kept going through a time warp, through the same area time and time again, even though I was driving for miles in one direction.

Everything reached a point of insanity when Greg moved out and came straight with Mom and Dad about our drug dependency and I got another girl pregnant. I went through the same process as before—meeting the parents, planning for marriage—only this time there was an abortion based on medical reasons regarding the young mother. She and I drifted apart, and my apartment turned into a real shooting gallery, as they called it back then. Today, it would be termed a crack house.

DESCENT INTO HELL

He who walks on water walks down that hard road with you...

| From "Walks on Water" produced by Richard Bell

These are words to a song I have written recently for an incredible soulful singer named Shelby-Lynn who has experienced life at its cruelest, but they are applicable to this time period in my life because had it not been for the miraculous, I would not be here today—simple as that.

By now I was dealing speed to support my habit, and selling it opened me up to a very wide variety of interesting people. People started bringing me hot merchandise and I became a fence for stolen goods.

Some of Greg's friends who were junkies would come over to shoot up their heroin. I can recall them saying in their laid-back voices, "Danny, Danny, look at you, you're climbing walls on that speed. You need to relax, slow down a bit, come on man, have a hit of some scag, and take it easy, take it ease" (slang of the day in these circles).

I took their advice and the first hit of heroin I took made me vomit, a common thing to happen to first-time users. After the initial sickness I did feel calm and I liked the "stone" and spent the rest of the night shooting heroin.

One night I met a girl who was also a heroin addict whom my brother's friends had brought with them. What a pair we turned out to be: a junkie and a speed freak. Talk about mixing oil and water; we fought all the time. She was probably six or seven years older than me—I was nineteen then—but I guess there is truth to misery needing company.

Rod Stewart's "Maggie Mae," in which he mournfully sings, "Wake up, Maggie, I think I got something to say to you, it's late September and I really should be getting back to school," made me wonder what I was doing with this older girl and with my life. We had a love-hate relationship. She eventually moved out and found someone else to trip with and I think she also felt a little guilty for stringing me along as she didn't have the same feelings I did. Drugs or no drugs, you can't stay forever with someone you don't care for. With every relationship, I was learning more about the blues. You can't really sing the blues unless you've had someone do the watusi on your heart. Then you're singing from a hurtin' place and that adds the high-lonesome soul to your song.

Soon, I started copping heroin by the bundle (twenty-five caps) and was shooting up on a regular basis, but I still remained a speed freak. Speed was my drug of choice.

CREATURES FROM OUTER SPACE

Ain't nothing in the world like the power of the Lord…

| From "Nothing Like the Name of the Lord" by Danny Brooks

One night I had about a dozen people in my apartment and we all hit up. Some were preparing to do another hit when there was a knock on my door. Not an uncommon sound as I was dealing drugs those days; a knock generally means making some coin. Right after a hit, though, you can be a little shaky, and I'd just done a big whack of speed, which made me paranoid about going to the door. I had a lot of drugs and hot goods in my apartment.

"Who is it?" I asked, and I heard someone say, "Danny, it's Dad," so I opened the door, keeping the chain lock on, and peeked out. It was my dad. With him was Pastor Ross Ingram from Rexdale Alliance Church, which I used to attend as a kid. I wondered what to do. I was buzzed out of my mind and had an apartment full of freaks.

"We've come to pray for you, son, open up," Dad said, and I took the chain off the door and let them in. They walked right past me and entered the middle of my living room and looked around at all the stoned people on the floor. As I walked in behind them I saw the astonished looks on everybody's faces, and they were all speechless, staring up at my dad and the pastor.

It took a lot of courage for Dad and that pastor to walk in and stand there in the middle of a room full of addicts. It is the most unpredictable situation in which one can put himself. Some of the people in that room were violent and, coupled with the unpredictable nature of drugs, we could have had a dicey situation on our hands. Looking back now, though, I know Dad and the pastor had been prepared for the unpredictable—the worst, even—and they had had the faith to leave it in the hands of God. Like Shadrach, Meshack, and Ebed-Nego in the Book of Daniel going into the fiery furnace, they had known God was with them and would protect them.

I walked over to my dad and the pastor, and they laid hands on me and prayed loud and fervently. I remember thinking that not only everyone in the building heard, but the whole block. They weren't just praying politely as to not offend someone not used to this, but beseeching their God with utmost urgency. Literally, crying out with all their might. I get shivers even now thinking about it. As they called on God and His mercy to protect me and bring me out of the depths of the prison I was in, I could feel something in that room. I looked around at the mesmerized and shocked faces. Everyone was silent. It was as though they were all temporarily paralyzed. Dad and the pastor finished praying and Dad hugged me and said, "I love you, son." I saw a pained expression on his face as he and the pastor left.

I locked the door and went back into the room, where you could hear a pin drop. "What was that all about? Who were those guys?" someone asked in a very subdued and shaky voice. Before I could answer another one said, "I thought they were creatures from outer space just beamed down." There was a collection of heavy sighs. "Man, that blew me away," someone said and there were murmurs of agreement from everyone in the room. No wonder as they had never been on a trip like that before and believe me, under the influence of speed that was a heavy trip. It was even for me and I was raised around this; they weren't.

A Life Force entered that room and gripped everyone that night. Everyone was given a chance to make a choice and all our lives hung in the balance of that choice. That Force filled the room to the point that no one could move even if they had tried. When it left, it was very noticeable.

Sadly, only one made the right choice, albeit in the future, but God knew it, as He knows the outcome of things beforehand.

Sixteen years later, in 1987, after I got out of the Donwood Institute, Dad asked if I remembered that night he and the pastor had come to pray for me. "Yes, Dad, I could never forget that night. I remember it well." Dad looked at me intensely and said, "Well, son, you are the only one alive today of all those in that room." I recalled then the various newspaper articles about some of their untimely deaths, some of the car accidents, and I remember some of the overdoses. I said, "Dad, I think you're right; I'm the only one alive out of all of us that night."

I believe God told Dad this and He wanted Dad to tell me; I would not have even thought about it. I was too busy back then trying to figure out how to live in the next breath, keep my sanity, and stay straight. Knowing this was humbling and it gave me an understanding of God's provision and the power of prayer.

chapter eight

The Profits of Crime

If you do the crime, you got to be ready to do the time.

| Jail Proverb

If the washing don't get you, the rinsing surely will.

| From "Payback Time" by Danny Brooks

EVERYTHING TAKES its toll and there is a price tag for everything you do. We do reap what we sow. It is a universal law, and they who sow to the wind reap the whirlwind. My dad had a sticker on the "Glory Wagon," a truck I inherited when he crossed over to the other side of the Jordan River, that said, "The Devil gives you pleasure in sin, but he hides the price tag."

As each day went by I was getting more and more messed up. My thoughts were a fragmented mess of fear and twisted perceptions, and I knew I was losing it. I will share an incident that happened in early 1972, while shooting speed at Bart Clark's house. It was a turning point of sorts in the road to recovery. I had done a big whack of speed and I started thinking that Bart and his brother were out to kill me with a machete they were hiding down in the basement. I was convinced they were waiting for an opportune time, and I was really freaking out and trying hard not to let them know it. When you're freaking out, a casual glance from someone can have catastrophic hidden meanings and a whole incredible scenario of what that person is really up to can unfold in your head. Put bluntly, you are literally out of your mind.

Bart and his brother were looking at one another and then me because they saw a weird expression on my face and feeling the effects of the speed and my vibe, it would have a negative affect on them as well. Glancing at one another led me to believe they were signaling to one another to leap at me at any moment. I was becoming frantic and agitated, and thinking fast, I asked them if they wanted any more stuff for later and they said yes. I told them I had to go get it and that I would be right back. I bolted out of there and remember their baffled looks. I figured I had tricked them into letting me go because of their need for speed, but I'm sure they were relieved to see me go.

I went to Greg's apartment in the Jane and Woolner apartment complex but couldn't get him to answer the door. I looked through the mail slot near the bottom of the door and could see him passed out on the couch, but I couldn't rouse him, even pounding so hard on the door that the neighbors were coming to see what was going on. Taking one look at me, a dazed and crazed-out speed freak, they quickly went back into their apartments. Maybe it was because I was so freaked and couldn't trust anyone that I went to my parents' house and told my dad about my condition. After a word of prayer he took me to the doctor's and I was given something to calm my nerves.

I had been so freaked out—and I mean petrified—that that was the last time I ever stuck a needle in my arm, and I'm sure I wouldn't have been able to even if I tried. I can't stand the sight of a needle to this day and have sweated it out going to the doctor's and getting a blood test. God did this to save me, putting me through a living nightmare that night, as the only way to separate me from such a seductive, deep, slippery pit. At one point I counted around forty people I knew from the neighborhood who had died in one way or another because of drugs. Too many others were sent to prison as well, and many more with mental health issues.

I had been just as addicted to the ritual of handling the needle and preparing the drugs prior to the injection that to get over everything all at once is miraculous. Later, I replaced the needle with booze and although I still smoked pot, I didn't enjoy it as much because it made me feel jittery and I would sometimes get paranoid from it. At this juncture it would have been very helpful if I had spoken to a doctor about some of my problems, drug related and otherwise but, sadly, that wouldn't take place for another fifteen years. I was on my way to becoming a serious alcoholic, cross-addicted to Valium and cocaine, not to mention the then socially acceptable and extremely addictive cigarettes.

Bill and Greg often visited my apartment to keep an eye on me, and each time, it seemed, they got me at the end of a run when I was totally crashed out. Once when they couldn't wake me, Billy looked through my bedroom window, at the back of the apartment building. Since I was in a basement apartment, he could see into my bedroom through the slightly open venetian blinds. He saw I was not moving on my bed. He got the landlord to let him and Greg in. They revived me, found my drugs, and flushed them down the toilet. I was really gaunt and sickly and they wanted me out of there, to take me to Mom and Dad's place. I guess they figured taking me there even temporarily was better than leaving me alone at the apartment until I started my next binge.

The look on my poor mom's face, seeing her son almost unrecognizable from the little boy who'd followed her to church dressed up in a little suit and tie, broke my heart as well as hers. It is not easy looking into the eyes of a grieving mother and feeling her pain, and I couldn't look at my mom. I remember sitting in the living room, kind of hunched over in the big couch chair, and my two sisters Kristin and Karla, who would have been eleven and eight then, peeking around the corner from the hallway. I remember the frightened look in their eyes as they took in this skinny, jaundiced, and shaky shadow of a brother they once knew. I was anything but the overconfident, gregarious brother they may have remembered. It got to me, seeing their reaction, and it occurred to me that I had to do something with my life or I could die.

My family tried to get me help through the doctor's office and the Addiction Research Centre, but there is only so much one can do. I wasn't ready. You can lead a horse to water but you can't make him drink, they say. I ended up back at my apartment and by about the third time my brothers caught up with me and flushed my drugs down the toilet, I was falling behind with my pusher and he was not too happy about it. I bumped into him at a popular drinking spot and he took me outside for a little chat and quietly, very politely, told me what perhaps had to happen to certain limbs of my body. He let me know that it hurt him to have to tell me those things as he had a lot of respect for my brothers.

I began to think about pulling robberies to make money to pay off my mounting drug debts. I convinced myself there was no other way out and I didn't really have many options. I did not possess a clear enough mind to consider much more than that. My first break and enter was into a leather goods store in Mt. Dennis. I hit that store twice in a week's time, making three trips each (I didn't have a car) crossing Weston Rd, a main street, and going down to a house on Rutherford Avenue where a friend let me stash the stolen leather coats, belts, vests, and leather accessories.

There is no honor among thieves, and a week later a drug user in the neighborhood tipped the police off as to where the goods were. The day the police came was the day after I had robbed a gas station and I had been identified as a hippie with a colorful patch on my jeans above one of my knees. I was taken to the police station for questioning and, of course, I told them I knew nothing about anything. I felt I was quite convincing and that they didn't really have anything but circumstantial evidence. They knew it was me, I'm sure, but they could only try to bluff and scare me. When the cops told me they were going to charge a friend of my Dad's for the break-and-enter, I owned up to them and the possession of stolen goods. I couldn't allow my dad's friend to be charged. They pressed me on the gas station robbery, but I held my ground, saying that tons of guys wore patches on their jeans and there were a lot of guys who looked like me.

I ended up in the Don Jail for a two-week presentence report before I went to court. It was an in-depth report that checked my background to make a proper assessment of my character. I was very fortunate: I ended up with such a good report that when I was finally before a judge he said he couldn't imagine that I was the same person in the charges and chalked it up to the evils of drug addiction.

The old Don Jail took a lot of flak over the years as being outdated and cruel to prisoners. Let me tell you, it worked its charm on me and went a long way in scaring me in the right direction. The open homosexuality and perversion among the inmates was one thing. The shared dorms and tiny lockup cells at night were another. If I touched my knuckles together, my elbows just about hit the walls. That's how wide my cell was. There was maybe an inch to spare on each side of the wall. Barely enough room to get by the small cot, you had to slide sideways for this maneuver and at the front near the barred door there was just enough room to use the pot to do your business in, which was never easy, regardless of the task. Once finished you put the pot down and waited till morning before it was removed. Needless to say, the nightly aroma in the place could get a little unpleasant.

While in jail I started to read more and heard from various "professionals" that, it being my very first offense, and if I got a good presentence report, more than likely I was going to get probation and no jail time. I was starting to feel confident and actually forgot about the gas station robbery as I thought they had nothing on me. They had tried to scare me, which didn't work, and they had no evidence, so I would walk, simple as that.

Unbeknownst to me, however, there were other powers that be that saw it otherwise. You don't mess with those powers; when they deem what's going down, that's what's going down, and that's that.

ROY MCMURTRY

...ain't nothin' he can't do,
and he wants to blow the socks off you...

| From "Ain't it Amazing What God Can Do"
Danny Brooks and Greg Martin

My two weeks in the Don Jail were up and I was happy to get out of there. I went to court and I was confident that things were going to work out. My name was called and I took my position, and before the proceedings got very far it was brought to the attention of the judge that I was now charged with another, more serious, crime of armed robbery with violence. Things went quiet in my little universe and I was stunned into silence. "Son, I think it's best you get a lawyer," the judge said. He told me that if we carried on with the current charges and then came back to court on the more serious charges, it had the appearance that I was moving up the ladder of crime and I would be dealt with much more severely and could then be looking at serious convictions and time in jail.

I took his advice. My positive presentence report helped me at this time in my life. I wasn't a bad kid as much as I was misguided and lost. I met people who were bad and I could see the difference. They were kids who had been severely mistreated as youngsters, beaten and raped. Some were bad to the core, who got off putting cats on fire and tying them to railway cars. I knew I was doing a lot of wrong things: drugs and selling them, the crime I had gotten into. I knew all that was wrong and I even knew my mom and dad's belief system was right and mine was wrong. Maybe that was the difference in my catching a break at this juncture: that I could admit my error.

I did get out of jail on bail set by my brother and I got a lawyer. I picked one of the top lawyers in the business, a Mr. Roy McMurtry, who was an ombudsman at the time. McMurtry would go on to great achievements including becoming Attorney General of Ontario and Solicitor General in the Cabinet of Premier William Davis, being appointed Ambassador to Great Britain and, in 1996, being appointed Chief Justice of Ontario.

When I was ushered into his office on University Avenue, he asked what he could do for me. I told him about the break and enters and the armed robbery with violence charge and that I was guilty as well. I think he found that sort of refreshing because prisons are full of innocent people done wrong. He smiled at me and very respectfully said, "Danny, your case sounds very interesting and I would love to tackle this problem with you; however, I am caught up in a very time-consuming murder case and won't be able to give you the attention your case deserves." That case happened to be the very high-profile Peter Demeter case, the Mississauga businessman accused of hiring a hit man to kill his wife. Mr. McMurtry escorted me into the office of Bruce E. Scott and said, "Danny, Bruce is one of my finest, new young lawyers and I believe he is the man for your case."

Mr. McMurtry was smooth and he knew how to make a person feel important. The Good Book says, "If you want friends, show yourself friendly." It has been my experience that when people are very busy with time restraints and heavy workloads, they can be abrupt and rushed and they would not give me the time of day, much less show me the consideration that he did, but then, he wasn't what most lawyers were made of; he was a cut above the rest.

So was his younger associate Bruce Scott. Bruce made an incredible impact on my life and I owe a great deal to him for my current well-being and outlook on life. Sadly, I attended his funeral just before Christmas in 2005. He was only sixty-three.

BRUCE SCOTT

Some people go crazy trying to hold on; you can't make it in this world on your own.

| From "Waiting for Your Ship to Come In" by Danny Brooks

Bruce, like Mr. McMurtry, got a kick out of my admission of guilt and we became fast friends. He ended up hiring A. Bill's Express when he needed our services, and his word of mouth helped my brother's little moving company grow. Bill and I spent time sitting around and having a few drinks with Bruce every now and then. He was a fan of W.C. Fields, too, and we had a lot of fun some nights recounting our favorite Fields movies and doing imitations of the beloved comedic curmudgeon.

Bruce really impressed on me the need to get off drugs and be clean of them before our trial date, which was looming in September of 1972. He was a true friend, being very blunt about my pending trial. He said, "Danny, if you plead not guilty and lose you get a minimum of five years, maybe more. You plead guilty—because you are and if you really do want to start over, you can't start over with a lie—you will get a reduced sentence and maybe get a year or less." I did want to start over; I was getting tired of it hanging over my head, so I decided to take Bruce's advice.

The day of the trial, outside the courtroom, Bruce met the man from the gas station that I robbed and as a result, the armed robbery with violence was reduced to just robbery. Later, I asked Bruce what he had said to this fellow and he responded, "I can't remember but I pleaded with him to give you a break and told him that you were sorry." I would still be punished if that's what the man wanted, only less so if he would give me a break and not come into the courtroom.

The judge told me to take the stand and asked how I pleaded, to which I said I pleaded guilty. It was Judge Clooney, whose nickname at the time was "Rosemary," after the famous singer, because he had heart and was known to shed tears sending young people to prison. He shed no tears for me but still gave me a break and he mentioned my presentence report as being instrumental in his decision. He pounded the gavel and announced fifteen months, to be served in the Guelph Reformatory. I say he gave me a break because it's easy to see it that way now. At the time it hit me pretty hard. When you're twenty years old, fifteen months seems a whole lot longer than it does when you've seen fifty.

chapter nine

Guelph Reformatory

They can imprison your body, Danny,
but they can't imprison your mind or soul.

| Mrs. Brundage (Neighbor)

THE NIGHT BEFORE I went to court for my trial, I had gone to see Mrs. Brundage to thank her for the kind words she'd spoken on my behalf in the presentence report. I had thanked her earlier but wanted to see her again, as she seemed to have a calming effect on me. In her own words she believed in a Supreme Being, just a little differently than the churches, and that was all right with me. Her son, Jack Brundage, better known by his pseudonym John Herbert, had written the play *Fortune and Men's Eyes*, which was made into a movie starring Sal Mineo, and was based on his experience in jail. She shared a little of this with me. She told me to read as much as possible when I was in jail and to write down my thoughts, to keep a journal, and make the most productive use of my time as I could.

She was right on, and coupled with my dad's advice to read the Bible, I was equipped and advised in the best way possible. I can still see Mrs. Brundage's long silver hair gently blowing across her peaceful face, lined with wisdom, as we sat on her front porch that warm autumn evening. We were sipping tea and eating biscuits and she looked at me and said, "It's up to you, Danny, how you do your time in jail. They can imprison your body but that's all they can do. They can't imprison your mind or your soul. Use your mind, Danny, be creative and let your mind soar."

I WAS TAKEN BACK to the Don Jail in September 1972 and was there for just over a week before I was taken to the Guelph Reformatory on the "Blue Goose," as the jail bus was called. I remember my dad came to see me after the sentencing took place and he prayed with me in the holding cell. He could tell I was worried and tried his best to reassure me that I would be okay, and he turned out to be right. I told him I thought I was like a little lamb among a lot of wolves. He told me there were going to be a lot of lambs there; that I would not be alone. He was right again. Jails may have a lot of bad people in them, but there are a lot of innately good people, too.

The morning I went on the bus that was called the Blue Goose with about another dozen guys, I was pretty hyped up; the fear of the unknown and the tricks your mind can play on you if you let it wander too far! I remember asking God to protect me and help me get through this ordeal, and as I looked out the window on the highway watching freedom whiz by, it hit me that I finally had to pay the piper. There was no turning back. It was payback time; it was time to reap what I had sown. This was a real "valley moment." Sadly, it wasn't the last time.

WE ARRIVED AT THE Guelph Reformatory and were taken into a holding area and then down to a basement where we had a communal shower. It was very strange and I felt as though I was gliding along in a dream I didn't want to be in, but I was powerless to change it and could only go along with it; in fact, I was pulled into the flow of it. The basement was like a dungeon with big brick and old pipes, and I was reminded of a medieval castle. What really hit home, bone jarringly and soul shatteringly so, was the loud clang of the huge iron door we walked through to get into the main prison area. We jumped. I think they purposely put a little *umph* into closing that door. It let us know where we were and who was in charge and there was nothing we could do except our time in the best way possible. Fifteen months is not a long jail sentence, but it's not so much the length; it's the waking up those mornings knowing you're not free to do what you want and that anything could happen. It was long enough for me. Little things we take for granted such as a cup of coffee, certain smells in your kitchen, and answering the phone become very noticeable in their absence.

After the shower and processing, I had an appointment with a guard who was also a social worker. We sat in his old office and he read a file on me while I looked out the window, thinking of another window in L.A. where my dreams vanished with the clouds. After a while he looked up and said, "It says in your file that you're actually a very decent person who just got mixed up with drugs and the wrong crowd. What do you say to that?" I said something to the effect that I didn't know how decent I was, but I knew I did wrong and wanted to make up for it some way and I wished that I hadn't hurt my parents so much. He looked at me and nodded, then said, "It says you're a pretty good musician as well, and I've brought the harmonica you had in your possession. Would you play something for me?" I was surprised by this but took my harmonica from him and moved back my chair so I could assume the position. I started with a mid-tempo train groove and the acoustics in that old place seemed to amplify the sound of the harp to the point that it seemed to fill the whole building. It sounded great to me and I wanted to hear how my voice sounded. Changing the groove somewhat, I broke into Sonny Boy Williamson's "Don't Start Me Talking": "Da da da da dum [blown on the harp], Goin' down to Rosie's stop at Fannie Mae's, (Da da da da dum) Going to tell Fanny what her boyfriend say, now don't you start me talkin…" When I finished the song, the guard clapped and so did a number of unseen hands, accompanied by whoops and hollers.

I have Holy Ghost shivers thinking about it even now as I hear those sounds of approval echoing through those old stones and reverberating through the halls of time. The Good Book says, "A man's gift makes room for him and brings him before great men" (Proverbs 18:16). That day, my gift made room for me.

The guard said he enjoyed my music and that something would have to be done about me being able to practice and play music while

I was there. He said I probably wouldn't be able to have the harmonica, though, because of the metal sides that could be taken off and filed down into a sharp blade. Later, they made an exception for me, which was unprecedented, and I was allowed to carry my harps with me (I ended up having more brought in).

We talked about my drug use, and although I held back my paranoid thoughts for fear of being put into a padded cell in a mental institution, I shared enough that he put me in the prison hospital for a few days for observation. Here I got a glimpse of Mental Institution Hell, and I'm glad I held back from telling the social worker everything, as I would have hated being in an institution full of the types in this wing of the prison. I would soon learn this was an assessment wing and that some inmates were later sent to various hospitals or institutions, including Penetanguishene, for the criminally insane. I told no one that I heard voices and hallucinated, and that I suffered from paranoia. I will never truly be able to tell anyone how difficult and terrifying this period of my life was. It went on for many years, and I was so crazed I attempted suicide twice. I fought so hard to appear to be normal when I was anything but. I also suffered from agoraphobia, a severe fear of open or public places.

Perhaps I was borderline schizophrenic or even manic, I don't know, and maybe I never will. I called these dark and scary moods "blue funks" and I thought they were just a reaction to all the drugs I had taken and that some day I would get over it. It was so bad I knew that I was in a daily fight for my sanity and I knew that I might lose this battle. I didn't trust anyone and in a way I am glad I didn't. I have seen what some in the medical profession have done to "help" certain people I know with similar problems. Today these people are on an endless merry-go-round of drugs and therapy and maybe they need to be, but maybe not. Some of them are now just above a vegetative state because the drugs they take zap the life out of them, making them zombielike. I know people are used as guinea pigs for the medical profession to test new drugs, and certain types of personalities are needed for this cause. We have proof of this with film footage of testing people with clinical LSD and other drugs. Some of this footage is very difficult to watch and many, many lives were destroyed, many died.

I don't mean to use a wide negative brush, and it would be absurd to, as there are many well-meaning and caring people in the medical arena and we need them. But even well-meaning people can get one into trouble. No one with an addictive personality should ever be given mood-altering drugs.

THE PRISON HOSPITAL

Reach out and touch the hand that wants to see you win,
that will keep you from falling when you get back up again.

| From "Waiting For Your Ship to Come In" by Danny Brooks

I was soon interviewed by the prison psychiatrist, who felt I should be on a mild sedative, as I had been given Valium in the Don Jail. Considering I was shaky from the booze and years of drug use, it was probably a good move at the time even though I would have been addicted in no time at all had I stayed any longer than the week I was there—in fact, I did develop a certain dependency on them. The drug quieted the voices I heard, I found it helped regulate my "blue funks," and I wasn't nearly as jumpy.

There were about a dozen of us in the hospital. I swear I was the only reasonably sane person of the bunch—and I was pretty messed up. That first night trying to get to sleep in the hospital dorm was very difficult—a night to remember. One guy started mumbling about something and the next guy had to top that by having a conversation with invisible aliens; another sang a lullaby of sorts, and two other guys were arguing about who had the cutest cat back home; another was going, "boo, boo, boo, here comes the bogeyman, he's going to get you, ha, ha, ha, boo, boo, boo," and I was really wondering what I was doing there. I had problems, yes, but these guys were real nut bars. At times a guard would come in and gently say to keep quiet. He'd receive a chorus of giggles and soon after, the moronic outbursts began again. The guards knew these guys had serious problems so they handled things a bit differently than in the rest of the prison, which I soon found out. I was afraid to sleep that first night in case something weird happened.

I was shaky the next morning till I got my morning blue pill (a number 10 Valium) and was relieved that nothing untoward had happened other than the crazy *Twilight Zone* chitchat. We had breakfast; some of the inmates were in their own little worlds: some were robotic, others secretive, peering around as if to catch some unseen person lurking somewhere ready to pounce on them. This was probably good for me because it convinced me that I wasn't nuts; therefore, I wasn't as bad as I had first thought I was.

Later that day, we had a group session and the doctor asked us questions as we sat in a circle around him. He didn't have a real lively bunch and he must have felt a little like a dentist, because it was like pulling teeth to get us to respond the way he would have liked. Some people were sullen, others made faces, and one guy kept looking at me and saying, "I don't like you." It was our first day together like this, and it was probably par for the course. We needed something to break the ice, and finally Doc came up with the idea for us to write an essay about ourselves or a favorite topic. This produced results and it also clearly showed where the lights were out, maybe never to be turned back on again.

That day people started uniting to a degree while trying to write, asking how to spell certain words or just helping one another in general terms. We got through the day without any major problems, just minor quibbling about missing crayons or pens.

At night the moronic chatter started up again: the bogeyman was coming to get everybody and some were singing, but this time there was also crying, and that was unnerving. One of the poor guys wanted to go home and see his mom. I guess we all did and for a while it was quiet except for the guy sobbing. Then someone started jeering, "Crybaby, crybaby," the way children tease and things erupted as people sided with "Crybaby" and those on the "meanies" side kept jeering. I had to get out of there, but I was enjoying my blue pills.

The next day, during our session with the doctor, he asked us to read our essays and we went through them. Some talked about aliens among us that were hiding and waiting, others about their pets, which prompted the cat quibblers, who started up again about who had the prettiest cat.

But there was one that took the prize, and I will never forget it. It was written by the most sullen guy in there, who was eventually shipped out to Penetang for the criminally insane. His essay and "artistic" delivery, albeit it fraught with lunacy, was what made up my mind to have a one-on-one with the doctor and get the hell out of there.

Sullen Guy told the group his story was called "Pucks to Pies" and I can remember it as though it were yesterday. His essay was about hockey and his favorite player, Bobby Orr, who went from playing hockey ("pucks") to owning pizza parlors ("pies"). He tried to explain the game of hockey as if we were from another planet, slowly describing the appearance and dimensions of a hockey net, and what a puck and a hockey stick were and their sizes. You get the picture. We were all a little uncomfortable, including the doctor. At times, when someone snickered as he read, he gave a look that chilled, which stopped the snickering immediately. I listened in stunned silence for I was in the presence of King Nut Bar, who would at times speak quietly, then loudly, sometimes leering at us and sometimes like a professor teaching a class of hungry-to-learn students hanging off his every word.

The way he read that essay—shouting, maniacally, laughing uncontrollably, and, at times, whispering eerily—was a sure testimony to his instability and unpredictability, and a thoroughly frightening experience that has stayed with me to this day. I had never witnessed such madness, and being that close was an experience I never wanted to go through again. It made me think this guy was demon-possessed. I'll bet he rated on the doctor's top-five list of all-time prison wackos. One of the things that stick out in my mind was how he said, from a quiet voice to a shout, eyes bugging out of his head and every blood vessel in his neck and forehead ready to burst, "Do you get it, pucks to pies, PUCKS TO PIES, DO YOU GET IT! HAHAHAHAHA!"

I think we all realized, doctor included, that this guy was a special piece of work and people left him alone in his own little world. I was so shaken up by the experience that at night I had a difficult time getting to sleep. My mind raced thinking about some of the madness around me. I realized that, pills or no pills, I had to leave and get into the main population of the prison. I had heard while I was in the hospital ward that we psychs would be given a hard time in the "normal" population, but I figured it was better to take my chances there than to lose my mind in the hospital and quite possibly face even graver danger such as kitchen instruments being stuck into me at night.

The doctor and I met, and he understood how I felt and even warned of the possible retribution in the OR (Ontario Remformatory), as the main prison area was called. He asked if I was sure that I wanted to go there and I told him that I really didn't belong in the hospital, that my problems were different than those of the other inmates there. He agreed with me but he also knew my nerves were fried from my drug and alcohol abuse and he thought staying in there might help me better come to grips with my straightening out. I persisted, though, and he seemed to admire my wanting to go. He had me transferred in two days. He wanted me to think about it for another day and I did and still wanted to go, so we parted ways and he wished me luck. Then, to my pleasant surprise, he said, "You're going to do all right, Danny." That made me feel pretty good because he meant it, I could feel it, and it had reassuring power. "A word fitly spoken is like apples of gold in settings of silver" (Proverbs 25:11).

I had to go, and as it turned out, it was for the best, even though I got off to a shaky start. The first night in the OR I learned how to pray fervently.

chapter ten

The OR

Sometimes this world is a cold, cold place
and you feel like you're all alone...

| From "Nobody Knows You Like the Lord" by Danny Brooks

AS I WAS LED into the main prison and other inmates sized me up, I wondered if I should have let the doctor talk me into staying in the hospital a little longer with my pills. They led me into a dormitory that held at least thirty inmates, with cots about ten across, three deep. My bed was right against the wall by the dorm entrance and that suited me just fine. I put my stuff on the bed and took a look around, not looking at anyone in particular but taking everything in. I had just got settled when we had to go for work detail in the kitchen.

I spoke when I was spoken to; said little with just a hint of a friendly attitude. My job was to mop and keep the kitchen clean. Before too long one of the main cooks from the civilian world took a liking to me because he saw that I was not afraid of work and I took my job seriously. He showed me the ins and outs of cooking and running a kitchen and told me I could make good money anywhere in the world if I wanted to take this up as a vocation. He was a decent man and had been a cook in the navy. Every inmate in there respected him because he treated us as people and not as inmates. He cut an imposing muscular physique and had many tattoos all over his arms and chest.

During that first day in the kitchen, I just tried to work hard and mind my own business, and I got a feeling that maybe everything was going to work out all right. Time seemed to pass quickly.

That night after work we went back to the dorm. I kept to myself then and during "jug up," or dinner. I went to bed and said a prayer of thanks and asked for protection, because I had been told the first night was when someone would try something on you. But the boys in the dorm had someone else marked out that night. It sickened me. About five of them had one of the guys and they abused him. He whimpered and cried and begged quietly for them to leave him alone. The guards must have heard it but nothing was done about it. I lay there in silence and steeled myself; if anybody came near me I was going to flip out—turn into a Tasmanian devil and do whatever it took to protect myself. You make up your mind to be ready and you picture yourself going crazy and fighting them off, but you still feel the fear.

The next morning this poor kid was an emotional mess and he was taken to the hospital. He didn't return to the dorm. Just as well. I felt bad for that kid but I minded my business and spoke to no one and no one spoke to me. But they were watching.

That day in the kitchen a guy from another part of the OR approached me. He told me that sometimes the guys in his dorm got a little hungry at night and if I made a few sandwiches for him, he'd give me some "tailor-mades"—slang for filtered cigarettes—not "rollies." I figured there was no harm; he didn't try and pull a heavy on me, and it turned out it was a wise move on my part. When you enter a prison, you're known by the inmates who run things there because they pay the inmates who work in the administration to furnish them with your rap sheet: what you did, how much time you got, what happened in the court, how you handled yourself, things said about you—everything.

It turned out that one of the guys on the receiving end of my sandwiches was from my old neighborhood, a guy named Mike Cooper, and we had always got along well. He was older than I was but we'd tripped together a few times at parties and concerts and had respect for one another. He was on the inmate committee and was in a position to help me shake good time. He asked if I was interested in putting a band together in the prison to perform for the inmates. Of course, I said yes, and he said, "Leave it with me and I'll get back to you in a few days." Mike was an easygoing guy and I was very saddened to hear that not long after he was released from prison he died in Jamaica of alcohol poisoning. It was because of him that I shook good time in jail.

It doesn't hurt when other inmates see you getting along with one of the prison heavies. It makes you look good and people figure you are connected and are therefore not to be messed with. In two days' time I had the go-ahead to start a band and word got out that a new inmate, a musician from the street, was looking for players. Five of us clicked in no time, and the drummer, Frank, and I were given permission to leave early from the kitchen each day to rehearse in the music room. Frank and I were more or less the leaders, so we called ourselves The Kitchen Blooze Band. In two weeks we were to put on a Friday night show and the place was buzzing about it. Sometimes bands from outside would come to perform and it gave us something to look forward to. People got really excited, and everybody would put on their best "blues" (blue jeans and shirts) and get duded up. When the Downchild Blues Band performed once, it was a very exciting time for everyone. My old singing partner Steff Remollo also performed once with his band, Jawbone, and it made me feel a little bummed out. It wasn't his band; they were great. It was just that he was leaving at the end of the night and I wasn't. I felt pretty homesick that night wondering what my friends were up to.

After about a week, the head of my dorm approached me and sat on the edge of my bed as I was propped up reading (which was a common sight; I was always reading). "How's it going, man?" he asked.

"Can't complain," I said, looking up at him.

He said, "You don't talk too much. Don't you like talking?"

"Not really," I told him.

He smiled and said, "Danny, you're all right. My name's Boston," and he extended his hand. I shook it and he added, "I've been watching you and you're all right. You mind your own business, you're not a loudmouth, you're okay, so you can relax a little. No one's going to bother you. What I say in here goes and I say you're all right."

I said thanks, and then he asked me if I knew what people in the dorm had nicknamed me. I had no idea.

"They call you 'the prof' because of all the books you bring in," he said, and asked if I really read them all. I told him I did. At that time I was reading a Leon Uris novel called *Mila 18* and I explained to Boston the fascinating way the Jewish people fought the Germans and even won their respect.

Boston and I became good friends, but I still kept my guard up with him and everybody else in the dorm, and allowed myself to relax only a little. Even at the best of times in Guelph I could still feel and sense the uncertainties. People were given to doing the unexpected. That was why I was in prison.

Getting ready for our concert in the prison we rehearsed hard and diligently and had a great repertoire of Taj Mahal, Sonny Boy Williamson, Hank Williams, Jimmy Reed, Muddy Waters, Solomon Burke, and a couple of our own tunes. We were as excited as the rest of the prison population. In some ways this gig was similar to my first paying gig at the Bala Avenue Public School. There was anticipation in the air; the prison population was hootin' and hollerin', and our nervous energy peaked when we hit the stage and were announced. "Ladies and gentlemen—I mean, gentlemen!" the announcer shouted and everyone went wild. Right then we were free men caught up in a moment of glory.

We started off with Solomon Burke's "Everybody Needs Somebody to Love." The place went wild and by the end of the show no one in our band could do wrong in the eyes of the prison population. In a sense we were prison stars.

I was asked to join the inmate committee and was given the roll of picking the TV show lineup for viewing and, of course, voting on other inmate issues. Just like that, overnight, I was allowed to go almost anywhere in the prison. Even most of the guards liked me. We were already getting ready to put on more shows. I was allowed to have more harmonicas brought in and was trusted to keep them on my person. I still have trouble believing it.

Never in my wildest dreams could I have imagined that jail was going to treat me so well and that I was going to have such an experience as this. I will make this perfectly clear; it was only because of God's providence and mercy. I knew it then, even though I had only a "foxhole" type of religion, named so for the prayers in wartime uttered only in times of peril. I look back now and see how He protected me.

Even the prayer of a person who is really just using God has power. He knew when I got out of jail that I was going to put Him on the back burner, yet He delivered me nonetheless. Amazing grace.

THE POWER OF LOVE

Make a blind man see, a lame man walk, deaf begin to hear and the dumb begin to talk about the love, the power of love...

| From "The Power of Love" by Danny Brooks

As the newly appointed member on the inmate committee and given free reign to pick the TV shows for us to watch, I went about my new task studiously and wanted to pick shows that everybody would like. One show I picked just because I had a crush on the pretty actress playing Marcia, the oldest sister on *The Brady Bunch*. On the first night, pandemonium broke out among the inmates in our dorm as the station identified the upcoming show, *The Brady Bunch*. Hoots of derision and "Who put this crap on?" continued as the show's theme song played. They all looked at me and suddenly pillows flew and they started razzing me. But a funny thing happened when the show started.

Silence, and I mean quiet. Everybody watched the program and even got into it. When a commercial came on the shouting resumed, "Danny, what are you trying to do to us?" (They had an image to uphold, after all.) But as soon as the program was back on: silence. As I looked around the room I saw things I'd never before seen in those guys. They were watching something that reminded them of home and more. Even the guards were somewhat surprised as they looked around our dorm and saw these violent types drawn into a family sitcom.

Every time that show came on they razzed me. "What are you trying to do to us, Danny?" But as soon as it started, you could almost hear a pin drop. Every time! And I knew it had something to do with home and the love and interaction of family members; I just didn't know to what extent until many years later, and what a revelation it was.

I didn't say anything to anybody and nobody brought it up, either, about what the show meant. When I looked around at the guys I saw quite a few misty eyes but no one dared say anything except to yell at me during commercial breaks. There is nothing like the power of love; it stays even in the hearts of criminals.

For some reason, and I'm not sure why although I have some ideas about it, the sexual assault incident that happened the first night in my dorm with the young kid was never repeated with anyone else. Our dorm became a decent place to do our time and more than a few guys whose sentences were up were kind of sad to go. I'd settled into a routine of doing my kitchen chores, rehearsing five days a week, and doing a show at least every three weeks.

I did read voraciously, too, just as Mrs. Brundage told me, and I read the Bible and prayed and wrote my thoughts. Going to jail was the best thing that had happened to me thus far, and it was exactly where God wanted me to be. I started to truly get an education through my reading. I had read in Dr. Dennis Whaitley's book *Seeds of Greatness* (one of the best motivational books I have ever read) that the word "education" comes from the Spanish root word *educo*, and it literally means to "learn within," which is what I started to do in jail. I was learning from a few authors but Leon Uris was my favorite. I've always had love and respect for the Jewish nation as Dad had always taught us to respect God's chosen. I was also improving my vocabulary and learning amazing things regarding Jewish history and even my own Jewish heritage.

Working in the kitchen I learned how to make homemade hootch, although I never made any on my own, but I helped a little, and I saw how they made it with yeast, sugar, and fruit and let it ferment in a drum, then strained it with a clean mop head. I tasted it once and it was pretty strong stuff.

There were drugs in our dorm and people had needles. Some were shooting up Novocain, a freezing agent used in dental offices. There was acid to be had as well. It was still all I could do to keep my composure because of some of my problems stemming from my past such as my "blue funks" and my paranoia. I chose somehow to stay straight; it was the only way I could do my jail time.

chapter eleven

My Time Is Up

When the storms of this world try and beat you down,
just remember the sun is always shining on the other side of the cloud.

| From "Other Side of the Cloud" by Danny Brooks

BEFORE I HAD MY major freak-out with the giant whack of speed that scared me off the needle and soured me on pot smoking as well, I would have joined in those illicit jail activities. I would have been a different person coming out of jail and I certainly wouldn't have learned some of the lessons I needed to learn while I was there. I got out of jail and still messed up for another fourteen years—and I know this may be hard to fathom—but God did reach me during this time of sobriety and I believe that the things I learned, coupled with putting a distance between me and the needle and the wrong crowd, prepared me for God's ultimate plan for my life.

I also learned something about the power of love and got much-needed structure and discipline. I learned to pray and rely on God and was able to see firsthand His making a way where there seemed no way. My experience also started me on a journey of reading that, to this day, is a thrill for me. I am never without a book to read; I never even leave home without a book in case I get some reading time. I love watching a good movie, but there is nothing that can match the movies we can see with our imagination. WOW! We are fearfully and wonderfully made! Greg Quill, music critic for the *Toronto Star*, once said regarding his songwriting that reading is the basis for his ability to turn a phrase, and I credit this time spent in jail reading as the bedrock for my writing ability today.

Christmas came and I applied for a Christmas pass and was saddened when I didn't receive it. I felt that maybe I wouldn't receive the national parole I had applied for, too, to get out on good behavior. Soon, though, the gentleman who had come on the Blue Goose with me to Guelph, and who went by the name of "Numbers" (never did find out his exact vocation, but I can venture a guess), gave me great news. He worked in the administrative offices, and told me I would receive national parole in late February. At first I was uncertain, but he assured me and also said that was why I hadn't received a Christmas pass; they were reserving it for people who would be there longer. I was very happy about this, but it also created a new problem: my mind was focused on getting out of jail, and this can cause an anxiety that makes your time harder.

Boston noticed this and sometime in mid-January of 1973 he said, "Danny, I can get you work in the tower running the coffee shop. You'll be on your own, and after serving the hacks [guards], you can do a lot of reading."

It was interesting meeting some of the guards and hearing their point of view on various subjects. Some thought the prison was cowtowing to the inmates by giving them TV and other privileges; some thought it was a decent balance, and some thought even more could be done for the inmates to help them get more education. One guard, upon noticing my books, opened up about his interests in the civilizations of 2,000 years ago. "Men were men back then," he said, "and could swing swords with one hand that we barely could even lift today with both hands." Every day he griped about the inadequacy of modern man.

One day when I mentioned some of the breakthroughs we've had in medicine, and the current modern inventions, he just lifted his hand in the air, swept it down on an imaginary fly, and said, "Ah, that's stuff we could do without—look what it's done to us. We're weaklings today, all of us!" He stormed off.

One guard told me he had taken a little flak going to see my band shows on his days off. This man encouraged me to follow my music, stay straight, and go places with my life. He assured me I could do it and mentioned a few self-help books to read. He was one of the guards who thought the system could do more in educating the prisoners. Thank God for guards who are more than just guards putting in their forty hours.

I'd been officially notified: I had about two weeks to go, and was chomping at the bit. I had one more show to do and that helped a little. One night at dinner a guy was upset that I was leaving and tried to pick a fight with me. As I said earlier, anything can happen and people can be unpredictable at times. I was told later the guy didn't really want to hurt me but instead wanted me to stay longer! This is strange love, not tough love, and in a crazy kind of way I understood where the guy was coming from.

There was a party in my dorm the night before I left. The next morning as everyone hustled off to work after breakfast, I said my goodbyes and embraced the guys in my dorm. Crazy as it sounds, I was sad leaving and it certainly gave me a weird sensation. I told everybody that I was going to return with my band from back home. Six months later we did just that and it was one of the performing highlights of my career. I still have the live tape of that performance that our bassist Alex Fraser recorded that night.

My brother Greg was coming to pick me up at Guelph and that morning when he came to the administration office to get me, the guard said to my brother as we were walking out, "This place is really going to miss your brother. It's going to be different without him."

I give credit to God who made a way for me in the wilderness, and brought me through the furnace of affliction and showed me firsthand His incredible grace and mercy. When I left through that big iron gate, the loud clang took on a different ring this time. It was the ring of freedom and of a new chapter in my life. I had spent only five and a half months in prison, had turned twenty-one, and I had learned valuable life lessons. I have never since used terms such as "being bored," or "there's nothing to do." There is so much to do and not enough time in our lives for us to be able to come close to experiencing what life has to offer. *Read*; it will give you ideas to pursue that will enrich your life.

My former pastor Dan Rogge's take on "As a man thinketh, so he is" is this: "If you can dream it, you can do it!"

part two

possibility thinking

chapter twelve

Many Rivers to Cross

Many rivers to cross, but I just can't seem to find my way over.

| Jimmy Cliff

I LABORED OVER WHAT to call the opening chapter of Part Two of this book. I started off with "New Beginnings" but thought that would be wrong. It implies that things turned out better, were brighter, and although in some ways there were bright moments, the truth of the matter and sad reality is that this marked the beginning of a long, arduous, and painful journey for too many people. I wish I could say it was painful for only me, but it wasn't. Sometimes you hear people say, "I'm not hurting anybody, it's my life, and I'm just hurting myself." Wrong! Our actions affect people in positive or negative ways. Always! I feel the pain of my past mistakes, and they weigh very heavily on me. I know I'm forgiven and I accept that, but that still doesn't erase all the wrong and pain I caused others. I am truly sorry.

When Greg and I left Guelph Reformatory that cold February morning, we stopped at a coffee shop and when Greg tried to pay for the coffee and doughnuts, I wouldn't let him. It was the greatest feeling paying for my own coffee and doughnuts and it was, in a way, my way of stating "I'm free! This is my money, my moment, my coffee and doughnuts, and I just paid for it—yes, I'm free!"

Greg took me home to visit Mom. While she had never come to visit me in Guelph (I knew it was too painful for her), she had written to me, and she bought clothes for me for when I got out. Mom was always there for me. On one visit Greg had with me in Guelph, he shared Mom's pain of my being there. Merle Haggard had a hit called "Momma Cried" and there's a line in it that says, "Turning 21 in prison doing life without parole ... Mamma cried, Mamma cried." My mom heard that song and she did cry.

Later, Greg and I caught up on things and I was set to start work again with him at the *Globe and Mail* and with my brother Bill at A. Bill's Express Moving Co. That night Greg had a surprise party for me at the apartment on Jane and Woolner. With all the people at the party, I had mixed feelings. I enjoyed the company but I was also afraid. I had trouble mixing in and part of it was this (which I didn't realize at the time): all the bad trips and the last freak-out had taken its toll on me and I wasn't the same person. I wasn't comfortable with drugs anymore because they made me feel uneasy and I guess that crowd had the same effect.

As I sat looking at everybody coming into the party my unease started to grow, until someone passed me a shot of whiskey. I made short work of it and although I wasn't a stranger to booze prior to going to jail, I got acquainted with it that night in a way that dictated my lifestyle for the next fourteen years. I was still having my panic attacks and I knew something was not right with my head, but I was afraid to approach a doctor for fear I would be locked up. I didn't know how to tell anybody what was wrong with me. I was afraid and it was a powerful fear. Nothing made sense and I suffered in silence.

After drinking that glass of whiskey, I felt a warm and burning new confidence come over me and I heard this smooth, comforting voice inside my head say, "You don't need to speak with any doctor, Danny. This is the answer, and you've found it. This will give you all the confidence you need." I swallowed that lie hook, line, and sinker, or perhaps I should say "snifter"! I drank every day to keep the demons away. Everything was fine looking at the world through rose-colored glasses, and I soon found out it was not so rosy when I wasn't wearing them.

For the next year I worked hard with Greg and Bill and even started saving a little money. Greg and I drank a lot but we still managed to do our jobs well and take care of business. Drinking for me was a way of survival and I always had to have a drink at certain times. Eventually I solved that problem by always having booze in a carry bag.

Dad was involved in real estate and Greg and I bought a four-bedroom semidetached house in Mississauga, where we moved in the summer of 1974. My bass player Alec Fraser and another mutual friend named Dave moved in with us and for the most part we had a pretty good time and got along well as four steady-working, hard-drinking bachelors. Man, did we drink. That lasted for about a year, and then Alec and Dave moved out.

SETTLING INTO A GROOVE

I've got whiskey on my mind, I got troubles I want to leave behind,
Please Mr. Bartender, bring another double on time.

| From "Whiskey on My Mind" by Danny Middlebrook

I was settling into a groove all right, working hard, playing hard and writing music, performing and keeping my sanity in check by drinking enough alcohol to remain in a comfortable buzz. I didn't realize the answer I thought I had found was in fact slowly robbing me of my faculties and fooling me at the same time. A treasonous friend indeed.

One night Greg and I were doing the *Globe* route (from one a.m. at the docks to about a six a.m. finish on the later edition. The bulldog run, or earlier edition, started at ten p.m.). We were at a large plaza in Etobicoke and we saw a bunch of black garbage bags piled up, but nowhere near a garbage bin. We checked them out and discovered new Reeboks, Nikes, and other brand-name running shoes. We did notice a large sporting goods store nearby, and figured someone had pulled a burglary and somehow left these shoes behind. We made a decision to put them in the truck (at least eight full bags), and did the rest of our run in stealth, getting jumpy every time we saw a police cruiser.

Finally, we got home and quickly carried the bags into our sparsely furnished dining room while under the cover of darkness. We opened a couple of beers and started to rummage through all the shoes and boots. We had dumped the bags onto the middle of the floor and after a while Greg said, "Hey, Danny, I'm only getting a lot of left shoes and I can't find a match." I was having problems finding a match, too. Suddenly the lights clicked on in our heads that these were store display shoes ruined in whatever way, and we had just picked up the store's garbage! We were disappointed but got a chuckle out of it. We couldn't throw everything out all at once in our area as that might raise suspicion in the local garbagemen, so we threw one bag out at a time over the course of the month. (In retelling this story later with friends it became The Great Shoe Caper, and we were asked repeatedly if we had any new shoes for sale.)

At this time I started a band called the West Side Blues Band, which featured a hot guitarist, Peter Boyko, and incredible harp player, John Bjarnason, from the original Whiskey Howl band that rivaled the Downchild Blues Band in its day. Rounded out with Ronnie Runch on bass and Eric Clipsham on drums, we had a hard-hittin', groovin', rockin' blues band. Peter Boyko encouraged me to pick up the guitar and start playing it in the band, which I did, and it paved the way regarding my songwriting. I'm grateful for his advice and support. Sadly Peter passed on recently but he will always be remembered as one of best "Telly" players I've had the pleasure to perform with. I was really getting into the blues and starting to sense that I was afflicted with something of a curse. I also called it the "Hank Williams Syndrome." I came up with a line at the time that sums up what the curse is all about. Many people in the arts succumb to this malady: "Woe unto me, for unfortunately adversity is the main ingredient to my creativity." I sought out troubles living by this credo, and justified it by being creative with it. Even though I realized I was destroying myself, I still justified it. It was easy.

chapter thirteen

Married Life

Youth, bright lights and marriage don't mix well.

| From "Nobody Knows You Like The Lord" by Danny Brooks

IN 1974 I STARTED dating a girl who would later become my wife. She was seventeen; I was twenty-three. When I met Donna we were both young, and apart from our youth the biggest thing we had in common was the party lifestyle. We started living together early in 1975 and soon after that Greg and I sold the house in Mississauga. Donna and I got an apartment in the Weston area in west Toronto and we were married in the spring of 1977. We had had the first of three children, Kyla, in 1975, a beautiful girl who has since made me a granddaddy three times. Kyla lives up in the Muskoka area north of Toronto, but we are close and have much in common. She is a very talented actor and musician. Not too long after, we had another beautiful daughter, Nicole, who is a gifted songwriter in the urban street music scene and (I may be little biased) one of the best story-telling rappers I have ever heard. A couple of years later, our son Justin was born.

In 1977, I took over A. Bill's Express Moving Co., which became our primary livelihood. I was still performing but not as much as I would have liked and I didn't go back into music full time until 1979.

Things started slowing down in the moving business and the truck was becoming too expensive to run and fix all the time. I set out to help our financial difficulties by trying to sell the goodwill of the business to one of the major van lines. I phoned a United Van Lines company called Bird's Transfer. Bird's was based out of St. Catharines,

Ontario and they were expanding into the Toronto area with a new office, under the name of D. Armstrong Moving & Storage. My call was timely as they had just acquired an office building with storage space. I met with their newly appointed operations manager and while I tried to sell him A. Bill's Express, he sold me on the idea of become a moving consultant. I told him I was a truck driver but he said I was a salesman. His name was Star Hefford, Star being short for Starriet. Star had been an army sergeant. We were like two pieces of sandpaper rubbing together, but we developed a mutual respect and worked well together. The company was so new it was just him and me, but for the first couple of weeks it was actually just me. We had an old, run-down building in New Toronto and I had to go to the corner restaurant to use the washroom facilities, as the one in the old building wasn't working and it would be a few weeks until we got it up and running.

One day a woman called the office and Star handed the phone to me. As I was earnestly selling the lady on our company, I told her of our special "coagulated" boxes, which would ensure the safety of her prized china.

When I got off the phone Star barked at me. "What kind of boxes did you say we have for her prized china?"

"Coagulated," I emphatically told him, wondering why he didn't know anything about our boxes.

"You nitwit," he said, chuckling, "it's *corrugated*, not *coagulated!* Sheesh! How do you get so many sales, Middlebrook? *Coagulate!*" He chuckled some more and shook his head. I guess I come by the Fieldsian humor naturally.

I learned a great deal as a moving consultant and it was an interesting time in my life. I was successful at it and met successful people and moved them all around the world, but primarily around Canada and the United States. I started to book corporate moves and Star wanted me to join the prestigious St. George's Golf and Country Club in Etobicoke. I told him I couldn't play golf and he said it didn't matter. He knew I had a fondness for the bottle and told me that just drinking there would be fine. Playing a rotten game of golf and losing to the operations managers of the corporations would only make them feel sorry for me, and they would make up for it by giving me more moves. Can you believe it? I can just picture some of the outlandish reasoning behind some of today's corporate strategies.

Even though I was doing well at the moving consultant business, it wasn't filling the void I felt by not pursuing my music. I started writing again, some real heavy hittin', hurtin' country tunes in the vein of ole Hank Williams and Gram Parsons, whom I considered the modern Hank. At that time Donna wasn't pleased, and she wasn't positive about my direction and the possibilities of getting back into the music business. All things considered I guess I couldn't blame her for feeling that way. I decided to enter the CKFH Radio talent search of 1978. I spent a whole year going through the process of eliminations (kind of like these Idol contests today), performing in all the top country rooms. By the year's end, I was performing at the Black Velvet Room in the now defunct Orchard Park Tavern in the Beaches (it is now a Days Inn), a top show room in its day.

On the night of the talent search finals, they had Whiskey River as the backup band, which consisted of some top session players: Al Borisko on pedal steel and John Gulley on guitar. Top luminaries in the country music field were there, including Carol Baker, who was quite popular back then, as well as Walt Grealis of *RPM Weekly*. They were to pick the top three out of the ten performers. The winner would receive $1,000, a brand-new stereo, a recording contract with a small label to put out a single, and a ride anywhere you wanted to go that night in a limo.

The excitement was mounting as they got ready to pick the top three artists. I was very nervous but although I was an alcoholic at the time I knew how to keep things in check and only had enough to drink to maintain my front as a happy-go-lucky fellow without a worry in the world.

Donna and a few other people told me I was going to be in the top three, but while I knew I had put on a good performance, I wasn't so sure. We were sitting with our friends Dennis and Wendy Russell (still dear to me today), who kept saying that I would win it all.

Any of the performers there that night could have walked home with the top spot; after all, they too had just come through a year's process of eliminating a lot of very talented people. The drumroll began and the announcer cried, "Danny Middlebrook!" and then the two other winners' names. I was tingling all over.

We had to do one more song each and it wasn't easy for any of us. I wore a dark blue three-piece pinstriped suit with a gold watch and chain crossing the vest pockets, and a black felt Texan cowboy hat. I was emulating the "Country Gentleman" I saw as a kid at the Grand Ole Opry. Fortunately, the song I performed really clicked with the crowd. I was the first to go up, and that put the pressure on the other two. One faltered from the pressure and I felt bad for him. The other, a girl, decided to do a slow number, which didn't connect with the late-night, pumped-up, and slightly inebriated crowd that wanted to be pushed into a down-home, barn burnin' foot stompin' frenzy.

After we performed, in one of those magic and exciting moments of my career, I was announced the winner. I won! It got me thinking about getting back in the business full time.

Donna and I rode home in the limo, drinking champagne. The stereo was in the trunk, I had $1,000 in my pocket, and a date at a studio to record two songs. I was feeling pretty good, quite "bubbly" in fact! Shortly after, I did the sessions, which turned out mediocre, and the "deal" fizzled—if you can call it a deal; it was more like an arrangement—and I was already back to square one. But the creative juices were flowing, leading to the big decision of getting back in the music industry full time.

MIDDLE-AGE CRAZY BEFORE MIDDLE AGE

I quit my job at the moving company…

| From "Quit My Job" by Danny Middlebrook

After winning the CKFH talent search, I was back to needing the performance void filled as I was no longer involved in performing, even on a semi-regular basis. It hurts not to perform when your heart yearns to do so.

My sales were getting better as a moving consultant, though, and it turned out I was the main reason the company was steadily increasing its market share in the long-distance moving industry. In a moment of celebration over my sales, Mr. Armstrong, the owner, said to me one day, "Danny, if you cause me to put another trailer in the long-distance pool, I will give you a thousand bucks." I did; he gave me the thousand bucks; Donna and I were off to Florida!

We drove down. I loved driving then and I still do today. It's one of the most creative times I have; there's just something about a wide open road where one can unwind and be inspired. Many of my songs have come while I was driving!

We stayed in Daytona Beach. The first night there we drove along the strip and I noticed that Little Richard was appearing that night! I had to see him; I loved this guy's music and energy. We ended up at a table almost in front of the stage. I'm telling you I was as excited as I had ever been to see a concert. Suddenly, the band walked on stage. Tension mounted in the audience. The musicians got their gear together, someone counted in, and they started playing. They were really rocking and I was about to burst, when Little Richard came running across the stage in a milk-white shiny suit and ruffled shirt. As soon as he was center stage the band stopped on the drummer's rim shot, timed perfectly to Little Richard's spin. Facing the audience, Little Richard smiled and shouted, "A wham bam a loom bam a wham bam boom, tutti fruit aw rootie …!" The place went berserk as he ripped it up. He got into it as if we were the greatest audience in the world and it was the first time he had ever played it.[3]

When we left the club that night I knew something had come over me and had changed me, but it wasn't until the following night that the metamorphosis was completed. The next night we were driving along the strip and we saw a sign that read, "Appearing tonight, Sly and the Family Stone." The band's song "I Want to Take You Higher" is still one of my all-time favorites and that groove to this day has to be one of the biggest "in the stink" grooves recorded!

I was tingling all over when we got in the club, and I couldn't believe that in two nights I was seeing both Little Richard and Sly and the Family Stone. Twenty-seven years later I still haven't seen such back-to-back performances from such watershed artists. These guys were as important to the music world back then as they are today.

Sly and the band took to the stage, and Sly seemed a little out of it but he was still able to perform. When they did "I Want to Take You Higher," something happened in my spirit. It was a soul cry from the depths of my being to get back into music full time. My eyes welled up. When I get hit by the Spirit that way I am joyful, sad, and tearful all at once. Poor Sly couldn't do another set and the band took him off stage and performed without him, but he still, along with Little Richard, convinced me to get back into the music business. With my new mission in life cemented, Donna and I walked out into the balmy Florida evening.

Later I shared my feelings with Donna and she was understandably not as certain about it as I was. When we got back home and I gave my employers two weeks' notice, they were flabbergasted and made me promise that if I ever returned to that line of work I would contact them first. Over the years and going through lean times, which has been often, I've thought of the good money I made and have been tempted to give them a call, but I've never been able to bring myself to do it. I would be making well over six figures today had I stayed. Both my parents thought I had lost it. I guess I can't blame them; how do you convince somebody of the pull that music has on your soul? [4]

I called my old friend Alec Fraser, and we put a band together with Kevin "Lightning" Higgins, whom I also affectionately called "the Higmy" because he was only a little over five feet, but he played like a giant. We teamed up with Vic D'Arcy on keyboards and Wayne Wilson on drums. We had one cookin' little band; we should have—and could have—gone somewhere. We were fusing rock, blues, and country before that was even popular in Canada.

We were playing one time in Pembroke at Pembroke Hotel and I was staying in a room where, several weeks earlier, pianist Ray Smith had left a written note of despondency in the top dresser drawer and then blown his brains out. This was not the first or last room I had stayed in where something like this had happened and the thought did cross my mind that the same thing could happen to me one day.

On this particular trip I told Alec and Kevin that I was an alcoholic. It was the first time I had openly admitted this. I also told them that I would probably die that way. I've been wrong about a lot of things, too many things, in fact, but this was the absolute best time I was wrong! That weekend, Alec asked me where I got my ideas from and I had never given it any thought before. I said, "Sometimes it's like a light coming from up above and it shines on me and the next thing you know I got this song." Was I ever surprised years later reading James 1:17: "Every good gift and every perfect gift is from above and comes down from the Father of lights."

By this time, Donna and I weren't doing so well, and our marriage finally came to a crash near the end of 1980 when I started seeing another woman. Donna and I didn't really have much by then, but I will not make excuses; I was wrong to do what I did. We did try and patch things up on a few occasions but that never lasted for very long. It was during this time that Justin was born. Justin grew up to be one of the nicest kids you would ever want to meet; then he hit a bump in the road and got into trouble and ended up in jail, like me. Now he's sorting out his life and is learning that he has a natural talent in stonemasonry. Like Nicole, Justin is one hot rapper and I believe one day will be known for his talent. The song "You Won't Show" on the *Soulsville* CD is about Justin. It is one of the worst feelings in the world, knowing you shortchanged your children. Yes, I am forgiven today by God's grace and mercy, but that still doesn't erase what I did. We don't see each other that often but we have patched things up and I look forward to us drawing even closer and believe we will.

chapter fourteen

Road Stories

Old wheelin' willie had the pedal to the metal to hit Chicago on time...

| From "Carolina Shine" by Danny Brooks

AROUND 1980, our new band was performing at the "Great Canadian Chili Cook-off" held in the Milton Fairgrounds, a town west of Toronto. It was styled after the big one in Terlingua, Texas where folks such as Willie Nelson, Waylon Jennings, and other "outlaw" country artists of the day performed for the "Chiliheads," who had started this zany tradition there in 1967. Today I am friends with and write with Will Callery who was on Willie's Lone Star label and performed at this festival with Willie. He also wrote one of Willie's biggest songs, "Hands on the Wheel." He has an amazing story and I am encouraging him to write it.

Our good friends Dennis and Wendy Russell and Lone Star Bob knew the people putting on the event and had landed us the gig. We performed on two flatbed trucks, and to get us out of the sun the good folks at Molson's provided a beautiful air-conditioned trailer full of their cherished product. We were loyal, defiant "Molson men"—that day, anyway! There were at least seventy-five entrants in the chili cook-off, and Mr. King-Snozz himself, Eddie Shack, one of the hockey greats from the sixties, was one of them. I took it upon myself to taste a little from as many of the contestants as possible, as I figured it was part of my paid duty. It was not a good mix: playing in the hot sun (there was no tarp over us), drinking cold beer in an air-conditioned trailer, and then stretching our stomachs to the limit with chili made from buffalo, deer, moose, rabbit, cow, snakes, various birds, and so on. I literally had a dead zoo in my stomach.

Alec had nine relatives visiting that day from Scotland and they wanted to see "wee Alec" and his band. During our second performance I lost all that great chili. Trying to be discreet I turned my back to the audience and released the food between the gap of the two trailers, then urinated to wash off the mess. I returned to the mic and finished the set. Alec wondered what his relatives had thought, and to his surprise they told him, "Alec, that lad Danny is something else, he can really sing, he's quite good." Either no one had noticed or all those close up were in the bag too.

THE HOWLING MUMBLE

Sometimes you just have to go for it.

| My brother Bill

I also did some gigs with the legendary David Wilcox. He was a real gentleman, and I thoroughly enjoyed my time spent with him. He had a great sense of humor, and will remain one of the most distinctive characters I have ever met, as well as one of the greatest guitarists on the planet. Back then, Alec gigged with him often too. David was rather fond of his stimuli then and on many occasions he would ask me to sing when he needed to. (Today David is clean and doing well and I hope to partner up with him again some day.)

It was a case of the blind leading the blind; I was just as bad as he was. However, I was more adept at the "howling mumble" than he was, which is the fine art of singing nothing but twisted vowels, purporting poetic significance. Hence "the howling mumble," which is mainly used for when the lyrics escape you or you just plain forget where you are, who you are, and what you are doing. It was a good thing that I became a master of the howling mumble, as a state of confusion would often take its sudden grip on me. Bob Dylan was good at the technique, too. It was not a talent appreciated by the lyric police, who were listening intently to the songs they knew. They always made a point of coming up to you afterwards and letting you know the error of your ways, and that they found it off-putting, as my British friends would say. Then they would proceed to tell you the right lyrics. I remember Alec looking at one of these people one night and saying something like, "Oh, shut up, have you nothing better to do with your time than to interfere with artistic expression?"

KINDNESS AT THE JUNCTION HOTEL

Can't judge a book by looking at the cover.

| John Hammond

I remember I was hustling my music around downtown Toronto and stopping at various record label, management, and publishing companies and some booking agencies. Donna and I were separated but it was my day to have the girls, so I had Kyla and Nicole with me, who were eight and four. We did a lot of walking, only using the bus and subway system sparingly, as I was low on funds. I remember the girls telling me they were hungry. We were walking up Jarvis and came to the Junction Hotel on the southeast corner of Jarvis and Gerrard Streets. It was what some folks would call a seedy joint, but it has been my experience to meet some real people in places like these. We walked into the restaurant and the woman behind the counter sized us up. Figuring out people in a flash would have been this woman's talent due to the neighborhood we were in. She must have noticed our tiredness and the hungry looks on the girls. She would have noticed how sweet and beautiful they were, too; possibly they reminded her of her grandchildren. She would have seen the resigned "up for grabs" look on my face. As a matter of fact, that day gave birth to the tune "Up For Grabs" in which I sing a line that poignantly says, "…this weathered old heart ain't for sale no more, it's up for grabs."

I was beaten down and I felt like throwing in the towel. I would have accepted any deal, no matter how bad, and that's pretty bad, but sometimes life can get you down. I knew I had enough for the bus fare home and for one plate of fries and a Coke to split for the girls and a coffee for me. I placed our order. She told me the amount and I counted out my change. I had 25 cents left.

Our order came with another waitress. We received three large plates of fries, two large Cokes for the girls, and my coffee. I told the waitress there'd been a mistake, but she assured me that no mistake had been made and went back to waiting tables. I walked up to the woman I'd given the order to and told her that we had received more than I'd ordered. I saw a mother's heart shine through those eyes set in the hardened face she'd developed over the years of service in a hard neighborhood. She smiled and said, "Yeah, I know," and offered no more explanation. I smiled back and thanked her and walked back to the table, a little misty-eyed, I'll admit.

As we ate and talked and the girls looked around the place, I thought about the predicament I was in. I had no money—the gigs were sparse at that time—I had a failed marriage, I felt like a rotten dad, and I was thinking about selling out.

Taking the bus back to Weston, I vowed that one day I would make it and provide for my children and set them on strong financial ground. I am still working to that end, but with over 500 songs written I am getting closer to making it a reality.

Those who aren't familiar with the music business see a musician perform and think he's just having fun and living out a hobby. Many times I meet people who ask me, "So, what else do you do besides this?" and I tell them this is what I do full time. They look thunder-struck and say, "This is all you do? You don't work? You don't have a real job?" I remember the look of shock when I enlightened one of these people by telling them about the hours of rehearsal, the hours on the phone trying to get gigs because they don't fall out of the sky, the hours of songwriting, constant making of demos to shop to labels, and, in general, running a band and a business. An eighty-hour work week is nothing. In his book, Quincy Jones tells of the time he was asked, "What does it take to make it in this business and what is it that you see in this type of person?" Quincy said that the people he saw making it in the business had both work ethics that made them seem "possessed," and natural abilities with endless reserve.

All business is tough and competitive, but you would have to give the nod to the music business as the toughest and even cruelest busi-ness out there. The regulations in the general workplace in society do not apply in the music world. Artists and record executives alike are dumped unceremoniously all the time in ways that would never happen in the regular workforce. The late Hunter S. Thompson's description of the television industry has frequently been applied to the music business. He summed it up as "a cruel and shallow money trench, a long plastic hallway where thieves and pimps run free, and good men die like dogs."[5] (There's also, subsequent writers have added humorously, a negative side.)

LONDON, ONTARIO

You think you found a good friend because they treat you nice,
take away your dignity with a heart as cold as ice.

| From "Tested Tried & True" by Danny Brooks

I was very busy in London, Ontario from '82 to '85. It was the last real musical period before I went into rehab in early spring of '87. In many ways I met my Waterloo, as the saying goes, down in London. The name of our band then was Middlebrook and the Wasters and we lived up to it. My friend Johnny had a club called Saskatoons and it was a rocking hangout, busy all the time. The first time we walked in with our gear, Johnny grabbed our booking agent by his tie, dragged him across the bar, and said, "What are you doing booking these clowns in my room, they look like the five stooges!" "Wait till you see them play," our agent said. Johnny told him that if we weren't good he was going to kill him. The agent had a few stiff belts of whiskey.

The reason for Johnny's outburst was this: we didn't wear rock clothing or have the trappings or looks that most rock bands had cultivated. I walked in with no front teeth and looking very much the hungover drunk that I was; Vic was taller, a little on the heavier side, and looked like Larry Fines of the Three Stooges; the "Higmy," Kevin Higgins, was all of five feet; and then there was our beanpole drummer and the one rocker look, Alec, because he had a leather jacket and wild, long hair. Now, to be fair to all of us in the band, we did have a stage look when we came on to play and a band looks much different in full performance mode. When we took to the stage that night we rocked. A band will sink or rise depending a lot on the front man. Energy and commitment can be contagious and I was a fireball. One entertainment writer there referred to us as "The Explosion." This became a name we would perform under for a while, until we basically imploded.

I love walking onto a stage, picking up my guitar, going to the mic, and then letting it all out. It's confession time; you lay your cards on the table—no BS. It's as real as real can get and is as serious to me as being on my knees before my Maker, which is a position I now take before every gig.

In no time flat we had Johnny's place rocking and I was jumping so hard on the front part of the stage that I went through it. My leg went down a foot and a half, and I jumped back up and went through again, and people just loved it. I got the notion to bust up what was left so I at least had an even surface. Pieces of wood flew all over the place, and the crowd thought this was just great. By the end of the song, the cheers were deafening.

To my surprise the person who loved it the most was Johnny. At the end of our first show he called the band over and said we could have whatever we wanted, on the house. That night after our performance he cooked up steaks and we partied till early morning. He wanted us to play exclusively for him, in London, and hired us on a fairly regular basis.

"Waiting for Your Ship to Come In" is a song I wrote based on Johnny; I could write a whole book on my experiences with this man. He had quite a life and was one of the hardest characters I have ever met but also one of the most genuine. He was fearless. Once, I thought the jig was up when he challenged eight bikers during a card game, which made them reach for their guns. [6]

Johnny was raised by Mennonites as a young teenager and knew all about salvation. Prior to that, his upbringing had been one of incredible hardship by a man who was a trained assassin for the military during WWII. Many years after our experiences together he called me early one morning on the CTS show *Nite Lite*, a late-night call-in show, and we prayed together. Yes, God can touch the hardest of hearts.

CITY HALL / THE HAWK'S NEST

Sometimes this world is a cold, cold place and you feel so all alone

| From "Nobody Knows You Like the Lord" by Danny Brooks

One night we were performing with Long John Baldry in a club called City Hall, then partially owned by Rompin' Ronnie Hawkins (hence the upstairs room's name: The Hawk's Nest). Poor Long John; we opened up for him and we ripped it up. By the time he went on stage the crowd wanted to be rocked again. Long John was performing solo and if it had been him at the beginning of the night, it would have worked, but not this night. The crowd was yelling to bring us back on. To Long John's credit, he was not put off and called for us to join him. We worked well together, connected with the audience, and got an encore. Later, Long John ordered a round of Heinekens with a shot of whiskey for each of us. Sadly Long John passed on in July of 2005 at sixty-four and is missed by all who appreciated his sincere and direct approach to the blues.

That night, I met Tracy, with whom I would have a love-hate relationship for about two years, which almost destroyed both of us. For every heart I had broken along the way, I was paid back, with interest, and it probably looked good on me. I didn't see it that way back then, of course.

Over time I was becoming more of a mess, getting into fights and drinking heavily. I once overdosed on pills and woke up two days later in a different city. I had no idea where I was. When I finally got back my faculties, I returned to London only to work on losing them again.

Johnny was bringing in girls from Montreal as he had a license for strippers and he figured it would do me good to go up to Montreal with him on business. I went. The whole weekend was a blur of cocaine and booze and craziness. I had been snorting cocaine off and on since 1980 but booze was my choice of drug—it was my lifeline and kept me from cracking up. Why I started doing cocaine is a mystery because it only added to my "blue funk" periods; it's an upper, like speed, and causes paranoia. Maybe I was thinking I could capture the old buzz without going through the process of the needle. Still, I could do without cocaine and the Valium but I could not do without my bottle, my treasonous friend; it was with me at all times.

THE TALBOT INN CRAZINESS

So many nights alone in my room,
waiting for someone to take away my gloom…

| From "I'm Blessed" by Dennis Keldie

Tracy worked as a waitress at the Talbot Inn, an old, run-down place where I performed many times. This was not a five-star hotel and there had been talk for years about tearing it down. Today it no longer exists.

One night Tracy left the club with some other guy. She and I were in a constant state of breaking and making up, and I didn't take her leaving with him very well. I was staying in a run-down part of the hotel at the time, and I destroyed about five or six of the rooms. After that night they were never used again. The dust was so thick from all the walls I had torn down that when the manager, Brian, arrived in the morning, the dust had filtered down to the main floor and he wondered where it was coming from and what was going on. He came upstairs and found me sprawled out on the floor. He woke me up with a long pole, not knowing what to expect. I came to with a 40-pounder in my hand, maybe an ounce left in it, and I had a mouth as dry and sandy as a desert floor. It seemed as though I was looking through a fog at someone vaguely familiar.

My eyes were full of dust and I heard a voice say, "Danny, did you do this? What happened?"

I looked at him sheepishly because I realized what had happened and why I had done it. All I could say was, "I'm sorry, Brian."

Brian had compassion because he knew about my alcoholism. He told me to wash the dried blood off my hands and to get them looked at. I have scars and odd-shaped knuckles to this day from that period in my life. I've hit cement walls so hard that I've fractured one hand and some fingers.

At one point I tried to quit drinking and drugs cold turkey. I was sick for days and could barely move off the couch. After about the fifth day I was climbing the walls, shaky and miserable as can be, and I fell back into my old ways, hanging with Johnny and getting into more trouble. I knew by now that I was in real need of help and that one day, perhaps soon, I was going to die if I didn't get it, but help was still about three years away.

Often there were periods during which I had no place to stay and on some occasions I stayed out on the streets, or crashed wherever I could. Some people were very kind and I would stay with them for periods of time when I was in their neighborhood. Without them, who knows where I might have ended up. One woman who welcomed me had two lovely little girls for whom I tried to be a good influence, but I sadly fell short. I guess I was sort of substituting them for my own two girls, to show that, in spite of my mess, they knew that I had love for them.

chapter fifteen

Me and Brownie McGee

Son, fo' a white boy, you sho 'nuff got a suntan on the inside.

| Brownie

FINALLY, BRIAN SAID, "Danny, you need help and if you want to try and kick your habits I will let you stay at the hotel for free, but you got to stay clean." I agreed because I knew he was right but also I was hurting and needed a place to stay. I was clean for three days there, going through really bad withdrawals, having the shakes, nausea, and the sweats and it's a miracle that I didn't die from convulsions, as I was later to learn. It was obvious to anyone looking at me that I had a major world of hurt. It is one thing going through withdrawals in a hospital or even with other people around, but it is very scary and incredibly lonely when you tough it out alone.

One of those nights, in the Talbot Inn's Fire Hall Room, which was in the back of the hotel and featured the best in local and international blues artists, the legendary Brownie McGee was performing, one half of the famous Sonny Terry and Brownie McGee Duo. When you get folks like James Cotton, Brownie McGee, Luther Allison, the Neal Brothers, and the locals who are preserving the history and integrity of an art form and way of life, you can't help but feel that in a room. The walls whisper to you of the people who have come through. It's as though a residue of their soul and life experiences has been left behind to mingle with the other stories, creating a library of soul sensations and vibrations. I know it may sound weird but that's how it feels to me. Everything has a voice.

The night Brownie was performing with his band (Sonny was ill), I was not well at all, but something inside me said I couldn't miss that historical moment. The impact that these two W.C. Handy Hall of Fame artists have on the folk and blues world is immeasurable. I must have had some kind of intuition, because it did turn out to be a historical moment for me. As Percy Sledge sang, "… when least expecting, fate tumbles in."

I walked into the club and sat down at the very back. I wanted to be alone and as inconspicuous as possible because of my "delicate" condition. If it hadn't been for Brownie I would have been up in my room hiding. Now I was publicly hurting. Brian came up to me and asked how I was doing. Even though I had caused him some grief over the years, Brian did like me and I liked him. He was a fan of my music and supported me and the band with gigs over the years. He caught me off guard, however, when he said, "How would you like to play and sit in with Brownie?" I looked at him, thinking he was joking, but he said, "I mean it, Danny."

Sick or not sick this was something very special. Although part of me wanted to do it and the other part knew I wasn't well or near my peak form, I reached for the incredible opportunity. I still said to Brian that I didn't think Brownie would go for it, and I wasn't too sure how well I could pull it off, but he said, "You'll do fine, just leave it with me."

Before too long the place was jam-packed, with a lineup to get in. Brownie and his band entered the room and went to the stage area to prepare for the show. I made my way over to see what kind of gear the musicians were using. I was about fifteen feet away from the stage. At this point Brian went to speak to Brownie and during the conversation Brian turned around and nodded at me. Brownie took one look at me and then looked back at Brian, saying something while shaking his head "no way." Looking back I don't blame him; after all he was a legendary professional and I was a sickly looking, lost down-and-outer. I would have responded in the same manner. I don't like it even today having someone sit in, even if they look good. If I don't know that someone is not going to be a liability, why take the chance? You invite known and proven players, simple as that. That's the professional attitude. On occasion you bend the rule, but that's very seldom.

Brian and Brownie continued to talk and their discussion became animated. I don't know how Brian had the nerve to put something like this to a person of Brownie's caliber before his show. The last thing any artist needs before showtime is a hassle. It can throw you off and negatively affect your performance. I must add that it wasn't that Brian lacked consideration for the artist, he never has; he just wanted to do something he believed would be good for all, especially for me. Brian has since, these twenty years later, booked me on various festivals and special event gigs and as far as working for event planners, they don't come any better.

By then I was uncomfortable and headed back to my seat at the back of the room. Though I was a little disappointed I was also somewhat relieved. There is something to be said about knowing where you stand. Now that I knew I wasn't performing, I wasn't on edge as much. Brian and Brownie were still talking and finally Brownie and his boys got together at the side of the stage and prepared for their show. Brian walked toward me with a bit of a smile and said, "Brownie's going to do a few numbers and then he's going to call you up." I was absolutely stunned. "How did you manage that?" I asked, and I couldn't believe what he told me. He said, "I told him I would never hire him in this room again and that he should give you a chance and that he would see why." I was happy and sick with fear and nerves at the same time.

Brownie's band started to play; they were seasoned performers who played effortlessly, setting things up superbly for Brownie's entrance. Brownie came on and the people cheered enthusiastically as though there was no place in the world they would have rather been at that moment. Even I was enjoying myself, I was sick, and on pins and needles knowing I was soon to join this legend on stage. People loved him; what were they going to think about sickly me up there with him? I was enjoying Brownie enough that I didn't care if he never called me up.

After about six songs, my heart leapt into my mouth as Brownie suddenly announced, "We have a special guest tonight, folks. Please put your hands together for Danny Middlebrook!" I noticed a few surprised looks at me as I made my way up to the front of the room and stepped up onto the low stage. Brownie asked what I wanted to do and I looked at him and the band, and said shakily, "'You're Going to Need Somebody on Your Bond' in the key of A, a mid-tempo shuffle by Taj Mahal." They knew the tune. I also caught their knowing look. They'd seen people in my predicament many times before. Thinking about it now, I guess it probably told them, "This kid ain't no wannabe," and maybe set them up to play the way I ended up singing it. I sang it as a cry out to God; I needed Him on my bond that night and probably never sang this song better before or since. Something happened to all of us on stage that night. I always look around at band members when I'm feeling the song; it's like paying respect to them for helping make the song so powerful. This night they looked back at me and I knew the look. They accepted me as one of them and that's the highest praise I could ever have received that night. I finished the song and said thank you and I turned to say thanks to Brownie and walk off. Instead, Brownie ended up having me sing another three songs.

When I was leaving, he grabbed my arm and looked at me with soulful, penetrating eyes, eyes that had seen it all, and said, "Son, fo' a white boy, you sho 'nuff got a suntan on the inside." I said thanks and he wished me luck.

His wish came true. I found myself. I found God and discovered He had been there all the time.

BERNIE SOLOMON / DALCOURT RECORDS

I've slipped on the floor of a sure thing, oh one too many times.

| From "Daddy's Got An Angel" by Danny Brooks

I went back and forth from London to Toronto, staying at Alec Fraser's place in Port Credit when I was in the Toronto region. I met Ross Munro, who became my lawyer and new manager. Ross and Bernie Solomon, owner of Dalcourt Records, came out to one of my gigs one night, and I'll never forget Bernie saying, "What are you, Danny, the Rich Little of the music industry?"

"Variety is the spice of life, Bernie," I replied.

We were constantly digging at one another but there was a mutual respect between us, and I can genuinely say I liked Bernie. There are colorful stories about Bernie being hard and so on, but I have fond memories of him. Bernie spoke his mind, and I appreciated that. Eventually I had a meeting with Bernie and Ross about recording. Ross warned me not to goad Bernie and I said, "I won't, but if he digs at me, I'm digging right back." Bernie had a wooden leg and it was said that after an argument in his office once he pulled the leg off and hopped after the person to clout him over the head with it. Makes for quite the picture, eh? I promised Ross I would not refer to Bernie as "Hoppy." Bernie often referred to me as the "toothless wonder" or other more colorful epithets depending on his mood.

We worked out a deal: Bernie would pay me $10,000 up front to publish ten songs and Ross was the administrator for those funds. We recorded the ten songs at Manta Sound (Bob Seger recorded *Hollywood Nights* there not long before our session) and the sessions went very well, as we were in good hands, and we got great performances from Michael Pyn (from Swinging Blue Jeans), Lightning, Vic and Wayne, and Jim Lawless. Things were looking good. Dalcourt had a record release celebration at a fancy hotel in Ottawa after our gig at Barrymore's, a beautiful old theater converted into an incredible nightclub.

We had a great gig and quite a celebration, although I got so high on mushrooms I had to leave to vegetate in my hotel room. "Hide" was more like it, really, because I went into one of my "blue funks," feeling there were people lurking in the shadows ready to spring out of nowhere to do me harm. I was like the nut bar back in the Guelph Reformatory's hospital ward who was freaked out about the bogeyman.

My blue funk periods were terrifying, and I say this now, remembering, even after putting all those years behind me and having been healed. People who suffer from this malady need understanding and help. I do have some reminders of those days. They mirror the Apostle Paul's thorn in his side, for when he asks God to take it out, God says, "My grace is sufficient …" (2 Corinthians 12:9). Like Paul's thorn, my reminders are to make me never forget from where God has brought me, and so I can relate to others with relevant understanding.

We went back to Toronto the Sunday afterwards. I felt the future was looking really bright. Hot Toronto guitarist Dominic Troiano (Mandala, James Gang, Guess Who) was the A&R representative for Dalcourt Records and he advised me to purchase the Tokai copy of the Fender Stratocaster guitar. The Tokai was such a great replica of the Stratocaster that Fender sued, lost, and then bought the company. I feel sick to think that I traded that guitar in to beef up my PA system! [7]

TORPEDOED

It's going to take a miracle to melt this Missouri heart of mine.

| From "Daddy's Got An Angel" by Danny Brooks

On Monday morning I woke up and shook the cobwebs out of my head. The phone rang. It was Ross Munro, who asked if I had read the newspapers yet that day. I hadn't and he said, "Take a look and call me back." I went straight to the entertainment section, figuring there would be a review and press release for our upcoming Dalcourt Record release. I found no such article and called Ross back. "Go to the front page," he said. So I did. There was a heading about the Cadillac Fairview Apartments being sold three times in one week for $200, then $400, then $600-odd million dollars. I asked him what that had to do with us. "Don't you know, Danny?" Ross asked. He told me that Lenny Rosenberg from Greymac Trust was Bernie Solomon's cash pipeline and since the government had now frozen Greymac's assets because of their part in this real estate fiasco, Delcourt was forced to cut corners. I was one of those corners.

I was stunned and numb. I couldn't believe it! Every time I got close, something happened to take the wind out of my sails. I went on a bender for a week—and I mean the bender of all benders. I was the perfect picture of drunken oblivion for an entire week. I felt as though my world had caved in and there was absolutely nothing more for me to do.

After my week-long bender I tried to deal with my situation the best I could, but I was sinking fast. Then I hooked up with a gentleman named Patrick Johnson and entered a new chapter in my life, one in which God made me open my eyes to the big change that was just around the corner.

chapter sixteen

Me and Mr. Johnson, 1985–1987

Sometimes we're all runaways, running to be free.
But I stopped running when I realized I was being chased by me.

| From "Come Home" by Danny Brooks

JUST PRIOR TO MEETING Pat Johnson, it finally sank in that my relationship with Tracy was not a healthy one and I brainwashed myself to be angry with her and to completely despise her. I would never think like that today but at that time it was the only way I could survive and give myself the distance needed for healing. That's how I thought, then: learn to hate to overcome love lost in order to love again, if there ever would be such a time.

Soon I bumped into an old friend, Uve Volkner (who died of heroin complications in 2001 at the age of forty-nine), and we started to hang out and party and reminisce about old times. One night he took me over to Pat Johnson's place where we spent the night drinking and carrying on. Pat was an interesting man and we hit it off well—he was a lover of the Fieldsian sense of humor—and if misery needed company, then we needed each other.

Uve and I crashed at Pat's and in the morning Pat asked if we would do a beer and liquor store run for him. Uve and I obliged and off we went after our morning beer. That day I got to know Pat a lot better and he found out I was not living anywhere in particular. He told me I was welcome to stay the week if I wanted; I ended up staying almost two years!

I become somewhat of a nurse for Pat; he was in the advanced stages of alcoholism. He was jaundiced and a hemophiliac because of alcohol abuse. In the later stages he developed what is called "wet brain," a condition that causes your body to reproduce the beer you drink so that having one beer is like drinking three or four. Pat had already been told that he was going to die in a few years, and he had outlived the doctors' predictions. But he moved around like an ill seventy-year-old man, slow and unstable in his movements. He was only in his mid-thirties.

Pat had been active with folks who were involved in international trade, and he had "retired," so to speak, because of his ill health. One day some of these people paid us a visit, primarily to check me out as they had heard Pat had a guy staying with him. I guess they thought it important to see who I was and what I was about. I could feel a certain vibe in the air and it wasn't a "good ole boy" vibe, let me tell you. Luckily, they came to like and trust me over the next little while. Eventually they set me up in their "trade" business on a local level.

Waking up first thing in the morning and having a beer and a vodka Popsicle was how Pat and I started off our day. Then I'd tidy up and look after doing the laundry and shopping. We watched TV, went out for walks, and I tried to keep active with my music and was still writing songs.

Our address was 666 Willard Avenue and, thankfully, we were right beside a black gospel church, which Pat and I attended Sunday mornings on a semi-regular basis to offset the demonic curse we felt because of our address. As the music spoke to us, Pat and I shed a few tears. The congregation knew we had problems but they welcomed us with open arms and even hugged us; they could smell the booze and they could see we were seasoned alcoholics, but still they made us feel wanted and important.

I think they appreciated our letting loose; at times we stood on the pews clapping, shouting, and singing. Sometimes this got a little hairy because Pat didn't have the best balance and I would have to make certain he didn't fall from the pew onto the floor, as he could easily be seriously hurt and, being a hemophiliac, could bleed to death. We were a sight to see, I'm sure.

THE FINE ART OF COMPLAINING

The bigger the complaint, the better the result.

| Pat Johnson

Pat and I had a ridiculous pastime that was both bizarre and hilarious. Pat seemed happiest when he was railing against the system and complaining: that boy loved and lived to complain. It's what kept him going and probably why he lived longer than the doctors had said he would. Society being what it is, Pat found fertile ground to launch great and lovely complaints to grow and develop.

It became commonplace that on a weekly basis large firms such as Labatt, Molson, Frito Lay, Hostess, Kraft, Sunfresh Eggs, Pepsi—you name it—dropped by with products and coupons for free goods. This was a good way for us to save money on food. It had started off as a joke that grew as we took turns calling companies using absurd, outlandish names and complaining about their products (sometimes it was legit).

We called Hostess, for example, and asked for customer service, and, when connected, we introduced ourselves as Og Ogilvey, Horatio Hornbuckle, or Arthur B. Twimble, sometimes Zerubbebel Hoople or Horton Floomberg or Olliver E. Crump, which was my preferred alias. We tried to match the voice to fit the name and sometimes there would be a slight snicker on the other end of the line. This always worked in our favor, as our feigned indignation always compelled them to look after us with an added zeal, especially when we threatened to lodge a further complaint to their immediate superior. Pat was in the zone when this took place and I remember him talking and complaining to at least three supervisors at one company, from whom we received a large box of products.

Our grievances usually included bugs, mice, or flies. The complaint that started this avalanche of Fieldsian silliness was a legit one to a certain brewery because we did find a little mouse in a beer bottle! When the representative from the company brought us a twelve-pack of beer, he saw all our empties (generally five or six cases before we

My grandmother on my dad's side: her name was Annie and she died in December 1954. This picture was taken in our backyard in 1952. She is holding my brother Bill.

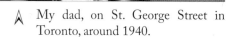

My dad, on St. George Street in Toronto, around 1940.

Mom with Dad: Julie and Bill Middlebrook, 1946.

≪ My brother Bill with his arm around me, 1954. It looks like we're on a train ride.

ⱴ Me playing with my favorite toy record player in 1956.

≪ Danny the Cub Scout beside my sister Shannon, in 1961.

Me in Fayettville, North Carolina, in 1965.

At the "wrong table," 1985.

Me at Pat Johnson's apartment in 1985, holding a poster announcing a major concert.

May 1987. I had just gotten out of the Donwood Institute from treatment for drugs and alcohol. I am holding my recovery cat named after Winston Churchill. "Churchill" was a stubby cat with six toes on each foot. He would always come to me if he sensed I was anxious, and take his leave after I calmed down.

My "tough guy" pose outside The House of Blues. in Cambridge, Massachusetts.

Jamming on the beach with Michael in 1995, in Port Dover, ON.

≪ With my mom—and best fan.

∨ Caitlin, who loves animals, is holding her pet roosters in front of our barn. It's the summer of 2000.

∨ At the CD release party for *It's a Southern Thing* in 1998 at the Silver Dollar in Toronto. That's Dennis Pinhorn on bass and Mismo Acevedo on congas.

⋀ At the Ottawa Blues Festival, in the beautiful St. Mary's Church. Amoy Levy is accompanying me on vocals.

I hope I hit the note. ➤

⋁ The CD release party for *Soulville: Rock This House*.

The Rockin' Revelators perform in Port Credit at the 2005 Southside Shuffle, Ontario's big blues fest.

My good friend and mentor, John Donabie.

My wife Debra and son Justin, backstage at the Southside Shuffle in 2006.

Richard Bell.

cashed them in), and of course was happy to service such good customers. He came by about twice a month!

It was wrong to do it, but at the time—and I know an excuse is the inside skin of a lie—we were not in our right minds. I believe some of the representatives knew this, too, especially the beer reps, but that was their job and, to be honest, they didn't seem to mind. They even grew fond of us complaining, good-natured kooks.

LARRY'S HIDEAWAY

Lonely and hungry when she left that night, another evening in the fast life,
with a borrowed smile, she might get away for awhile.

| From "Running from the Mirror" by Danny Brooks

For the most part I stayed with Pat, but I did spend time elsewhere, sometimes in London, and at a club in downtown Toronto, where I hung out with Danny K., the manager. Larry's Hideaway was a premiere underground rock room featuring the latest in bizarre or punk rock. It was also a well-known brothel to the police, and why it ran so smoothly and so long can only make one wonder.

I befriended Danny K. by performing at the club and staying to party with him on many occasions. He was funny and witty and we shared many laughs and tears together. We got along on both a business and personal level, and many nights we got talking about the Divine Purpose. Danny had been a Jehovah's Witness so we had some interesting chats.

We also kicked around a few ideas about things in the music business and he told me about an idea for doing a Woodstock show, but he hadn't yet got it together. He had been speaking with clubs and agents who'd shown a keen interest, and to other artists who were doing well "cloning" other musicians, to see if they would be interested. He was getting a good response. He told me he thought I would make a great Joe Cocker.

The area harbored a lot of old-timers who were very heavy drinkers and were at Larry's day or night. I befriended many of them, and we spent time drowning life's sorrows and finding things to laugh about in our "pickled haze" existence.

One Sunday morning at Larry's I was sitting with five or six other seasoned alcoholics watching Jimmy Swaggart (before his fall from grace). Beer in one hand, whiskey chaser nearby, all of us were in our usual state, listening with rapt attention to Jimmy preach. He was really laying it on. Jimmy could really preach.

Incredibly, Jimmy suddenly told us that it was okay to drink! We were all broken-down, lonely alcoholics in that room and we knew what booze was doing to us and that we would probably die that way, down and out—but here was this world-class, famous preacher telling us it was okay to drink! We were glued to the TV.

Then Jimmy shouted, "I like to drink!" The TV camera panned the stunned congregation. We were stunned, too, but in more ways than the church group. We looked at each other. Then the ultimate happened. Jimmy further confused us all over the world, shouting, "The Lord loves to drink, too!"

What was going on? Was this guy going nuts and losing it on international TV? Jimmy, still railing and looking straight at the camera, eyes bulging and jowls shaking, said in his hushed tones, "It's okay to drink, we neeeed to drink, oh hallelujah, the Lord just wants you to change brands!" This last sentence was delivered with old revival meeting fervor, and you could see the relieved faces on the TV church audience. I don't think Jimmy had brought his followers that close to the edge before. I'll bet his producer was on the verge of pulling the plug, perhaps thinking Jimmy was losing it in front of millions of people.

We were relieved, too. It's kind of funny that we hardened alcoholics didn't want to be told we were doing the right thing. You can spend a long time in denial defending your alcoholism, but there comes a time when you know that it's got you in its death grip and you don't deny it because you can't. You start to feel the pain in your liver and stomach; you see the yellow skin, the nose capillaries, the blood in your urine and stool. You look in the mirror and see only a shadow of what you were before. Drinking takes precedence over everything and anybody. There is nowhere to run anymore because you have already run the race and here you are, at the end of the line. Way beyond denial.

Jimmy kept on preaching and we watched him often, always with our eyes welling up. Like the guys in my dorm watching *The Brady Bunch* during my jail experience, no one here said a word or joked about it. I learned that God's love can reach even a hardened alcoholic; that a tear can come from the hardest of hearts. There is hope. When there is nothing else, there is always hope, because God is hope; always.

SENSE OF DOOM

It's a jungle out there; you're hard pressed to find someone who cares.

| From "Tested Tried & True" by Danny Brooks

One night after a party at Pat's and everyone had left, Pat was crashed out on the couch and I was alone, my head buzzing. I was still a little high from the blow I had done that day and my thoughts were racing. I started to tell God how sick and lonely I was. I took a few Valium and had a beer and a shot of whiskey. The last thing I did before I crashed was cry. I was calling out to God.

The next morning, I had a beer and a vodka Popsicle first thing, and then, as this more or less made me feel normal, I remembered my conversation with God the night before. I thought about it for a minute and then went on to something else, and it was forgotten until the next night.

There were mornings when I had to help Pat get in and out of the shower because his health was up and down. Several times I took him to St. Joseph's Hospital and on occasion they kept him overnight for observation, but there was really very little they could do. He was in the last stages of alcoholism; quitting then would likely have killed him due to the shock and body convulsions that result.

I started paying closer attention to Pat and I remember thinking that maybe God had put me in front of him to show me something. It had worked because I started telling myself that this was not how I wanted to end up. But I also knew that I would have to clean up in order to avoid it and that was a scary thought, too, as I had tried quitting before and knew I had quite a battle ahead. I was not looking forward to it. One of the worst feelings in the world for an alcoholic is to wake up one morning without a drink and have to face the world with the shakes, craving a drink so you can normalize. Outside of sleeping, I had trouble going over an hour without a drink and I would start getting antsy. Some mornings when this happened and there was no booze around, I would go to a Chinese corner variety store in Parkdale and buy a few bottles of bitters to take the edge off.

I remember asking myself, or maybe God asked me, what I would do if there was a radio warning of an incoming nuclear strike. Would I go to help and be with my estranged family, or would I look for the basement of a nightclub stocked with booze? I was ashamed by my choice and if I never fully realized how despicable alcoholism was, I realized it then and it rattled me. I knew I was going nowhere and that I was sick and if I didn't do something about it, soon it would be too late. I sensed an impending doom and had an unnerving vision of myself in the future as being a serious, sober person. I remember thinking, "There will be no more fun in my life. I don't want to dry up and find no joy in living by being too serious and not knowing how to laugh." It rattled me but I wasn't seeing the big picture. Yes, I would become a serious and sober person, but I would also have joy and fun among the serious moments. Life is like that. I think the Book of Ecclesiastes puts it best in 3:1–8, the verses that gave Pete Seegar the inspiration to write "Turn! Turn! Turn!" Everything has its time:

> To everything there is a season, a time for every purpose under heaven: a time to be born, and a time to die; a time to plant, and a time to pluck what is planted; a time to kill, and a time to heal; a time to break down, and a time to build up; a time to weep, and a time to laugh; a time to mourn, and a time to dance; a time to cast away stones, and a time to gather stones; a time to embrace, and a time to refrain from embracing; a time to gain, and a time to lose; a time to keep, and a time to throw away; a time to tear, and a time to sew; a time to keep silence, and a time to speak; a time to love, and a time to hate; a time of war, and a time of peace.

For me, it was time that I started thinking about getting well. Just those beginning thoughts constituted taking the right steps to a new beginning. We gravitate toward our most dominant thoughts, and the right thoughts will eventually be our saving grace. I was on my way; I was getting closer to finding the way back home.

WOODSTOCK REVISITED

I was praised for being artistically together
even though I was more screwed up than ever.

| A lesson on human nature

Danny K. finally got together the Woodstock revival he'd been talking about. "Woodstock Revisited" was a musical show put on by Danny, who was a keen wrestling observer, and he applied some of the bizarre traits of the wrestling world to help promote this show. In this musical reenactment of the famed 1969 Woodstock event, I took on the persona of famed British rocker Joe Cocker. I also added John Belushi's antics from *Saturday Night Live*, much to the delight of a crowd that was hungry for the bizarre and dangerous.

An agent had already told me I was committing professional suicide being caught up in drugs and alcohol. Then along came the Woodstock Revisited show and there I was, more buzzed out than ever, crumpling beer cans on my head and pouring beer all over myself in my maniacal portrayal as a "Belushioid" Joe Cocker. I even tumbled a few times off a four-foot-high stage using last-second on-the-spot training in stunt techniques to prevent certain injuries. To this day I find it hard to believe that I didn't hurt myself. I was a nut bar being paid to be nuts and that fostered more bizarre behavior: my Belushi–Joe Cocker character was taking on W.C. Fields traits. I was really out there. Everyone was laughing at the clown while the clown was crying inside.

Agents and other music industry people came to my dressing room, saying, "Danny, you have finally put it together, this is great, you're going places, I always knew you'd get it together," and on it went. I remember one night sitting alone by myself, buzzed out to the point that I could hear my brains "fry," a loud electrical-sounding hum with white noise. I sat there crying, wondering if everybody was nuts or if it was just me. I heard the agents' voices echoing in my mind: "You finally got it together, Danny, you're going places, Danny, this is great, Danny," and I wondered, "Can't they see I'm killing myself? I'm sick and I'm dying and nobody notices it but me. Or maybe they do and just don't care." It was a real eye-opener to human nature, I'll tell you, and in more ways than one. I needed off the crazy train; I was on my way to rock bottom and I needed to change.

part three

change is going to come

chapter seventeen

Empty Inside

We need a change, oh we need a change, a change in the way we love.

| From "We Need a Change" by Danny Brooks

I WAS DOING WHAT I wanted for the most part, but I was so empty inside. I remember calling out to God for a change. Pat and I had just moved into our third residence at High Park and Bloor, overlooking the park, and I was sitting on a park bench one day having a little talk with God. I told Him that I couldn't do it alone, that I needed someone who could love me in spite of myself and my condition, and who could help me get on the right track.

I haven't mentioned some of the parties and the crazy stuff I did under the influence, but suffice it to say, they are not things I am proud of, which is furthermore what brought me to the point of calling on God that day in High Park. I was in trouble and I needed someone who could help me. Exactly who, I didn't know; I just knew that I needed someone because I couldn't do it alone anymore. [8]

In October 1986, I got a gig at the Genosh Hotel in Oshawa and I needed to hire a sound and light man, so I called my old guy, John. A woman named Debi answered the phone. Debi had been dating John years earlier when he did sound and lights for me in the early eighties and she had also been a friend of my first wife, Donna, so I'd seen her around from time to time, and she would come to our gigs when John was doing the sound and lighting. I'd been attracted to her back then but I had never hit on her, which was very unlike me. For some reason, though, I'd developed a conscience. I wouldn't hit on a band member's woman.

Now here we were, a few years later, and Debi was on the phone. We said our hellos and she let me know that she and John shared the house, but he lived upstairs and she had the downstairs area. Well, I was messed up, but I wasn't stupid. I told Debi that I needed to speak with John but that after I was finished I wanted to speak with her again, if it was all right. She said it was.

John was no longer very active in the music world, so we talked about old times and I politely ended the conversation quicker than I normally would have, asking him to put Debi back on the line. Debi and I spoke for a while and she agreed to meet me at the Hotel Isabella the next night.

We had a good time together when we met. Debi noticed how much I drank and I noticed how little she drank. Turned out that Debi wasn't a drinker, though she'd have the odd glass of wine, and that's what she had that night.

DEBI

You are my new world girl, you are what makes it turn.

| From "New World Girl" by Danny Brooks

After that night, Debi and I saw a lot of each other over the next few weeks. This also gave Debi an insight into who and what she was getting involved with. Later on, she shared that she could see the real me through all the crud and that I was salvageable. She could still see the old me (bad) and figured that, in time, she would be able to see the old me again.

Within a few weeks, Debi moved in with Pat and me. Pat enjoyed having a pretty face around the place and I felt I had a soul mate now. Debi realized that I needed help but was careful in her approach, which is to say she was silent about it, waiting for the opportune time.

I was still doing my Joe Cocker thing in the Woodstock Revisited show and Debi and another girl became my background singers. I named them "The Cockerettes." The opportune time was fast approaching for Debi as she saw firsthand the sickness and madness I was slipping into. I did my crazy Belushi–Cocker character on stage, which was total unbounded foolishness but the crowd loved a clown and wanted more. Now that I had two women on stage I figured I needed to include them more in the act so they were not just singing. I grabbed them and swung them, and, while they were singing, came from behind on all fours and tried to crawl through their miniskirted legs, sometimes knocking them over. The crowd loved it, the promoter loved it, the agents thought I'd finally gotten it together, and I was sinking, sinking, sinking.

Many times Debi saw me being sick during my comedowns after these shows. I also shared my thoughts with her regarding the distorted agents' viewpoints. She saw our lifestyle at Pat's and how we drank. She knew the time was ripe to speak… and I listened.

It would be months, however, before I would even consider getting help. My opinion at that time was that people who were supposed to be in a position to help people needed help themselves. We tried to get help a few times from one major addiction center, but we didn't have much success with them, as they didn't seem then to realize how much danger I was in and continued to ask questions to which the answers were blatantly obvious, and then failed to act. I was very sickly, a real mess, and truth be told, I probably should have been rushed to a hospital. But protocol seemed more important than my rapid state of decline. I admit it was my fault for becoming such a mess, but I say now to those in positions to help: in these cases, look into the eyes, the window of the soul, not at your textbook questionnaires.

Anyone with experience and heart should know a bona fide seeker when they see one. After all, nobody pushed me on them. I was a walk-in; I was by then desperately seeking help, for crying out loud! It angers me to think of it even now because I almost did die, and someone more concerned with tidy, institutional thinking would have been partially to blame. When I was finally admitted into the Donwood, I was diagnosed as being near death because my heart was going to give out.

chapter eighteen

The Painful Beginning

Sometimes this world is a cold, cold place and you feel so all alone.
When the chips are down and you have no place to go
Nobody knows you like the Lord!

| From "Nobody Knows You Like the Lord" by Danny Brooks

DEBI AND I TOOK A lot of walks in High Park. We traveled with the Woodstock Revisited show and went to Ottawa, London, and Windsor. For the most part Debi was keeping an eye on me and we were getting along very well.

Concerned for my health, Debi finally got me an appointment with a family doctor, who also assisted her in getting me an appointment at the Donwood Institute for Addiction and Mental Health. The doctor advised Debi to take me off the hard liquor but to keep me on the beer, saying that if I was to try and stop everything at once, I would go into convulsions and could die.

Over the next two weeks prior to the Donwood appointment, I did suffer from convulsions, which left me in a state of absolute confusion, and even blackouts. One day Debi came home from work and found me sitting at my desk with a bleeding cut on my nose. I was chewing cigarette butts and blandly staring out the front window overlooking the park. Debi called to me and I was unaware of her until I noticed her concerned face in front of me, asking me what I was doing eating cigarette butts. I had no idea what she was talking about. It was very frightening for her. Eventually I came around but I was still confused regarding what had happened. There were times during that period when I would feel as though I'd been judo-chopped on the back of my neck and my body would jerk.

Debi arranged for an appointment at the Donwood, which did not go well. I was already soured by my previous appointments with the other clinic and, coupled with being nervous and scared, I was on edge, to say the least. When I arrived at the Donwood, the admittance officer said to me, "You've been drinking, haven't you?" I said yes, and of course she said that I was not supposed to be drinking. I lost it. "Look, I'm an alcoholic. I drink. If I could prevent myself from drinking, I wouldn't need you, and I wouldn't be here now, would I!" Upset, she told me that she didn't like my attitude and that I had better leave. I was escorted out of the clinic.

I don't understand some people, purported experts who deal with addictions every day yet don't understand the mindset of a messed-up substance abuser. Serious substance abusers are not rational; thus, nice, tidy little meetings are probably not going to happen. Expect a little shit to go down; we're messed up, not dressed up for Sunday school! If they can't handle the unexpected, or the emotionally charged and frightened people, then they should find employment working with plants in a greenhouse or in a library, where most people have it together!

Needless to say I stormed out, escorted. I was steaming. I figured, "That's it. If this is what getting help is all about, forget it. They don't know what they're doing anyway, so I'm going to have to figure out something on my own." Debi came running after me, told me to wait in the car, and then went back to the center. She was able to talk them into letting me go back in another two weeks by convincing them that I would be all right by then.

Two weeks went by and while I was trying my best to stay off hard liquor, I wasn't totally abstinent; I just didn't have any at the house where Debi could see me. For my next appointment, I was nervous, but not as bad as I had been earlier, though I was hoping not to see the same admittance officer again. I didn't; this time I met with the doctor who was the head of the clinic. He knew the score and I soon found out why. He had been a heroin addict for fifteen years, a cocaine addict for two, and a Valium addict for another two years. This was while he was a practicing surgeon at one of the major Toronto hospitals. This may sound unbelievable, but some can go on for a long period of time maintaining their habits while still doing complex procedures. There are many people from all walks in life who are in this very state.

This doctor was very congenial and discussed my background regarding what I had done and how long I'd be using. Similar to the simple but effective wisdom of Solomon, he wisely tested me, saying, "Danny, how about you come in here for the daytime classes and go home at night? You can carry on this way for the duration of the month and get everything sorted out this way." He said this as though there was no major problem at all with me. I looked at him with desperation and determination. "Doctor," I said, "there is no possible way I can do it like that. I will abuse this method. I need to get away from everybody and everything; I need to hide away. It's the only way I think I'll kick it. If I go home at night, I might as well not come here at all because I *will* abuse this situation." He'd got the answer he wanted from me.

Time and beds were at a premium and he could see the look in my eyes, the desperate hunger. He gave me my entrance date, shared a bit on what to expect, and we shook hands. I had two more weeks before I was admitted. It is not an overnight process and sadly too many do not make it.

I was taking one of the biggest and most important steps I had ever taken in my entire life. I guess in some ways I knew the import but not to the extent I know now. Everything about me now—my faith, my family, my music, my writing, absolutely everything—is directly tied to it and exists the way it does because of that one decision and giant step. *Get help!* You can only get the help you need by first admitting you need it or it will never work.

THE DONWOOD

I've known a lot of people, but the best of all
is the love of a friend when you've had a fall.

| From "Payback Time" by Danny Brooks

First Debi, then the folks at the Donwood. I never would have made it without them, and I am a strong-willed person. I have to be; I'm in the music business. But the bottom line is, you need people in your corner—good people—or you will not succeed at anything. The best people are those who love you and care about your well-being. That is what I got from Debi and the folks at the Donwood.

The night before going to the Donwood I became very anxious. I had a fear of the unknown, the kind I got before going into jail years before, and I was starting to think and feel as though I was going into a sort of prison. I had been good those two weeks and had stayed off the hard liquor, but I'd gotten a mickey for the night and morning before going into the Donwood.

Debi found my mickey of whiskey hidden under the kitchen sink behind the cleansers and other assorted junk we kept under there. Of course, she felt it was her duty to pour it down the sink, so she did just that and said nothing about it to me. That night I went looking for the bottle. I was freaking about the next day and wanted a stiff belt of whiskey. My plans had been to have half that night and finish the rest before entering the Donwood the next morning.

When I discovered it was gone, after a frantic search, I lost it. And I don't mean a petulant little fit. I literally lost my mind. I snapped, simple as that. I charged into our room, which was adjacent to Pat's, grabbed Debi by the throat, and started strangling her. Her eyes were bulging; she was terrified. "Why why why, how could you do this, you shouldn't have done this!" I hissed at her.

I don't know how long I was choking her but something stopped me because I let her go and she collapsed. Suddenly, I realized what I had done and I picked her up, crying, telling her how sorry I was. We hugged and she said, "It's all right, I'm sorry, too. I should have told you I'd thrown it out before you started looking for it."

I am extremely lucky I did not get put in a jail cell that night, or maybe even a padded cell. I shudder now, thinking how my life would have been changed forever in that instant. I might have killed the one person in the world who was there for me, to help me. Where would I have been after that if God Himself hadn't stopped me from choking her to death?

The next morning Debi had me packed and ready to go. It was like a small move. I had two guitars, a large bag and a small bag, and a briefcase full of music and songs. Greg Johnson, a friend we knew from the music industry, drove Debi and me that morning to the Donwood. I had had a couple of beers with Pat that morning and, while part of him was happy for me, I knew he was sad to be losing his comrade in arms.

The drive to the Donwood took about fifty minutes, but it seemed much quicker than that. Part of me was worried that I was going to lose ground in the music business—that I was going to miss my break, or be perceived as damaged goods. In short, I was afraid it was all over for me. This lie is what keeps a lot of people from taking this important step. But it's the best thing to admit your problems. You're not perceived as damaged goods but, rather, as a brave fighter. You are going to get your break when you are ready for it—with a clear head. *Breaks happen when a clear head acts in ways that make way for the break to happen.*

We pulled into the Donwood parking lot and I immediately noticed some strange but familiar behavior. A guy had his trunk open and was glancing around stealthily. I made my way over because I knew what he was doing and wished to partake. I said hello and next thing we knew, we were sharing his bottle and a couple of Valiums. Debi, rubbing her neck, said nothing about my tippling but made a comment about the Valium.

I hugged Greg and he waited in the car for Debi, who walked me up the front steps and into the admission area. I was processed and was asked to wait. Debi hugged me and told me she loved me and would call and visit when she was allowed to.

As I watched her walk out that door, I felt alone, really alone, more than I can ever remember feeling before, and I wondered what life had in store for me. This was the day the laughter died in sorrow. I have always been upbeat and as a kid I was a thinker of possibilities, a motivator with a sense of definite purpose long before I even knew what that meant. I could soar with my mind, but at this particular moment, surrounded by all my earthly possessions—two guitars, two bags of clothing, some books, and a briefcase of songs—all I knew was despair and a resigned feeling that I had failed.

After Debi left I sat and looked around the room. I thought about leaving and going to see someone in the city for a drink, and then I looked at all my stuff. Suddenly, a light came on. Debi must have anticipated that I might do that very thing and had purposely saddled me down with all my things. She knew how attached I was to my guitars, songs, and books and that I would never just leave them because I couldn't live without them, either. With grudging admiration I reflected on her cunning and stayed put. Finally, my name was called and a friendly nurse helped me to another holding area in the building where I was processed again, this time into "Happy Valley." Whoever came up with that name had a warped sense of humor. The so-called Happy Valley became my nightmare.

HAPPY VALLEY

I cried out Jesus, won't you help me please...

| From "Nothing Like the Name of the Lord" by Danny Brooks

My first few days there, there was not one happy moment in Happy Valley; I was scared, vomiting, and very shaky. I came across some old notes I took during this time and I found that I had contemplated hanging myself from the shower bar on my first day.

To this day I don't know why I hadn't impressed upon the doctor who admitted me into the Donwood my more than casual use of drugs such as cocaine and Valium, as this played havoc with my (un)Happy Valley experience and my overall recovery. The only reason I can think of for why I didn't tell the truth was that I had been more frightened by waking up to no booze than anything else, so that's where my focus was. I was asked if I used other drugs but I had quickly dismissed it, saying I had taken them but only very occasionally; booze was my main thing, I maintained, as it was the one I couldn't live without. Be that as it may, that still didn't mean I wasn't affected by the other drugs. Booze was my closest treasonous friend, but it wasn't my only one.

When I was admitted to the Donwood, I had bleeding ulcers, a triglyceride count in my blood of 5.9 (1.8 is normal, 3.5 is heart attack time) and my liver was very swollen. I weighed about 180 pounds. (At five-foot-six, 150 pounds was normal for me. What a difference from my speed freak days when I was 85 pounds.) I was told to refrain from any type of strenuous activity. I probably should have stayed two months instead of one.

On my first day there, there were about ten of us and maybe half a dozen who had been there a few days or more. Generally you were in this "valley of glee" for a week and it was where you experienced your comedown before entering the main program and clinic. This first day was a little more bearable because I was still a little buzzed from the booze and the Valium I had taken in the parking lot and from whatever else had been hibernating in my system in the last little while, but as the day wore on … oh boy. It was *not* happy time in the valley, let me tell you. To their credit, the staff tried to ease us through the next few days. For me it was four days of pure hell and only during the three to four days after that, albeit shakily, I did have some moments of levity and a faint hope that I might make it after all.

The first night was frightening; I sweat a lot and I thought I had wet the bed. They had given me some Valium earlier and that helped a little. I woke up the next day and I was already starting the harder part of recovery, during which the body starts to rid itself of the drugs and booze it's been used to, depends on, and is now deprived of. It was as though my body was saying, "Aw, come on, feed me, give me what I need, why are you doing this to me?" It was going through shock and my nerves were shot.

I spent that day very quiet and sullen and tried to grasp what was going on. It was not easy. There seemed to be decent people around me, which was not what I had imagined. I had thought this place would be like jail, with the hard types; it was anything but. I was surrounded by professional people, for the most part, from a couple of nurses and high-powered sales and business people to an undercover cop from Calgary, a doctor, and some writers and tradesmen. People were friendly and I tried my best to be friendly back, but it was an effort.

That night things were worse and I had nightmarish visions and hallucinations and had to be sedated. I went through the next day on shaky ground. People had the good sense to kindly leave me to myself. I floated on a stream of fragmented kaleidoscopic thoughts.

It was on about the third night that all hell broke loose for me. I had nightmares and I felt as though I was in water. When I came to, I thought I had wet the bed again but then I realized I was soaked with sweat. My pajamas, my bedsheets, and my blankets were completely wet. I started hallucinating, having DTs, as they are sometimes called. I saw ugly, hideous faces, distorted and evil, leering and rushing at me, and shark heads with snapping mouths trying to bite me. I rubbed my eyes and looked again but they were still coming at me. I was completely frightened and shaking.

In the wee hours of the morning, I got out of bed and shuffled and shook my way to the nurse's desk. She looked at me, concerned, and said, "Danny, come here and sit, are you okay? Tell me what's wrong." When I tried to talk to her, it was as though I'd just done a big whack of MDA. I had chills and my voice was vibrating and shaking almost uncontrollably and I managed to tell her, "I-I-I'm seeing th-th-things a-a-and I-I-I'm s-s-scared." She saw the terror in my eyes and comforted me. She got some medicine, which I appreciatively took, and she brought me back to bed. Someone had already changed the sheets, for which I was grateful.

The next day was rough and so were the next few nights. No matter how I felt, I got no pills, no helpers. It was sink or swim; get-used-to-it time. The staff did try and speak positive words of comfort, more or less seed planting, preparing us for the next phase. They were very kind, loving, and caring and I know it was this kind of attention that prepared me for the rest of the stay. I began to peck a little more at my food. Maybe I would get through this after all. The other clients were cool, too, and it was as though we all knew we really needed to be there for one another.

By the sixth or seventh day I was more sociable with people. I was not happy or enjoying myself, but I was starting to adapt and had the occasional moment of well-being. It hit me like a ton of bricks that I would finally have to face the demons I had not dealt with from my messed-up drug past as well as the new set of problems from cross-addictions to alcohol, Valium, and cocaine. Part of me felt as though it was hopeless and I would never amount to anything.

I was still feeling rough, but the worst was already over as far as going through withdrawals. I was getting ready to be reprogrammed—to start the 1,000-mile journey that was the next phase in my life.

chapter nineteen

The Three Wise Guys

God works in mysterious ways.

| The Bibb speaks of the mysteries of God

I LEFT HAPPY VALLEY still fragile but a lot stronger and I was ready for the next phase. I was taken to a nice, clean private room, small but comfortable, with a window facing a wooded area. I was told to settle in and get ready for the "new beginnings." I looked around the room, put my clothes away, and picked up my acoustic guitar for the first time since I'd been there. It felt as though I was meeting an old friend.

We had a class of about thirty people. We watched motivational movies, learned about nutrition and healthy eating, exercising to stay fit, proper sleep, and, in general, developing good habits, including keeping a journal and learning to write out thoughts and ideas. We were told we had to learn all over again to develop a disciplined daily lifestyle. This was what we learned for the duration of our stay.

One day I thought, "Can I go on forever being sober? Do I have to? Maybe I can kind of get rested up and get my health back, party again some day, but not as wild as before, just be more controlled."

God heard those thoughts of mine loud and clear and I guess He figured, "I'd better do something to set Danny straight on this one before he runs too far and gets himself in trouble again." You be the judge, for this is what I ran into that first day in the clinic.

That first night we lounged around in the communal area and before too long three elderly gents and I found ourselves talking about various matters in life, our vocations and expectations, about faith, family, and so on. These men were very bright and articulate and they certainly had my respect. I admire successful sales- and businessmen because I know it takes guts and determination to be at the top in their field and these men were—another lesson that alcohol picks no favorites; these men were pillars in their communities. They were very humble in their approach and attitude with me, but were crystal clear regarding their thoughts on total abstinence.

"So, Danny," one of the wise guys asked me on that day, "what do you think of this place? Do you think that you can come in and get a tune-up and then pop back out there and do things in moderation?" This surprised me as I had just been thinking this earlier in my room, growing comfy with the possibilities of indulging again. "Well, sort of," I said, "I was thinking about this earlier and I think it's possible that I could handle it at some point." Wise Guy #1 looked at Wise Guy #2 and said, "Tell him."

Wise Guy #2 said, "Danny, I've been here three times and each time I left, I had those same thoughts. At first I handled it and then, slowly but surely, it all blew up again and here I am."

Wise Guy #2 nodded to Wise Guy #3 and he nodded back. "Danny," said Wise Guy #3, "we wouldn't lie to you. We have no reason to. We're older men in our sixties, and we may never kick it but we're trying. We get flown up here in our company jets because we make a lot of money for our companies and they tolerate us because of that. We may never quit entirely because of our age. We didn't have someone like us warning us when we were your age. You're young and have a lot of life left in you. Don't blow it."

The three of them looked at me, piercing my soul, and the third wise guy continued, "Danny, you can't come in here for a tune-up; you might as well play Russian roulette. You are an alcoholic and you are here because you are an alcoholic. You have a chance to beat this now because you are still young and strong, with goals for your music. Quit now and you have a chance—you can do it—but if you think you can come in here for a tune-up and handle it, you're only fooling yourself. Look at us."

Wise Guy #1 piped up, "Danny, each time we started back thinking we could handle it, it was only drinking wine with a meal and with the lowest alcohol content. Then we went to stronger content, then right back to the forty pounder a day. Mine was vodka." (#2's was gin and #3's was whiskey.)

"Danny, you can never drink again," Wise Guy #3 said. "Don't let anything or anyone try and tell you otherwise, or you will fail as we did. Start telling yourself tonight and every day while you are here that this is the way it's got to be. Get used to the idea. It will strengthen you, and then you can make it work for you."

I thanked these men for talking and sharing with me, and that night I did more or less come to that realization. I believe nothing is by chance; there is a reason and purpose for everything—God arranged for those men and me to meet. It was by Divine appointment. Because of this I was immediately able to come to grips with the task and journey ahead and to prepare to become successful in defeating my addictions.

ONE STEP AND ONE DAY AT A TIME

Inch by inch, everything is a cinch; yard by yard is hard.

| Zig Ziglar

We were now on a daily regimen, checking our weight every night and morning, making our beds, doing light exercise, going to morning classes, then lunch, then afternoon classes, then reading time, and then dinner. Classes on religion and spirituality were held on Thursday nights, but I never attended. I thought I had got enough of it growing up and that it was probably secularized, anyway. I was still getting a lesson on the Spirit while I was there, that's for sure.

Two nights after my encounter with the Wise Men, I had an encounter with God Himself. The weight and guilt of all I'd done weighed heavily on me and I was sorrowful. I felt like a hopeless case. (Sometimes God's best work is done when we're at wits' end because then there is less of us He has to contend with. Man does have a tendency to get in the way at times!) Realizing my shortcomings and failed marriage, my rotten examples to my children, and so on, I cried out to God:

God, I know that You are out there because of what You did for my dad. I believe You exist. I am a failure and I am very sick and I don't think I can do this. I need help in a big way and I need You to help me, please. Take out this desire in me to drink and do drugs because I can't do it on my own. I will abuse alcohol and drugs again, I know it, so You've got to help me, please. And God, I have been a rotten dad and person, and I can never make up for all the wasted years and not being there for my kids, Kyla, Nicole, or Justin, but I can give them a gift, Lord, if You will take this desire out of me and I go straight. God, my kids have been told I am a bum, a no-good, who will never amount to anything. Please let me change this image they have of me, because up till now they've been told right. God, if they ever get suicidal and think there is no way out because of drugs and alcohol, I want them to be able to say, "Yes, there is a way out, Dad found it." God, let me be a light to them if they ever lose their way. God, let that be my gift to them to be a small token for all the wasted years. Let me give them this, O God, please!

Then I cried, "And God, if I'm not asking too much, could you please restore my health? I know I don't look too good. Could you please help me get better? Thanks, God, thank You."

I meant it. God heard it. He did it!

I AM SHOWN THE POWER OF LOVE

*What can melt away a man's pride when he's outwardly tough,
but tearing up inside, oh love can, that's the power of love.*

| From "The Power of Love" by Danny Brooks

That night God showed me something about the power of love. He heard my cry for help regarding my addictions and my health and I believe I heard Him speak to me in the quiet recesses of my mind. He said, "Danny, I'm going to show you something. In order for you to truly be successful at anything, you must understand the power of love. Do you remember the night in your dorm back in Guelph when you first had the *Brady Bunch* show on TV?"

"Yes, God," I answered.

"What did you see?" He asked, and I was brought back into the dorm and I saw everybody and the events of that night, fourteen years later.

I said, "God, I see young men who had a rough childhood, where love did not reside in their homes for the most part, and in others, I see that they missed the love they once had. I see what they yearned for and what they all hoped to have one day: to have a loving family, to be loved, needed, and wanted."

I saw the tears in the young men's eyes, but even more riveting were the tears I saw in their souls. I felt the quiet and unspoken respect in the silence when nobody dared then to make light of one another's emotions, save for the good-natured clowning around. This vision was very powerful.

Then God brought me into the room at Larry's Hideaway where I was sitting in the room watching Jimmy Swaggart with the other hardened alcoholics. He asked me again, "What do you see, Danny?" It was as if I could get right into their very souls and feel their lifetime of pain, and I saw what God was showing me. These men had spent a lifetime of running, hiding in the bottle (I know all about this running and hiding), but they still couldn't outrun God's love and care for them. They couldn't harden their hearts enough to prevent Him from entering. The tears that had flowed from their eyes had been tears of acknowledging God's love for them in spite of their feelings for Him. As they contemplated the possibilities of change even after so many wasted years, the tears they shed were mingled with the shame of their mistakes and the hope that still existed that God still cared for them. Love can penetrate the hardest of hearts, the most negative of minds, and the deepest pits of despair.

I didn't make any commitment to God that night, on a conscious level, but in my soul I knew that the power of Love was crucial for hope and that I was going to start governing my life on this power.

I AM SHOWN THE POWER OF PRAYER

Looking back over my life it's easy to see,
I shouldn't be in the spot that I'm in now,
I don't deserve the kindness shown or the love I feel today
and I know that it's because Mama prayed.

| From "Mama Prayed" by Danny Brooks

I started thinking of all the close calls in my life and how I'd fared and I realized the ball had bounced an amazing amount of times in my favor when it shouldn't have been. With God I reviewed my life, and each scene I saw left me marveling about how fortunate I'd been. There are so many incidents I haven't mentioned in this book.

There was that time on Bloor Street near Lansdowne when my old friend Johnny and I were involved in a fight with a bunch of street hoods. It was outside a club I was playing at and I took a pretty good beating—black and blue face, some chipped teeth—and someone pulled a large knife on me. Time stood still for a moment and I watched as the knife went slowly back and forth. Suddenly the guy threw it away and took off just as a cruiser pulled up.

There were car accidents, one in particular when the hood came through the windshield, slicing my friend in the forehead (Danny Ross, who died in a different crash later) that required forty stitches, while I got a broken collarbone and some broken teeth. We'd woken up on the side of the highway and then were rushed to the Mississauga hospital. We had been going southbound in a northbound lane and hit a car head-on. We had a small Triumph TR6 and we hit a big Oldsmobile. The doctor said if either car had been doing five miles an hour faster we would have been decapitated.

One night I totaled a Ford van, hitting a metal pole head-on. The van was a write-off. I had been very stoned on Valium. I was with a friend and we had just mainlined fifteen #10 blue Valiums each. They didn't break down well in water and kept clogging the needle but we somehow managed to get it into our systems. I walked away from that accident with a piece of my tongue split open. This still affects me even today as every now and again I accidentally bite my tongue and it splits open a bit, making it difficult to chew and even speak.

I had also tried to commit suicide and I took *over* the overdose limit of 600 mg of belladona. I got very ill and screamed at God for not letting me die.

I could go on with these examples. After God showed me these clips of my life He said, "Danny, you have been covered by the blood and the prayers of the saints and have been spared by the power of prayer." Quite a night I had, this night in the Donwood, a night to marvel at, because I didn't deserve the kindness I had been shown. Thank You, God!

After all this, I knew I was in for the fight of my life in more ways then one, and at times it seemed so daunting. Many things in life can seem daunting and overwhelming. You have to learn to look at things from a different angle and always, always, take it one step at a time. Inch by inch, everything's a cinch. You can do it! Just take the "t" off "can't." You have to *try*; you have to take the first step—you have to, that's it that's all!

Debi came to visit me as often as she could. Just knowing that she was there was a comfort. She'd almost gone on a tour out east with the Woodstock Revisited show but chose not to go in spite of wanting to. I needed her nearby and I was grateful for her choice. Upon learning of my desire to go into the rehab clinic, Danny K. had offered me much more money to stay with the show. I had been tempted and almost caved. I swear I heard the voice of God gently say, "Danny, if you go you may make all that extra money but you also may never come back again." It was the last part that got my attention and I got a shudder at the time thinking my demise had just been foretold. This was it. If I didn't get help right away, death was looming.

I had a two-day pass at one point and Debi and I were reunited at home. Soberly looking at my friend Pat for the first time, it really hit home that I had made one of the most important decisions in my life.

Finally, the one-month class was over and we had a "graduation." Debi and our friend Greg Johnson came and it was a beautiful sunny day. There was one thing they said at the celebration, though, that I found upsetting. We were told we were feeling good right now because of what they called "the Donwood high." It was the first time in a long time that any of us had been clean and sober and we were feeling good about this. But it was going to wear off soon and it would take around two years before we really got it together. *Wow*, two years! I couldn't even look beyond the next day or week; two years seemed so far away. (May 8, 2007 marked the twentieth year I have been clean and sober. Thank You, God! Sometimes it seems like yesterday and at times a lifetime ago.)

THE DONWOOD MIRACLE

Call on Me and I will answer you and show you great and mighty things.

| Jeremiah 33:3 (God's telephone number)

Just before leaving the Donwood, the doctor who looked after our medical needs while we were there brought me into his office and said, "Danny, did you really do all those things you said you did when you were admitted here?" It was a rhetorical question; he already knew the answer, but I said, "Yes, I did, and I'm not proud of it." And then I asked him why. He went on to tell me that my bleeding ulcers had disappeared "just like that" (he snapped his fingers). He also said my triglycerides, which were at 5.9 the previous month, had normalized at 1.9, the process of which should have between six months to a year. Then he said quietly, "Your insides are the insides of someone who has never done *any* abuse. There is no scar tissue anywhere, and given your drug past and jaundice, this is highly unusual."

I just looked at him because I was reminded of my prayer to God about restoring my health. The doctor said, "Do you know what I'm telling you?" I looked at him and said, "Yeah, that I'm going to be all right."

He shook his head, and said with a little exasperation, "Danny, what I'm trying to tell you is that this is a *miracle!*"

When I shared this news with the doctor who helped Debi get me into the Donwood, he said they must have made a mistake and told me to see him when I get home. When I went he gave me a barrage of tests, including blood tests. About a week or so later he called me into his office and told me, "Danny, I have one word for you: *Miracle!*" This was said with a certain amount of anger, believe it or not. You see, this doctor was an agnostic and this was outside the box of his thinking. Every time I went to see him after that appointment he remarked, "I don't understand it. Pat is dying and you are getting better—even *younger.*" When I told him it was because of my faith, he said, "Don't give me that." But that was what I gave him for about a year, until I'd had all I could take of his closed mind and negativity.

chapter twenty

Leaving the Donwood

It's a tough ole world getting tougher all the time...

| From "Give it Another Try" by Danny Brooks

MAY 8, 1987. Spring was in full bloom, summer was right around the corner, it was a new day, and I had my beautiful babe, Debi. When we got home the day I left the Donwood, I said to her, "I think God allowed me to go through all this stuff so I could help other people get through their problems one day. Does that sound weird to you?" Debi looked at me and said, "No, Danny, it doesn't." This was pretty cool because at the time, apart from my Christian upbringing, Debi and I didn't really share a faith of any kind together.

Everything looked new and different. Colors, scents in the air, the breeze through my hair—all my senses were heightened. I was really enjoying the Donwood high. I took up jogging and running. Before too long I could run ten kilometers without any problem. Later, I was doing fifteen, twenty, and twenty-five-kilometer runs. I enjoyed running; it was great thinking time and it helped me deal with issues. I recited motivational slogans and ideas of my own to write down while I ran. I was learning to build my house on the rock where it would stand, whereas before I had hurriedly built on the sand and in the sky, where I was tossed every which way. Today I am still active, and love to study the art of Shotokan karate with my daughter Caitlin.

I started reading self-help books one after the other: Og Mandino, Zig Ziglar, Dr. Dennis Whaitley, Norman Vincent Peale, W. Clement Stone, Napoleon Hill, Robert Schuller, and others. Most of them reminded me of watered-down versions of the Bible, so I started reading the Bible, too. I think most people are unaware that many self-help books, particularly *Think and Grow Rich* by Napoleon Hill, *The Power of Positive Thinking* by Norman Vincent Peale, *Peace of Mind Through Possibility Thinking* by Robert Schuller, and probably one of my all-time favorites, *Seeds of Greatness* by Dennis Waitley, stem from biblical principles and are centered on this passage from Philippians 4:6–8:

> *Be anxious for nothing, but in everything by prayer and supplication, with thanksgiving, let your requests be made known to God; and the peace of God, which surpasses all understanding, will guard your hearts and minds through Christ Jesus. Finally, brethren, whatever things are true, whatever things are noble, whatever things are just, whatever things are pure, whatever things are lovely, whatever things are of good report, if there is any virtue and if there is anything praiseworthy—meditate on these things.*

All self-help books stress the importance of the power of desire and due diligence. Proverb 12:27 says, "… diligence is man's precious possession." Be diligent and think "can!"

I told Debi that I wanted to write songs that said what these authors were saying. By reading these books, I was preparing myself to do this. I was also reading books on Zen, Zen Buddhism, Daoism, Taoism—any book I could read on enlightenment. One day after I had made my commitment to God, I went into the World's Biggest Bookstore in Toronto, and I reached for a New Age book on the latest personal development techniques. As I did, I heard in my mind, "Danny, you have the Book of all books. What more do you need?" I pulled back my hand and have never read another New Age book since. I've had no need to. I am fulfilled; I don't feel an ounce of emptiness.

When the Donwood high wore off and I started to go through a real tough time, the verses I had committed to memory kept my sanity intact and brought me through the Valley. There is power in the repetition of positive words but there is an especially incredible power when those positive words are from the Book sanctioned by the Creative Power of the Universe. The Power of the Living God!

I was still not yet spiritually grounded, but I was learning more each day about being accountable and doing right by people. I also started subscribing to the erroneous philosophy that it was my power of the mind that was bringing me this sense of well-being. I guess I was thinking I was God, which was becoming a popular thought in some circles of that day. I had been out of the Donwood around two months; this is where the rubber met the road, as they say.

I started getting my horrible blue funks again, and I was feeling as though the cure was worse than the ill. I was hearing things, seeing things, and really starting to come undone. I couldn't figure out why, and I was sick with fear, so we set up a doctor's appointment. I was diagnosed with floating anxieties and was offered a form of Valium. I told the doctor I couldn't take them; that I had an addictive personality and would abuse them. He reminded me that he was aware of my addictive personality, as he had also helped get me into the Donwood, but he insisted that it was better to take the pills than to freak out one day, possibly go out on a bender, and even take my life. He was very concerned for me. Now, of course, I was wondering what was happening to me. This wasn't supposed to be happening. I had gone to the clinic to get well, to straighten out my life, and it was unraveling. "Oh God," I thought. "What is going on? I'm losing it; no, no, this isn't supposed to be in the cards."

I didn't take the prescription. I was like a shell-shocked man, struggling for about a month, reading self-help books, praying, and trying to keep myself together any way I could. I didn't feel as though I was in charge anymore; I had come to the crashing, brutal reality of how frail and scared I really was and started to feel that I was not going to make it. Looking back now, I can see that this is exactly the spot in which God wanted me, to make me realize I couldn't make it on my own. Otherwise I would be lost in my own sense of self-accomplishment with no need for Him.

Fortunately, I started reading a book by Jamie Buckingham called *Power for Living*, a compilation of people's stories about how God helped them. Cliff Richard's story hit me most. Here was a fellow musician, so I could really relate. He had tried everything in life but still remained empty. One day, at wits' end, he called on God and let

God know that he had tried everything but Him. Now he was going to give Him a chance, to see if He could make the difference. God did. I was drawn by Cliff's admission to God of the pain he had caused others, the asking of forgiveness for his sins and for Jesus to come into his heart to show him the way. Cliff said it was not a spiritual Fourth of July show of fireworks in his soul but, rather, a quiet realization that he had done the right thing and that every day things got better.

Something hit home here. This was what my terrified and troubled soul needed. I needed this quiet realization that all was going to be well in my soul, because I was losing the battle for my mind.

I SEE THE LIGHT: AUGUST 3, 1987

Praise the Lord, I saw the light.

| Hank Williams

I finished *Power for Living* and looked around the apartment (it would be a month yet before Debi and I moved out and got our own place). Debi was knitting and Pat was watching something on TV, holding one beer for drinking and an empty for spitting.

I was about to say goodbye to an old lifestyle and way of viewing what was around me. We do see things differently through "spiritual eyes." I bowed my head and repeated what I had read in Cliff Richard's account and admitted my sin to God, asked His forgiveness, and asked Jesus into my life to guide me. I opened my eyes and looked around. Quiet peace and a realization that I had just done something of significance came over me. I remained silent about this new commitment till the next morning and then I shared with Debi that I saw the light.

I told Debi the next morning that I was "saved," to which she replied, "You're what?" "I'm born again," I told her. "You're born a what?" she asked quizzically, and then I realized I was using "Christianese," which Debi didn't understand. She had not been raised in the church as I had been, so I tried a different tactic. "You know how my parents are, right?" Debi had heard a lot about my upbringing, and she nodded.

"Well," I said, "I'm … one of them now." Debi looked at me strangely at first, unsure of whether this was a good thing or not. Then I saw it in her eyes that she saw something different in mine and at this moment she saw it was a good thing, this born-a-new-something business.

Overnight I had gained a new way of looking at things and a major change had taken place in my heart and mind—a spiritual surgery, you could say. I realize that the spiritual journey is a process, as is being a strong Christian, but the transformation necessary to begin that process had miraculously taken hold of me the evening before. Old things passed away and all things became new. I reasoned differently, and my level of morality increased, but I still had a fight on my hands regarding my blue funk periods. This was a battle I would have to deal with over the next few years. There are many ways of looking at why God had me suffer through this extremely difficult period, and I think it had a lot to do with my music. Foremost, though, it takes an irritated oyster to produce a pearl; a kite rises against the wind, and gold is refined by fire. Looking back now I really believe I benefited in ways I would not have if God had suddenly relieved me of all my anxieties and had taken away my blue funk periods. This not only forged a closer relationship with Him because I was so dependent on Him but it added something to my music: more depth, soul, and understanding. Did I enjoy the suffering? When revelations came, yes, but for the most part, of course not. Yet, my life was saved.

chapter twenty-one

Learning to
Get Down!

Coal turns into diamonds, gold refined by fire.
A kite rises against the wind higher and higher.
Life is a mystery you can't deny, but I get my strength from God above
who keeps me satisfied, under pressure.

| From "Under Pressure" by Danny Brooks

I HAVE ALWAYS WANTED to touch people through my songs, but I don't think that, at that time in my life, I fully realized the import of that desire and what was required of me to be in such a position to influence people. To write about subjects with depth and substance is one thing and one can draw on life's experiences. Say I had murdered someone and was sitting in a jail for my crime. I could sing something like, "I put a man down without hardly tryin' but now I'm sittin' in this prison and my soul is cryin'." That would be telling you a fact of what I had experienced and painting the picture of conflict and the resulting emotion from it. To write about conflict (which does take difficult life experiences plus a knack to say it poetically) is one thing, but now to write about conflict and *resolution*, whereby you give a parabolic message involving hope and answers that are life-changing, is a whole different dimension in writing. In the Book of Proverbs (18:21) we are told the power of life and death is in the tongue. I take this very seriously. Music and lyrics are incredibly powerful; if writers could truly see the effects they have on some of their listeners, I believe it would influence the way they write.

I had the tough experiences of jail, failed relationships, and twenty years of addictions, and taking my writing to a new level required new seasoning. I don't think this was all for just the music but for me personally, as well. I read this in *Our Daily Bread,* a monthly devotional, and it applies to all who have endured hardship and pain: "Sometimes God, Who knowest best, will give us sorrow as a test. Sometimes God will wound a heart, greater wisdom to impart." I didn't know at this time that I would be going into prisons on a regular basis and speaking and singing to men and women with harsh life experiences of their own, harsher than mine, but God did and I believe He allowed me to cry out to Him for the next two years as I have never cried out before in my life. What I learned I was able to share and I was able to make an impact. I know my songs took on new depths, but I had to go through a tested, tried and true process.

In 1988, I changed my last name from Middlebrook to Brooks as a stage name for a fresh start after rehab. Debi and I went back for a follow-up examination at the Donwood and when the doctor heard that we were still living with Pat, he was very concerned. He said to Debi, "You've got to move out of there, and the sooner you and Danny are out, the better. The longer Danny is around this environment, the greater the risks are of him relapsing. This is a very dangerous situation." He was right: Pat still had friends coming over and some of my old friends visited, too; I was the only straight person. Debi still smoked pot on occasion but, in about a month's time, she gave it up for me so I wouldn't be tempted with any form of stimuli.

THE MIRACLE APARTMENT

I believe in miracles and I want to jump and shout.

| From "Daddy's Got An Angel" by Danny Brooks

We took the doctor's advice and told Pat we had to move out. We felt for Pat because he was going to be alone but we had to think about my health, too. Pat was all right financially, but we knew he was going to be lonely.

We loved the High Park area so that is where we searched and we finally found a nice basement apartment in a newly built house on Quebec Avenue. Debi had $1,000 saved up and the apartment was $750 a month, first and last up front. We gave the woman the $1,000 and she said she would hold the apartment for us, but if on the first of September we didn't have the other $500, we would forfeit our $1,000 deposit. We agreed, feeling we would come up with the money somehow. At this point Debi was not working, which was by choice as she was more or less taking care of me. I was still in pretty rough shape.

We were getting close to the first of September and still we hadn't come up with the $500. Debi suggested I speak with my parents, but I knew I couldn't ask them after everything I had done to them in the past. (It would be another five months before I was close with my dad and mom.)

One week left and still no money. I remember telling Debi with my new, childlike faith, "Debi, the Bible says 'if we ask anything according to His will, He hears us. And if we know that He hears us, whatever we ask, we know that we have the petitions that we have asked of Him.'" I showed her this passage, 1 John 5:14, 15, and I said, "The doctor says we need this apartment for my recovery and I believe God wants me to recover, so I believe He is going to give us the $500. I don't know how, but I don't have to know how. I just have to believe and then I say a little prayer."

Back in May, when I'd got out of the Donwood, I had applied to the Society of Composers, Authors and Music Publishers of Canada (SOCAN) to which I am a member, asking for an advance of $1,500. I registered all my songs with them, so they were aware of me, but at that time in my life I was not a recording artist and no one was recording my songs, which would have been what generated the money, making an advance a viable situation. I didn't receive a response. I had given up and forgotten about them.

Three days before the end of the month and possibly losing the $1,000 deposit, I received in the mail a check from SOCAN for $500. No letter—just a check! Did that speak to Debi and me? You bet! Big time! It was our first major miracle together after my health miracle in the Donwood. I phoned Mark Caporral, who'd sent the check, and got his answering machine. I thanked him profusely and briefly told him what it meant to us.

Mark died in a small plane accident shortly after sending us the money. When I heard about this tragic accident, a few thoughts went through my mind regarding the last-minute timing in receiving that money. Sometime after this tragedy there was a benefit and tribute held in his name at the Diamond Club in Toronto, now called the Phoenix, and I offered to perform out of respect and thanks for his kindness to Debi and me. We met Mark's mom and dad and I shared the story of the check. I was able to tell them how important it was not only in getting the apartment, but in the drama of how we received the funds, and how integral this was in my recovery and our relationship. We all had tears in our eyes; they were so happy to hear and see the results of what their son had done on our behalf. God does work in mysterious ways.

Shortly after Debi and I moved out, to take possession of our new apartment September 1, 1987, Pat died from alcohol complications at the tender age of thirty-six. What amazes me is that Pat had never been into hard drugs. It was the booze that ended his young life, whereas I had been jaundiced from dirty needles and, of course, had messed up my liver from the effects of hard drugs, especially speed and MDA. These drugs are rough on your system! My liver had already had three strikes against it *before* I embarked on my heavy drinking period from 1973 to 1987. I truly am one of the fortunate ones but, as I mentioned earlier, I have my reminders, and they will be with me the rest of my days. However, what I have now is peace, joy, and an understanding that is incredible, which is far more than what I had had before.

THE LONELY BATTLE

The road I'm traveling is getting heavy, weary in my bones, feel like quitting, throwing the towel in, I feel like calling home, but I got one more mile to go...

| From "One More Mile to Go" by Danny Brooks

Though this marks a significant part of my life, I'm just going to touch on this phase here because I'm already working on a motivational recovery book regarding the lonely battle. It's not as negative as the title implies, but the truth of the matter is this: you can have a great support team around you, as I did—my old lawyer friend Bruce Scott, more or less captain of my team; my dad, a minister; my brother Bill; and Debi, without whose constant care and love I could not have made it—but at night, your head on your pillow, with all your thoughts, doubts, fears, and insecurities, you are alone dealing with the onslaught. Even if you believe in God, you can still have the feeling that you are alone.

This is where the battle for your mind is won or lost—right there on your pillow. You can pray all you want, as I did, and it definitely makes a difference, plus I had Debi, who was and still is the greatest, but you still come back to you. What are *you* going to do? You have to fortify your thoughts through positive thinking and by repeating memorized Bible verses, for example. There are forces hurling negative thoughts your way and they are relentless and want to see you fail. It's not just a physical battle; it's a spiritual battle and it's for your soul. What you think on your pillow determines if you fall or stand tomorrow. *I strongly urge people to fill their minds with positive thoughts before going to bed through reading or watching positive materials and prayer as the last thing you do.* This sets up your sleep time, protects you, and prepares you for the morning. I cannot stress the importance of this enough!

We need a team of supporters around us, every one of us: prime ministers, presidents, people from all walks of life, even Billy Graham. We need help and are wise to have good counsel surrounding us, but this doesn't just fall into place. It takes thinking, planning, and working the idea, and although we can think out loud sometimes with our supporters, it's mostly in the quiet of our minds that we conduct our battle. Maybe it's when you jog, listen to music, or drive, as well as when you put your head on your pillow, but you have to make decisions; you have to make up your mind that you are going to do it. You are going to be successful. Nobody can do it for you. The best help and support takes place when you have your mind made up, when you are determined to do it, no matter what! It is very difficult—but *not* impossible. *It doesn't matter who you are, what you have done, how far down you have fallen; nothing, absolutely nothing, is impossible with God, and there is nothing that you and God can't work out together to put your life back on a winning track.* It seems a very lonely battle, but God is always there. Always! Joshua 1:9 says, "Have I not commanded you?

Be strong and of good courage. Do not be afraid, nor be dismayed, for the LORD your God is with you wherever you go."

There *were* definite times when I thought I would lose it all. One night I was at my first gig after rehab, clean and sober at one of the top R&B rooms of the day. I still hadn't found my land legs yet (I was uncomfortable with sobriety and lacked confidence) and if it hadn't been for Debi, switching places and putting me on the inside of the booth we were sitting in, acting as a barrier or protective shield, I would have crumbled for sure. I also tried to convince her to let me have "just one drink" to calm my terrified nerves. Thank God she held her ground!

What worked for me in overcoming my battle was regimenting my day, and for someone whose maxim used to be "organization stifles me; chaos stimulates me," this was quite a change. I wrote down in a daily planner my things to do for the next day. This was seizing the moment before it slipped away from me, and by the next day's end I would feel good about accomplishing some of or all of the things I had set out to do. I would also project things I wanted to see happen over the next year and write them down in the calendar section of the planner. I started the day off by making my bed right away and immediately cleaning my dirty dishes at breakfast. Little things like that meant a lot and they added up in taking each day at a time. I read and exercised, and even though I still struggled with my blue funks, I knew I was becoming whole again—slowly but surely.

After reading about how animals can soothe people who are going through recovery and feeling stress, Debi brought me home a kitten. He was a six-toed kitten (on each paw) and because of his stubby feet and appearance we named him Churchill, after Winston Churchill. Churchill was great therapy for me in an utterly amazing way. Whenever I became jittery or stressed Churchill bounded onto my lap and started purring as if to divert my thoughts and calm me down. After the cat sensed my getting through the worst of it, he jumped off and went on his way. In this manner he helped me tremendously to deal with each day, each minute, at a time.

Nothing comes easily and nothing that took years to do is undone overnight, but the decisions you make now and your declarations of what your plans are will have lasting effects and will determine the outcome of your dreams. You will gravitate to what dominates your mind. Your goals are guardrails to keep you from falling; they also prop you up to reach higher. Every truly successful person about whom you read or hear had to dream with their sleeves rolled up and a determined desire to accomplish their goals. *Meditate on the right things and the right things will come to pass.*

Not long out of the Donwood I bumped into my old friend and lawyer, Bruce Scott. I was very happy to see him as we had lost touch; it had been at least ten years since I had last seen him. It was even more wonderful to hear of his coming clean from alcohol.

Bruce became a mentor, a friend and confidant, and was my best man when Debi and I got married in the spring of 1989. He was also like a coach, only in this case he was coaching me in the game of life. Bruce once said a very sobering statement to me: "Danny, if you never have another drink you haven't won the game; you've only tied." Wow, think about it. It leaves absolutely no room for another drink. At least that's what it has meant for me and I have been successful for over twenty years. I know some feel this is too hard a line and that you shouldn't worry too much if you relapse because things like that can happen. I agree it can happen, and if it does I don't think too much time should be spent beating yourself up; rather, apply that energy to getting back into the race and winning the fight. However, I feel if we start off with a "soft" view of a possible relapse, we are more or less bringing it on with our weakened stance. Remaining firm in my decision gave me strength but, once again, if I hadn't had Debi, I honestly don't think I could have made it. It certainly would have been a whole lot tougher.

ACTRA

A big boost in my recovery, as obtaining an ACTRA card is not easy.

| Danny Brooks

In the early 1980s I had done four Molson beer commercials (Duck Calls), which were national spots, and then I did a Rowntree's chocolate Aero Bar national commercial, which gave me five credits toward an ACTRA (Alliance of Canadian Cinema, Television and Radio Artists) card. Back then you needed six credits in a one-year period.

At this point in my life, four or five years later, I decided that I would apply for the card. The woman at the ACTRA office who interviewed me cut me some slack about the one missing credit and the time lapse because of my professional involvement in the music industry. Look at it anyway you want but I copped a real break here; I also didn't have the normally required letters of recommendation from two or more current ACTRA members.

During my recovery I was having such a rough time with floating anxieties and agoraphobia that I was unable to work but I needed something to financially sustain us. Debi had gone back to work but I needed something, too. I called the welfare office and the woman who came to interview me said, "You can't work anywhere in your condition." I told her I had just gotten an ACTRA card and felt that eventually I could start earning money this way. She told me to pursue that, and that I was allowed to make a certain amount, but I had to declare it. When I started doing better, I could go off welfare.

I collected welfare for about seven months and then was able to get by on my ACTRA card. I worked as a background performer in many movies and did some stand-in work as well. Standing in is when you do all the camera angles and set-ups for the star actors. You have to resemble them in height, weight, and hair/eye color. The one stand-in I remember most was for Dennis Boutsikaris in the Michael Keaton movie *The Dream Team,* a whacky film about four mental patients taken to a ball game by their psychiatrist, played by Dennis.

This ACTRA card was important to me and was such an asset during my recovery. I was often on set for up to sixteen hours a day and most of that time was spent reading, so I was educating myself and also slowly getting back into dealing with people, many of whom were decent and very helpful to me. I was involved in this for about three years and found that it was not only great for my recovery but for my confidence. Being a drug addict includes very antisocial behavior, as not many people in society stick needles in their arms, and you develop a sort of bunker mentality. Becoming an alcoholic didn't really improve my social standing, either. I had to reenter society and learn to cope on an altogether different level and it wasn't easy for me back then. Even today I find it difficult at times. Some people would say just being in the music industry can give you those feelings of alienation from the rest of society; you are cut from a different piece of cloth.

chapter twenty-two

The Test

I will show you great and mighty things you didn't know.

| Jeremiah 33:3

There's been times that I've been under, never like I'm feeling right now.
There's been times I've needed a shoulder, never like I need one right now.
Oh take my hand, let's get together…

| From "Take My Hand" by Danny Brooks

WORKING ON THE MOVIE sets I met the Langevin family, who were very talented IATSE (International Alliance of Theatrical Stage Employees) film union workers and who specialized in many things, including producing, special effects, camera, continuity, and lighting. One of the family, Andy, knew me when I was performing in clubs and had told me that if I ever straightened out one day, he would help me put together a video. At one time Andy had had a drinking problem, too, and he was very supportive when he met me on the set and saw me straight. He encouraged me to apply for a Video Fact grant and told me he would help with the process. Debi drew a storyboard, a first for her, of a song called "Take My Hand," which I had recorded at Greg Johnson's Tanis Productions Recording studio. After I got out of the Donwood, Greg had helped me record several songs and was a genuine supporter. Andy added the cost sheets and set up how the video would be shot. We applied and, to our great surprise, we received a $5,000 grant. What is remarkable is that we had no label back then, no record deal in place or interest from a label or management company, and these are major plus factors in getting a grant because you are competing with the major record labels and successful indies, and there is only a certain amount of funds to go around. Things like this—the miracle of the $500 in getting the Quebec apartment, the ACTRA card, the $5,000 Video Fact money, and so on—prompted

Debi to make her commitment to God in October of 1987. She was as overwhelmed as I was by the incredible way God was providing.

We shot the video and in addition to the $5,000, which we turned right over to Andy, he called in favors from his talented family and other IATSE workers and we got a $30,000 video made. We still have this video today. We were very excited because we felt that we could take this video and shop for a record deal, which we did. This eventually led to another major miracle.

DUKE STREET RECORDS/MCA

Dreams will keep you going when you feel like giving up,
'cuz that's what dreams are made of, that's what dreams are made of,
gravity from heaven to hold you up, they'll keep you reachin' when you feel like givin' up,
'cuz that's what dreams are made of.

| From "What Dreams Are Made Of" by Danny Brooks

The finished video was a great shopping tool. It was professional looking and well done, the song was a good one (or we wouldn't have been given the money otherwise) and so was the recording of it. "Look out world, here I come," I thought. "There's a new kid in town, looking for his new label home."

I shopped it around and absolutely nothing happened. I made callbacks and the answer was the same everywhere: "not interested." You have to be tough in the music industry; you can't take anything personally. The industry is a hard one, but sometimes it's hard to see past that. Let me put it this way: it is not easy hearing "no" all the time. I could wallpaper our living room with rejection letters from over the years.

In the meantime, it crossed my mind that my ACTRA card could lead to calls to do the beer commercials again, like the ones I'd sung for Molson earlier. Could I do them physically? Mentally? Could I do them with my newfound faith and my feelings about being the right example? I thought of Pat; we were encouraging him to quit drinking. Would doing these commercials be helpful to him or to others like him, or to folks in my current situation? The issue was something I knew I had to face and about which I had to make a decision. In my mind, God spoke to me very gently, "Danny, whatever decision you make, stick to it. If you are going to sing them, that's your choice to make, but if you decide not to, then stand by that choice." Wow, great! No condemnation from God if I sang a beer commercial! But I still couldn't feel comfortable about singing one.

One Friday afternoon, Debi and I went out to watch a matinee. Debi's friend's band was performing. Scoping out the room, I noticed an older couple in their sixties. I could tell they had been fond of the bottle for some time. They sat at a table drinking, and in times past I would have thought this romantic. This day I saw a different picture. I saw broken families, neglected children, fighting, heartbreak, and ruin, and that these two had progressed through this tide of sorrow to their impervious perch in the corner of this club. I don't mean to have an imperious or uncaring attitude here, either, for what I saw wasn't a judgment on them personally as much as it was an insight into what the bottle has done to so many families. I was sad for them and could feel some of their pain.

Right then and there I was galvanized in my decision to forgo any future beer commercials. That was it! I couldn't in good faith sing them with the feelings and pictures I had in my mind at that moment, and as I cemented this stand in my mind I recalled God saying to me, "whatever decision you make stick to it …" and I said in my spirit, "I'm sticking to it."

There was a message on our answering machine when we returned home that evening. It was from an advertising company that loved my voice; they had heard it in the recording studio that day and were very keen on having me for their national campaign. They said they would call me Monday morning. Yes, yes, yes! We were broke and Christmas was right around the corner so we were excited that money would be coming in; good money at that.

It wasn't until Sunday evening that it hit me and I said to Debi, "Hey, Babe, you don't think God would test me so soon after my making a decision not to sing beer commercials, do you? Do you think He would do that with us being as broke as we are? Naw, He couldn't do that. At least, I hope He wouldn't."

Monday morning arrived and I got the call. I was nervous; I didn't know what I'd do if it was a beer commercial they wanted done and I had to say no to a great payday with good residuals.

My heart pounding, I listened as the gentleman on the line told me they were heading up a national campaign for one of the major breweries and wanted me to come down that day to the studio. I was stunned and silent. He told me it would immediately involve several different TV and radio spots, all of which were to be updated regularly. On and on he went. I was physically shaking. Debi saw this and was concerned; she had probably guessed it was a beer commercial and that there would be no money coming in now.

The man told me they wanted to put a band together and have me travel in support of the campaign (large chunk of change there!). Suddenly I felt that if I didn't stop him right then I was going to cave; nervously I blurted out in a shaky voice, "I can't, I'm an alcoholic, I'm sick, and I can't sing this." "Would you like to think about it?" he asked, "this is—" but before he could finish I blurted out, "No, I can't think about it. Call John Dickie, he's a great singer. He's not sick, he can do it for you. I've got to go now, thanks for the call."

I hung up the phone, shaking violently. I was completely shocked. I couldn't even believe what I'd just done. I had just turned down what could have amounted to six figures. We were broke; what had I done? Debi walked over to me and put her arms around me. She said quietly, "I'm proud of you, Danny, I'm so proud of you. You held your ground."

I was shaky for three days. Three days—and then what mattered most sunk in: Debi was in my corner. In every relationship I had had before Debi, the girl would have said, "Are you *nuts*? Call them back!" They would have been thinking of all the nice things they could get with that money; then they'd slip away like the morning mist.

Not Debi. I suddenly realized what God had just shown me: more precious than gold, I had a real companion who was true blue and would stick with me through thick and thin. My recovery seemed even more doable at that moment. I had, in fact, just been shown I had something far greater than any beer commercial or any amount of money.

Yet, God wasn't through blessing up a storm!

Before the week was over, I got a call from one of the record companies that had turned me down when I was shopping with my video. It was Steve Thompson, Ronnie Hawkins's manager, and although he had his own label, he assigned it to Duke St. Records, as Duke St. had major distribution with MCA Records, before it became Universal. They said they had reconsidered and asked if I would still be interested in coming in to speak with them. It was all I could do to sound rational and professional. As stunned as I may have been over the beer commercial incident, it could not compare to the absolute jubilation in my soul at this turn of events. I had never ever heard of anything like this before. Talk about an emotional roller-coaster ride that week!

We agreed to meet first thing Monday morning. I got off the phone and Debi and I went wild with joy. Suddenly, something hit me again, and I said to Debi, "Hey, Babe, do you think God rewarded us because I said no to the beer commercial and held my ground?" I didn't wait for her answer. "That's what it is, Debi, it's got to be! I believe that's what He did." Thinking like that was real encouragement to always hold to what I thought was right and true.

We got the recording contract in 1988, which I agreed to and signed. We recorded with Duke Street/MCA, and the songs did well. *Billboard* had told MCA in Midem, France at the yearly music seminar that "Keep It In Line," the lead-off single, was a top five *Billboard* hit, hands down. MCA pushed this record in the beginning and we were number one and number two for two weeks on the "Top Ten at Ten" on the Q107 Rock radio network, based out of Toronto. We became one of the fastest additions to radio, and they brought me into MCA to meet the top brass. I was later nominated for a Juno for "Most Promising Male Vocalist."

I was on my way to where I am today, and although we had our differences and sometimes butted heads on issues, I am grateful for the opportunity provided by Ross Munro, Rik Emmett, Steve Thompson, Andrew Hermandt and the folks at MCA.

DENNIS PINHORN

You play like a catfish, man, you hug the bottom.

| Traveling musician from Florida on Dennis

I met Dennis Pinhorn back in 1984 during my Talbot Inn days, and we hit it off well. I was impressed by his dynamic, pulsating approach to the bass and by how he propelled the Downchild Blues Band with whom he was performing at that time. I thought it would be great to get a band going with him, and when I put forward the idea, he agreed with the prospect and said we should talk further. Several months after this discussion, Dennis finally tracked me down and called me at Pat Johnson's place where I was staying then. He recalls that I was in a bit of a "state" and rushed him off the phone, promising to call him back immediately. I had hung up without getting his phone number. After that we lost touch. Years later, we met up again.

After the first record with Duke Street/MCA, I wanted to put together a band that was there for my songs—one that would complement the style of my heart: roots music that mixed blues, R&B, soul, and country with a positive message. Later, I added healthy doses of down-home gospel styling to the mix, and that's when I finally found my niche. In putting this band together I met Joe Mavety. One day we were to have a rehearsal at his house to go over some of my music. When I got there he told me he'd invited a bass player and—wouldn't you know it?— there was Dennis Pinhorn. We were very happy to see each other after such a long time and Dennis humorously quipped, "I've been waiting for you to return my call; it's only been five or six years." Dennis was looking at the new me: clean and sober. We talked about how I used to be and he mentioned that he had seen me once at a club and had said hello but I had been so hopped up I hadn't even noticed him.

Dennis has been such a steady influence during my recovery; he is of the old "stiff upper lip" British stock and his playing on the bass reflects this attitude: rock steady and always there for the song. We started performing together in late 1990 and he is the only musician who has been with me on a full-time basis since then. He's been a constant encouragement to me, steadfastly maintaining that I have what it takes to go all the way and he wants to be there when it happens. More importantly, he loves and shares my taste in musical style.

Anne Murray's drummer Gary Craig, who has performed with us from time to time over the years, shared his insight: "You guys are so tight as a rhythm section you could go anywhere in the world and any drummer and guitarist worth his weight could join in. You'd have a band, just like that." That's when I realized I wouldn't be able to do what I was doing if I had any bassist other than Dennis. A drummer needs a solid bassist to lay the beat down and a guitarist or keyboardist needs to follow the bass to know the changes. Even if they don't know all the changes, they can "skate" or fake to some degree until they do know everything. The bassist, on the other hand, needs to know all the correct changes; there's no skating for a bassist or the song will sound terrible and throw everything off. He is part of the foundation; everything stems from the bassist and drummer. You can't have a house without a solid foundation; same idea here. I knew it wasn't by chance that this situation with Dennis came together. I believe it was by divine appointment, both for the music and because we all need a friend in our corner who is an encourager. Dennis has been that for me over the years and I believe he has been blessed and will be blessed further for his role.

chapter twenty-three

Demons and Angels

*And the L*ORD *said to Satan, 'From where do you come?' So Satan answered the L*ORD *and said, 'From going to and fro on the earth,
and from walking back and forth on it.*

| Job 1:7

I'M SURE THIS VERSE GAVE Stephen King the inspiration for
the Walking Dude in his book *The Stand.* This is another story of a
miracle, and it starts with a scary encounter with a tall man on Dundas
and Yonge streets in downtown Toronto. Debi and I were standing on
the southwest corner in front of the old Eaton Centre. It was a beautiful, sunny, breezy summer evening and the year was 1989. There was a
carnival atmosphere and excitement in the air. Apart from the throng
of people of all ages, sizes, and color, there were jugglers demonstrat-
ing their skills, juggling bowling pins, balls, and sticks. There were a
couple of fire-eaters and there was a three-piece rock band pumping
out the volume. Merchants sold their wares, ranging from clothing to
flags, trinkets, and handbags. Hot dog vendors added the sumptuous
aroma of fried onions to the perfumed air of the patchouli oil being
sold nearby.

Incongruously added to the mix were two preachers, and while
one warned of the wrath to come and that Jesus was coming soon and
we had best be ready, his partner handed out gospel tracts to people in
the circle listening. Everything seemed so surreal. The air was charged
with energy.

I saw him coming from the west on Dundas Street, on the south
side where we were, a head taller then anyone around him. He was
dressed like a businessman with a maroon suit jacket and gray pants.

He carried a black briefcase. I saw him in my peripheral vision at first as I took in the preachers and the fire-eaters, but I was drawn to his presence as he approached. As he passed by in front of us, he abruptly stopped, turned around, and faced me, coming closer and sticking his face right in front of mine. He looked like Ichabod Crane, with a long bumpy nose, large ears, a long, thin bony face, and a huge Adam's apple protruding just like his nose. A double affront! His unsightly, imperious mug jammed in front of me (I felt fear), he mockingly and malevolently sneered, "So what do you think of these preachers, Danny?" He spat out my name. All I could do was stare. I was shocked and frightened by his invasion. Ichabod attacked again. "Well, do you believe them, Danny?" he demanded. Part of me wanted to humor him, to make him go away, and say, "Yeah, they do kinda sound foolish, don't they?"

Suddenly I saw myself in an old arena and on one side there were angels and on the other side demons, all of them waiting to hear my reply. I saw this clearly in my mind as though I'd been transported to a different time and place. It was completely unnerving. In that moment I knew there was going to be lasting repercussions regarding which way I answered. What seemed like time standing still for a while was only seconds. I snapped out of my reverie and weakly and nervously said to this creature, "Yes, I believe them. They are speaking the truth. I'm an alcoholic, and God is helping me right now."

Ichabod seemed wounded, but then suddenly attacked Debi. "Do *you* believe as well?" Debi said yes. This fierce-looking manifestation of evil started to wilt in front of us. His facial expression was one of fear. He backed up and then scooted off, looking back once with a frightened look, as though he'd seen something we couldn't.

We were both weak from such an adrenaline release and a little shaky. Then Debi said, "Danny, do you know him? He called you by your name." I'm glad it had slipped by me earlier or I think it would have freaked me out and I would have crumbled. I remembered he had said my name when Debi mentioned it, but I had been concentrating more on my direct fear of who this Ichabod character was and what he may do. We reasoned that if it had been someone who knew my name from a previous performance in a club, the standard would have been, "Hey, I remember seeing you at such and such." No, this had not been someone who knew my name from an earlier show; this was someone who knew my name supernaturally and it wasn't one of the supernatural good guys, either. He had been a demon. We walked up Yonge Street and decided to take the next subway home. We didn't walk downtown for a while after that.

The repercussions of that decision in taking the stand with the demon were this: finances were pretty tight but the next day I got a call from Peter Lavender (God rest his soul) and as a result, steadily worked the next three weeks on *The Dream Team* movie. Just before Christmas we received a check in the mail for a fairly large amount that I hadn't been expecting that soon. Neither had I expected such a sum of money! It was from a movie I'd worked on called *In the Nick of Time* starring Lloyd Bridges.

THE GOLD COIN

God works in a mysterious way His wonders to perform.

| William Cowper

At a restaurant with Debi, I was sharing my fears of going into some of these buildings and relating the latest harrowing experience of being in an elevator with two other people, in a rough building on Islington. I had been carrying a crib. The elevator stopped on another floor and two more people got in. The next thing I knew there was an argument and shouting regarding a botched drug deal, and all I could see in my mind's eye was a headline: "Crib man shot in drug melee in elevator." I pulled the big crib box in front of me for protection and said a little prayer as the guys started yelling and shoving. Being confined to a small area with no quick escape made it all the more unnerving. I was sweating, expecting a gun or a knife to come out at any moment. Thankfully, they were too busy to notice me. Finally, I got to my floor and as steady as my voice would allow, I said, "Excuse me," and barged past. Having to return to make another delivery in the same building when things like that happened, which was often, didn't make my job any easier!

I told Debi about the guy shooting up speed sitting on the bed that day in the same room I was setting up the crib. I told her about the young girls in another project, in Rexdale, who were hooking, some of them only about thirteen years old. These girls were so hardened that they would have scared most tough guys. I remember leaving that building and seeing the young girls, one in particular with hardened and lost looks, her youth taken from her, signs of the uncaring treatment she grew up with. I didn't even realize that I was crying until my eyes started stinging.

There were children who were screamed at by a maniacal mother coming down from crack. There were roaming gangs looking for trouble. There were underground parking lots where parties, drugs, prostitution, and gambling took place, where, out of fear, nobody parked their vehicles. There were drug needles and used prophylactics in the stairwells, excrement and urine, and, in some buildings, the most graphic sexual graffiti written or carved into the walls. I saw all this in a day's work, every week. Once, I thought of reporting to the authorities the things I saw regarding the children and possible abuse, but was deterred when I realized that I would not accomplish anything by doing this. The problems were so impossibly rampant. The only way I could make a difference was by *being* the difference, by praying over the kids, their rooms, their moms and dads, the gangs, even the buildings. I prayed for young families that were living in those buildings who wanted to improve their lot in life and get out of these dangerous places. I prayed for the protection of the children, especially the small and picked-on ones.

In the midst of recounting to Debi all the things I had seen, I excused myself to use the washroom. After getting out of the stall, I went to wash my hands, and on the sink counter I noticed a gold-colored coin the size of a dollar. I picked it up. It had on it an image of an angel on one side and on the flip side it said, "No weapon formed against you shall prosper" (Isaiah 54:17).

Now you can draw your own conclusions, but seeing that coin after sharing my fears and concerns with Debi, I looked around half expecting to see an angel. That coin had been put there for me to find and pick up so that I could be comforted. It told me that I was being protected. There are angels among us. We are told "do not forget to entertain strangers, for by doing so some have unwittingly entertained angels" (Hebrews 13:2). Back at our table, I excitedly told Debi and she was amazed, too.

Debi and I lived on Quebec Avenue for a little over a year and then we found a bigger, nicer place on Humberside, still in our beloved High Park area. After seeing this thousand-square-foot apartment that was the second floor of a beautiful old house, Debi wondered where we would get furniture to fill it. It was much larger than our old apartment—almost three times the size. Debi said I would think and dream bigger with this extra space. She was right.

On the day we moved in, we noticed there was furniture left in the hallway to our flat. It was nice, old-style furniture: overstuffed chairs, a couch, and end tables and a coffee table, just what we needed. When our landlord came by that day, we inquired about the furnishings. He told us that the previous tenants had left it behind. We asked if we could have it, and he said, "Great! Now I don't have to get rid of it!" I love it when things come together like that! The Lord provides. We still have two of those old chairs today, eighteen years later.

Debi was working at A&M Records when we lived in our new place, and I started working for Bruce Scott's wife, who owned Dearborn Baby Furniture. I drove a truck part-time every Monday and the odd Tuesday, looking after a government contract, delivering baby cribs to folks on welfare. I became known as "de creeb man." It was an interesting job though not without its frightening moments as I had to deliver cribs in some very rough neighborhoods, to crack-house apartments and places in gang areas. Some of the clients were scary themselves. At one point I wanted to quit because I believed my life was in danger doing the job. I'm glad I stayed; I was able to witness the miraculous happen.

HARD TIMES IN THE LAND OF PLENTY

Children run and play on their way to school before they start to learn the ways of this world, why do we get so uptight about what we see in the news, why it's our example; They only follow after me and you, and the wheels keep spinning the wheels keep spinning around and around...

| From "Wheels Keep Spinning" by Danny Brooks

It is said that the will of God will never lead you where the grace of God won't keep you. I put gospel tracts in the elevators, sliding them between the metal plates, and left them in lobbies. I prayed over the cribs and the apartments I was in, pleading the blood of Jesus and even praying sometimes with the clients. Looking back, I know God was protecting me and had me there for a purpose.

Once, I was setting up a crib in Regent Park and in the living room (and this was around 10:00 a.m. in the morning) sat three very well-built men, drinking. I figured bodybuilders were not the type to be drinking at this time in the morning; they had probably recently got out of jail.

As I was leaving, I felt compelled to look them each right in the eye and say, "God bless" to them. Up until then I would say "God bless," but turn away quickly, sometimes before I even finished speaking, being shy but also in a hurry. These men, however, broke me out of my shell. I did as God had compelled me to do and a beautiful surprise resulted. Each man looked as if he had been touched by an angel. It was more than just the gratitude of a well-meant and powerful statement directed their way. It was as if they had been momentarily filled with hope and love and all things righteous.

Later, I asked God about what I had just witnessed and experienced, apart from me being instantaneously fortified with the courage to look anyone in the eye and wish them God's blessings. My answer was that when you sincerely say "God bless" to anyone, you are invoking all the Godhead power to immediately bestow that person with blessings. It changes the air around the person; I've witnessed this so many times! Psalm 46:1 says, "God is our refuge and strength, a very present help in trouble." This means immediately, not later—*right this very instant*—so when we say "God bless" to someone, it means *now*. It's a simple, small statement with all the power in the universe behind it!

I remember a distraught mother losing it on one of her kids as I was setting up a crib. I looked at her and said, "God bless." She stopped and looked a little dazed for a moment, then calmed down and left the room. When I said it again as I was leaving, I knew something positive had got a hold on her.

I also delivered many cribs in the Jane Finch Corridor in north-east Toronto. If around 1989–91 you had picked up your phone to ask anyone in authority such as the police, the hydro company, the pizza delivery people, or cab drivers (they wouldn't deliver or pick up there) if you should move to that area, they would have said, "Not if you can help it." It was a pretty rough area to live in and you could feel the tension and the despair brought on because of the drug problems. One day I delivered a crib to a building on Eddystone Dr. I was always a little tense going there. On this day I walked through crack deals to get to the apartment, and recited the spiritual riot act—Psalm 23—"The Lord is my shepherd; I shall not want... Yea, though I walk through the valley of the shadow of death, I will fear no evil." Garbage was strewn *everywhere*. You could cut the air with a knife it was so thick with the heavy vibe of despair, violence, and desolation; perhaps a sobering reminder of where I might have ended up had my life not been so miraculously turned around.

When I got to the apartment I noticed that the front door had been recently smashed into two pieces. It was held up with boards poorly nailed to hold the pieces of door together. A woman answered the door, and her image is forever etched in my mind; sunken, haunted, darting eyes and a constant body twitch. I took the crib inside and saw extreme filth; debris everywhere—a crack house with only a couch in one corner of the room.

The woman sat on the stairs leading up to the bedrooms and engaged me in conversation, which I thought a little odd. Suddenly I noticed something change in her eyes and I turned around immediately to see a guy with open arms as if to grab me in a bear hug. I also saw another guy coming out from behind the couch (I guess they had both been hiding there), probably ready to assist his friend in robbing me or something. Forcefully, I said, "God bless you." The guy in front of me stopped dead in his tracks, looking terrified, and the other popped his head back down behind the couch. I turned to the lady and said, "I will leave the crib right here, as you seem to have help," and I walked out. I walked out of that apartment building and I thanked God and said, "Oh God, you have got to send people into these places to minister." Kids born in these places have three strikes against them to begin with.

Once, I was in one of the Falstaff buildings, which run east off of Jane St. and are considered the beginning of the Jane Finch Corridor. Four guys were waiting for the elevator. I walked in and one of them said to me, "What floor you going to?" I just looked at him and he said again, "What floor you going to?" Something told me to go back and check the directory, so I just shook my head at the guy and turned around. In these types of buildings little round metal pegs signify the numbers of the apartments and floors. I needed to go to the twentieth floor but the metal peg for the "2" was pulled out, so I couldn't even ring the woman to tell her I was there. "Go up blind with these four characters?" I thought, "I don't think so!" and besides, I didn't even know if the woman was home.

So there was my dilemma: I was scared, I felt like a coward, and I was angry with myself for feeling that way. This woman needed a crib and I valued my life. One of the constant fears we crib men had (there were three of us) was of being robbed. Gang members could grab the crib and think we had money on us as well. We thought that way because the taxi and pizza companies had been hit all the time until they stopped going to certain places. The police didn't rush into these areas, either. In the Falstaff and Chalkfarm buildings especially, it was not unusual to find spent shell casings. This was common in all the projects as there was a lot of gang activity.

I didn't deliver the woman's crib that day at Falstaff and it ate away at me. I felt like quitting my job and that ate away at me, too. I was still having a rough recovery as it was, with floating anxieties and agoraphobia and I refused to take any kind of medication. Part of me said, "You've got a good reason to quit this job," but the other part of me maintained that if I was to run from the job I would be setting a precedent for running whenever the heat was on. I had to stand firm or lose myself, my dignity, and my self-respect.

That night I prayed, "God, you parted the Red Sea for Moses; you can part the sea of troubles for me in Falstaff and all the other buildings."

The next day was Tuesday, and I was "prayed up" and ready to do my job, albeit a little nervous. I drove fast and slammed on the brakes in front of the building, popped open the back doors, and grabbed the crib and mattress. I charged into the building as though I was defending the Alamo. No one was in the lobby. I made it up to the floor, delivered the crib, and set it up. I made it downstairs and out to the truck without a hitch. I said a big "Amen," and then, "Thank You, God, for parting the sea of trouble for me."

I was buoyed by His provision and I could look at myself in the mirror again. Looking back, I can say this job gave me a lot. Folks were blessed with prayers, kids and their cribs were blessed, gospel tracts were read, and, best of all, God was building and strengthening me. "Calm seas don't make good sailors," an old African proverb says, and God was trying me in the furnace of affliction then for other tasks up the road. More importantly, He was showing me His faithfulness in watching over me, affirming that I could trust Him. I still get scared at times but it is momentary, because I recall, "I can do all things through Christ who strengthens me" (Philippians 4:13). Here's another good one: "For God has not given us a spirit of fear, but of power and of love and of a sound mind" (2 Timothy 1:7). Even repeating Jesus's name has unfathomable power.

I told Debi that I was seeing kids grow up in an environment of R-rated films, drugs, violence, gangs, sex, parties, and constant loud boom-boxing, teeth-shattering music, and that consequently we were going to see an explosion of violence that would echo 2 Timothy 3, in which he speaks about "perilous times and perilous men." I started to notice when reading about crimes in the city that the perpetrators were usually from places to where I delivered cribs.

I was saddened by the kids growing up in these places, and sorry for them, seeing what I saw in the crib buildings; they never had a chance most of the time. I had once lived in those conditions, had once been walking down such a path of self-destruction and lack of hope. But with the help of God and others, I was able to change my life. Who knows how many people I'd influenced badly before then? It's our example, every one of us; we are either part of the problem or we are part of the solution. What we do, each and every one of us, has lifelong rippling effects. People are watching when we don't even realize it, people who are going to be led one way or the other by our example. Sobering, isn't it? Sobering, yet true.

part four

the best is yet to come

chapter twenty-four

Miracles for Breakfast

Miracle: 1. Act of God: an event that appears to be contrary to the laws of nature and is regarded as an act of God. 2. Amazing event: an event or action that is totally amazing, extraordinary or unexpected.

| *Webster's Dictionary*

SINCE I LEFT REHAB in May of 1987 and surrendered my life to Christ August third of the same year, so many miracles have happened in my life. I cannot possibly recount them all in this book, nor can I tell a lot of the other interesting things that have happened. However, there are certain memories that remain prevalent in my mind as indicative of God's love, mercy, and blessings. This part of the book is a compilation of several events God has allowed into my life to show me that if I only believe, anything is possible.

THE MT. MORRIS MIRACLE

HE shall give His angels charge over you.

| Psalm 91:11

This is probably the most profound and scariest lesson in my life and why I didn't have a cardiac arrest during the experience is only because God had me in His hand.

I went on a truck trip in 1989 with my brother Bill as he was having difficulties in his personal life. Someone close to him at the time was involved in reading books on witchcraft and Billy had been experiencing some bizarre goings-on. He asked if I would help him on his next long-distance haul because he felt he was coming undone and couldn't do it without me. I agreed, though reluctantly because I had stand-in work on a film coming up and also my nerves were pretty shot since it was still fairly early during my recovery. The morning I left, after saying goodbye to Debi, she yelled to me as I was about to get into the car, "Danny, don't you want to take your harmonicas?" I ran back into the house and grabbed my harp bag, kissed her, and off I went.

This trip turned into material for a Stephen King novel. Some very bizarre things started taking place and, caught up in my fears, I remembered an old Chinese proverb, "He who rides tiger does not get off until tiger lets him." I was stuck in a nightmare for almost a week—what should have been a three-day trip. Billy's attitude and demeanor were rapidly changing and I believe it was due to the witchcraft and spell book this person close to him possessed and that we were both targeted and affected on this trip by evil incantations.

At times Billy drove like a maniac, going down a mountain road once through rain at high speeds, a 3,000-foot-drop on my side. I was terrified, and he would sometimes glance over at me as if he was enjoying my fear. Other times he would break down, tears in his eyes.

Rubber from the truck wheels was starting to peel off. The air brakes went on the trailer. The bushings from the back tractor wheels started to go and I could see in the mirror how loose the wheels appeared, shifting from side to side. The engine developed problems that seemed to come and go. It was as though someone was practicing voodoo on a toy truck and we were on the receiving end.

Bill became unable to drive for longer than an hour and we were constantly stopping, which was dragging out the trip. On top of all these problems, he was relating to me the bizarre experiences in his personal life and we both felt convinced that we were the victims now of this person's witchcraft. Billy probably doesn't even recall this particular incident I'm about to share as he seemed right out of his mind.

It was late at night and we were going down a mountain. The truck wasn't handling well and Billy seemed hell-bent on ending in a blaze of glory, flying down the mountainside and buying the farm, as they say. He was saying odd things to me. I got the impression he was not himself and that it was someone else wanting to do me harm. I looked at this manifestation—because I couldn't believe it was my brother—and warned him, reciting a Bible verse from Mark 9:42: "…and whoever causes one of these little ones who believe in Me to stumble, it would be better for him if a millstone were hung around his neck and he were thrown into the sea."

Billy looked strangely at me and I felt the verse had the desired effect, but I was still fearful because I believed some kind of madness had come over him, his truck, and the trip.

Finally we pulled into a dilapidated gas station with a variety store and a restaurant on Mt. Morris. For anyone who has seen the movie *Deliverance*, this is what we walked into. We were exhausted from six days of weirdness and I was about to break. I had never prayed so hard for relief and by this point I was telling God that unless He got me out of this situation, I was about to start drinking again. I was starting to think that if I had a bottle I could take away some of the fear and that God would have to understand. My nerves were shot and I was at wits' end. I just could not take anymore. This truck was going to do us in, or Billy, in his semi-crazed state, was going to kill us both. The powers from this dark source hexing us were edging us on to an untimely demise. Hard to imagine things getting hairier and scarier but, boy oh boy, did they ever!

As we pulled into this so-called truck stop, I caught the look of a trucker coming out of his rig. "Billy," I said, "I'll bet this guy will know something about these truck problems." Something about the man reminded me of a Vietnam vet I had met in Los Angeles.

Billy had wanted to join the U.S. Army during the Vietnam war to learn to fly helicopters but had been turned down because he wouldn't renounce his Canadian citizenship, and also, I believe, because of his problematic ears. Bill had respect for the vets. It turned out that this guy was not only a vet but he'd flown helicopters. So now I knew Billy was going to listen to him and I thanked God for giving me the insight to instigate the meeting. Bill told him some of our problems, and he checked out the truck. "If you boys hop in this truck the way it is," he said adamantly, "I'll tell you what's going to happen. Yer bushings is so bad you going to be coming down a mountain, yer wheels is going to go and you are going off the side of the mountain. You ain't stopping till there's no more mountain." That was it. At the first opportunity in the restaurant I told Billy that we had to do something about getting the truck fixed and I was going to have to figure an alternative way back home for my film work.

Billy has a loud voice because of bad hearing in one ear and most people around us knew exactly what was going on. He called his trucking firm and they were going to decide what was best to do, but in the meantime we had to sit tight. The people running the truck stop told Bill they were going to have to be the ones to fix the truck because it was on their property and it was a hazard, and that they could get the sheriff to impound it there. Bill and I sensed a weird vibe in this place.

I figured I had to wire home for money and get a bus back home. A couple of guys from the gas station restaurant drove me to another, more modern, station, where there was a Western Union. I called Debi and she wired me $300, which had been intended for our rent. We got back to the station and it didn't take long for everyone to know what was going on and that I had $300.

I gave Billy some money, figuring I'd call a cab to take me to the nearest bus depot. Instead, a few guys in the restaurant heard my plans and offered to give me a ride. Eager to save money, I said goodbye to Bill, and squeezed into the pickup truck cab with a young kid and two men.

It didn't take me long to sense we were going the wrong way, especially when we crossed the state line. I asked the man closest to me where we were going. "We're taking a shortcut," he said. This did not sit well with me. Earlier at the truck stop I had asked where the bus depot was. It was definitely in a different direction than the one we were now taking, shortcut or not. The truck turned, crossing another road heading into a little town, and it seemed they saw some friends at the red light we stopped at. The truck booted ahead, and a car full of people followed behind us.

We were heading out to the middle of nowhere; I was in a truck with unsavory characters and a carload of their friends was behind. What's wrong with this picture? I got a sick feeling in the pit of my stomach and all I could think about was being robbed and my body being thrown somewhere in a bush. I was more scared than I have ever been before, silently screaming to God, asking what I should do. God said, "Danny, stay silent and look straight ahead. Trust Me. Just stay silent. I am with you." I was still petrified and wondered about God's terse reply, but it made sense later. I am so thankful that I took God's advice. At one point I was thinking I would just jump out of the moving truck but then I figured that with a broken arm or leg, I would be easier for them to finish off.

I remained silent although a big part of me wanted to scream out. I noticed one of the men looking at me and at his friend the driver, who would then look at me too. It was completely unnerving. This happened several times and I had no idea what it meant. Every minute I called out to God, asking for protection and what to do. I always got the same answer. "Stay silent, Danny, and look straight ahead." I guess I was hoping for something more dramatic (an angel with a flaming ten-foot sword swooping down to rescue me would have been great) but I was so stunned and frightened I didn't think or couldn't think about much beyond taking God at His word.

We were out in the woods now and I couldn't see any signs of inhabitants. The car was still behind us. Suddenly there was a clearing ahead, a sort of driveway. The driver of the truck pulled in and the car stopped around the bend behind us, out of sight. The two men in the truck got out, leaving the kid with me and commanding him to stay where he was. They went to the car.

I looked at the kid. He had long hair and an earring. For some reason I said, "You look like a rock star, kid, do you play guitar or anything?" "No," he said. "Would you like to learn?" I asked him. He beamed and said yes.

I pulled out a harmonica from my harp bag and started playing. Now, there were mountains around us and maybe that had some kind of effect on the acoustics because all I knew was that it sounded like a giant harmonica coming out of heaven; the notes cascaded down the hills. I played better than I'd ever done. I guess I was playing for my life. I threw myself into the music and so did this kid, who kept looking at me as though I was some kind of harmonica god.

Finally I stopped and said, "Would you like a try?" He gave an emphatic "Yeah!" I had an extra C harp and I gave that to him and told him to keep it. "Now, here's what I want you to do," I said. "Blow into the 2, 3, and 4 holes, twice sucking in and two blowing out. This is what I call the Memphis beat. Once you learn this you can start adding other little things. You'll learn to play in no time." We started doing this together. The kid was really getting into it, totally turned on to the music.

I guess the two characters and the carload of people wondered what was going on. The two men came back and told the kid to leave the truck. He not only refused but drew closer to me, it seemed, and said he wasn't getting out of the truck. After they tried a couple more times the kid refused and then I said, "Hey guys, I really have to make it to the bus depot." They looked at me and the kid, and said, "Fine. Let's go." The driver ran around the corner for a minute and came back, and then drove like the dickens to get me to the bus station on time. On the way there they mentioned how much they had dug my harp playing and singing and asked if I recorded at all. I told them I had just finished a record and that my manager was shopping for a deal. I was relieved to be making small talk like this, but would feel much better when I was out of their company.

We got to the bus station and I grabbed my stuff out of the truck. I pulled out a $10 bill and gave it to the driver, and as he took it our eyes locked. I felt I was looking into eyes full of malice and immorality; there was such a dark hole in his spirit. I quickly said goodbye to the kid and the two characters and ran into the bus depot with a minute to spare to get my ticket.

Once on the bus I tried to put everything behind me and started to snooze as we gently rolled down the highway. My last thoughts were that perhaps I had overreacted. Then I heard what I believe to be God's voice, jolting me out of my sleep, saying, "Danny, you were not overreacting. You were in trouble. I want to show you that I will never forsake you. Now let's go back." My eyes were shut but I was very conscious of what was happening. God said to take a look at things from the beginning: arriving at the truck stop, the types of people, how they managed to drive me to the Western Union, the offer to drive me to the bus depot, going the wrong way, crossing the state line, the car full of friends ...

"When I told you to keep silent, what happened?" God asked me.
I said, "It unnerved them, Lord."

"Why?"

"Because they had likely done this before," I responded, "and people had probably always cried out, and they were wondering why I wasn't afraid for my life. Then they became a little afraid."

God said, "Do you remember them looking back and forth?" and I said, "Yes, Lord. They were starting to wonder what kind of a person they had in their truck who wouldn't cry out for his life as others before me. This turned the tables on them."

Then God showed me how I had spoken to the boy, winning him over, and the sounds of the harmonica filling the air and even changing it. How when the two men came back, although they were somewhat impressed, they were still more or less out to do what they had planned to do, which was to steal and probably kill. But then the boy had refused to leave me and that helped save me as well as the timing of my statement about getting to the bus depot while they were still in a confused state. It was as though they had forgotten about the bus depot because they had never had any intention of going in the first place.

Then God said, "When you gave the man ten dollars, Danny, what did you see?"

"I saw the eyes of a man who had perhaps killed before, who was angry that he was only getting ten dollars instead of all of my money."

Little things always mean a lot, and as I was going down the highway in the bus I recalled Debi yelling out to me, "Danny, don't you want to take your harmonicas?" I believe they diffused the situation and saved my life, and I wondered what would have happened had I not had them. When I shared this with Bruce Scott later he pointed out another thing to me. He said it testified to the power of music and the effect it can have on people. That really blew me away. It showed me the importance of writing songs and how they can really encourage people and affect their attitudes and how they go through life.

I confirmed that I wanted to make a difference in the world through my songwriting. I want to touch people, to motivate them, to stir their emotions to think and reach for the higher calling in their lives and the lives of others. It worked on the Mt. Morris guys and it could work on others too.

I'm going to share some more miracle stories and then I am going to relate some divine appointments of people I have met in clubs, festivals, the prisons and churches. These appointments testify to the incredible way God is touching lives and how he brings people together and I am humbled and blown away how He works.

MT. MORRIS EIGHTEEN YEARS LATER— OCTOBER 5, 2006

His eye is on the sparrow.

| Martin/Gabriel

This is one for the Twilight Zone. It happened while I was returning home from a mini-tour performing in the south. I was working my way up from Atlanta, Georgia, where I played at Eddie's Attic and Blind Willie's. I had performed the night before in Thomas, West Virginia, at the Purple Fiddle. I just crossed the state line from West Virginia into Pennsylvania on Interstate 79 and saw a sign for Mt. Morris. My mind drifted back in time and the experience Bill and I had came back, and I felt a slight chill. I looked around and sure enough I saw this exit up ahead that looked familiar, and there was a Citco gas station. Part of me wanted to keep on trucking, as I had half a tank of gas, but I thought I could use a coffee, and for some strange reason part of me wanted to check it out.

Wavering, I pulled onto the exit almost at the last second. As I drove up the hill, I was sure this was the same spot my brother Bill and I were at eighteen years earlier. The winding drive and how the station was situated were the same, only this was a new gas station, not the old wooden one with the repair shop and honky-tonk.

I gassed up and looked around, positive this was the place. I could feel something, and then I saw the road leading further up the mountain in behind the station where I called out to God to get me out of here before I started drinking and losing my mind. I went in and paid for my gas and a coffee. I spoke to the young lady behind the counter and asked, "This is a new gas station, isn't it?"

"No," she said. "It's been here forever, or at least twenty years."

I told her I had been here eighteen years ago with my brother, and I described the old gas station, repair shop and honky-tonk.

"That's right. You're right; there was an old place like that. I was just a little girl of about twelve at the time, but I remember my daddy bringing me here."

"I thought so," I replied. "I'll never forget this place." She gave me a bit of a quizzical look as I said goodbye and God bless and walked out the door, sipping my coffee, looking at the mist rolling down from the mountain across the highway.

I looked around again and said, "God, did it really happen that way or was I just imagining things?" I hopped in my truck, took another look around and drove on up the highway heading for home.

About an hour or so up the road I looked at my watch and it said 11:11 a.m., and I thought that's wrong, that was around the time I stopped for gas. I looked at the truck clock and saw it was a little past noon. I then looked at the odometer and saw it had registered a little over a hundred kilometers in the past hour. That added up—but my watch? I then realized my watch stopped right around the time I stopped for gas. It's a new watch that my bassist Dennis Pinhorn gave me the previous Christmas.

I then said, "God, did you stop my watch as a sign to tell me that my life almost stopped eighteen years ago at this very spot? I questioned if it was my imagination back then, and today I asked if it really happened that way."

Man, I started to think about it and thought, "I wonder what time the gas receipt says?" I had put the receipt in the glove box before taking off and it was too difficult to reach from the driver's seat to check it out, and I had a small fridge on the passenger seat making it next to impossible. In truth also, part of me was reluctant to see it right away.

I drove straight home, and when I pulled into our driveway, Debi and Caitlin came out of the house and came up to hug and kiss me. I said, "Debi, remember Mt. Morris where Billy and I had our problems years ago"? She nodded and I told her about my stopping there, the watch stopping and before I said another word, I got the receipt out of the glove box. It said 11:11a.m.! Same as my watch!

We both knew what it meant. God does work in mysterious ways and I was moved once again in my soul that He does know the number of the hairs on our head and is watching out for us. His eye is on the sparrow and I know He watches over me.

CAITLIN

You brought light to my darkness, 'cuz baby I'm back believing again.

| From "Daddy's Got an Angel" by Danny Brooks

It is a miracle in many ways that Caitlin even entered into this world and Debi and I couldn't imagine life without her. I was the first roadblock to Caitlin's birth, which almost led to Debi having a hysterectomy, which would have been the second roadblock. Then the medical profession would have been the third roadblock—but let's start with me.

When Debi approached me about having a child together I was completely against the idea. I had recently come out of drug rehab and I was having a difficult recovery, one that took years to deal with and, in some ways, one I still deal with. I cited the fact that we each had three children from our previous marriages and also that I was in no condition to be a good dad. I said that pursuing my career in music would be too difficult with a baby on the way. Sounds very selfish now, I agree, but I was more afraid than anything. I really didn't think I could cut it already being on the edge all the time.

This went on for over two years and I guess Debi resigned herself to believing it just wasn't meant to be and made an appointment to have a hysterectomy to seal off any future possibilities of getting pregnant. The day she was to have the surgery she was lying on the gurney, waiting for the doctor to do the procedure, and that's when my frayed nerves from my recovery period came to be an incredible asset. Having jumpy nerves does not allow one to win any contests that involve being patient for long periods of time, or even short periods, for that matter. I became irate waiting what I considered to be too long a time and told Debi to get dressed, that maybe it wasn't meant to be and that we'd just be careful. We left.

Not long after this I felt God speaking to me about faith. He said, "Danny, you talk about faith to Debi, but are you showing faith to her with your fears about having a child together? This is important to Debi; give it some thought."

After thinking about it, I did realize that I was letting my fears dictate my actions. I went to Debi and said, "Debi, if you still want to have a child together, then it's all right by me." I told her how God had impressed this on me.

Debi became pregnant in early 1991 and during the third month, after a pregnancy blood test, they found her alpha-fetoprotein levels too low and made an appointment for us at the Genetics Department at the Credit Valley hospital. They asked us if we had any history in our families regarding mentally disadvantaged children. They told us there was a good chance Debi would give birth to a child with Down syndrome and that abortion was an option. We nixed that idea. They also mentioned that Debi could have an amniocentesis to check for Down syndrome; however, because of Debi's age at the time, miscarriage was very possible, actually more likely to happen than having a disabled baby. We told the doctor about our faith, and that we would rely on it. If we were to have a child with Down syndrome, then so be it.

Just prior to Caitlin's birth it hit me that I would have to hustle like never before in order to provide for my family, which ultimately made me the energetic person I am and need to be today in the music industry. I believe I am the competitive, diligent person who will not give up under any circumstances because of Caitlin. Today, Caitlin is a vibrant young teenager involved in music; she plays the piano, trumpet, and guitar, and is an excellent singer. She is a karate student and has won a gold medal at a tournament. She is a very bright and engaging young dynamo and we are extremely proud of her.

Caitlin aided me greatly in my recovery. Providing for Debi and Caitlin propelled me and I have never looked back. In speaking in the prisons, and where I perform and sing the song "Daddy's Got an

Angel," I tell people that sometimes your biggest fears, when turned inside out, become your biggest blessings.

Daddy's Got an Angel

Staring out my window, pouring rain is coming down.
Bills are pilin' up on the table, hard times again.
Another mouth to feed on the way, don't know how it's going to work out.
But somewhere there's a rainbow shining through these clouds of doubt.

I've slipped on the floor of a sure thing, one too many times.
Going to take a miracle to melt this Missouri heart of mine.
Sometimes, when least expecting, they say fate tumbles right on in.
You've brought light to my darkness, cuz baby I'm back believing again.

And I believe in miracles, and I want to jump and shout.
Daddy's got an angel now, shining through these clouds of doubt.
And I believe in angels that stand right by your side,
'Cuz I'm holding on to one staring me in the eyes.

Well from feelings of desperation rivers of victory often flow,
Like in a wild imagination where everything you touch turns to gold.
You are my heart, you're my inspiration, turning my fears inside out.
You're Daddy's little angel shining through these clouds of doubt

And I believe in miracles and I want to jump and shout.
Daddy's got an angel now shining through these clouds of doubt.
And I believe in angels that stand right by your side,
'Cuz I'm holding on to one staring me in the eyes.
Daddy's got an angel now and everything is going to work out just fine.

chapter twenty-five

The Nashville
Miracles

*I met ole Bootroots down in Nashville, Second Ave. and Broadway
He was singing with all he had, something 'bout respectin' yourself.*

| From "Hold Your Head Up" by Danny Brooks

IN THE EARLY NINETIES, after Dennis Pinhorn and I had formed our band and I had started performing under my stage name, Danny Brooks, we played mostly in the Greater Toronto Area. We had just completed a second CD for Duke Street/MCA entitled *Rough Raw & Simple*. The title track is a song about my dad, and the record is more of a roots-rock-oriented record. It didn't really get much support and we more or less fell between the cracks because radio didn't know how to categorize it. This led us to eventually go back into the studio and make demos to shop for a deal south of the border. I started making trips to do showcases and the "the asphalt boogie," hustling my music in Nashville, Memphis, New York, and Los Angeles. This particular story is of my trip to Nashville in 1994.

I was in downtown Nashville one day, after a week of hustling my music. I had probably hit at least seventy-five different record labels, management companies, song publishers, song pluggers, and booking agencies on Music Row and in the surrounding areas. I had about $3.00 cash left and enough on a nearly maxed-out credit card to make the trip back home. It was a beautiful, warm sunny day and I found myself standing just north of Broadway on Second Avenue, looking at the different colorful tourists and wondering where they came from. There's a lot of very interesting shops in this area, as well as eateries, cafés, and nightclubs. It didn't escape me that one of my heroes, Hank

Williams, had played the Ryman nearby and had walked these streets, probably thinking "song thoughts," as I was.

As I stood there, I thought about how long I'd been struggling and when my break was going to come and I was starting to work myself up into having a good little pity-party when I heard behind me someone singing an old Pop Staples tune: "You got to respect yourself … respect yourself …"

I thought, "Yeah, I should be happy I'm in the game and not sitting at home on the sidelines and wishing I was in one. I can feel good about being in the race and trying to do something. Yeah, I can respect myself." I moved closer to the street singer and I guess I was staring at him as I contemplated his message. Suddenly his booming voice said, "Yo, you lookin' at me?" I snapped out of my reverie and saw the big black blues singer, about six-foot-five, three hundred pounds. Mind you I'm not the tallest guy around and most people look huge. I decided to use the extra polite approach and say, "Yes, sir! You remind me of some of the great blues singers I saw as a kid, sneaking into the Colonial Tavern back in Toronto."

"Yeah? Who'd you see?" he bellowed.

"Muddy Waters, Willie Dixon, Howlin' Wolf, John Lee Hooker, Otis Spann," I replied, and rhymed off a few more.

He grinned and said, "Some o' dem was friends of mine, git over here." I walked over and he stuck out his hand and I took it. He told me his name was Bootroots and I told him mine.

Bootroots was a street person. He had a pushcart filled with belongings and there was a faint smell about him, but something told me he was no ordinary street person. He had pictures all over one of his tree limb-sized arms, which was covered with plastic to protect the photos of whom I guessed were loved ones from his past. I didn't go there; nothing needed to be said.

We talked about music and he mentioned the touring he had done. It seemed natural to start jamming, which we did, and people walking by put money in his big tip jar, right in front of the Wild Horse Saloon. As we played he suddenly said, "Danny, do you know dat music can hep people?" "Yeah, Bootroots," I answered, "I believe music can help people." Half a minute went by. "Danny, do you know dat music can heeeaaal people?" He drew out the word "heal" much like an old tent preacher working up the faithful. "Yes, Bootroots," I replied, "I believe music can heal people. There's a Bible verse that says, 'Every good gift and every perfect gift is from above, and comes down from the Father of lights, with whom there is no variation or shadow of turning.'" Bootroots paused, then almost knocked me over as he shouted, "And don't you fo-git that!"

We played more and had a great time jamming. He made some good tips. I was no longer feeling sorry for myself and actually felt good about things. But I had to get going and I bid a warm goodbye to Bootroots. We embraced and as I walked away from him (almost floating) he shouted to me, "Danny, if'n I don't see you down here in Nashville agin, I'll see you on da otha' side of the Jordan River!" (pronounced "Jooodan Ribaah"). I yelled back that I'd see him in either place.

I believe God puts a Bootroots in front of all of us when we feel discouraged and feel like quitting. Bumping into him had been no accident. Furthermore, I had been given another lesson on the importance and power of music. It helps and heals people. I was encouraged that day. Not only did the experience become a song called "Hold Your Head Up," but Michelle Sim of Northern Praise Ministries would later go on to write a whole play around the story, which was performed at the prestigious Oakville Centre for the Performing Arts. (Big Buzz Upshaw played Bootroots and did a remarkable job. Buzz passed on earlier this year, just two years after our performance of "Bootroots, A Christmas Tale.")

I had met Michelle in 1989, when she lived across the road from Ross Munro, my manager at that time. Ross introduced us and we have remained good friends. Michelle is an ordained minister under the Pentecostal Assemblies of Canada. Her Northern Praise Ministries is an outreach to Canadian artists and she is well known and loved for her tireless efforts in helping and ministering to their unique needs, especially when artists, like me, work mainly outside the confines of the church. Northern Praise Ministries has been a big part in my success.

THE LORD IS MY SHEPHERD

Dream your dreams and give them wings and watch them fly.

| From "Hold Your Head Up" by Danny Brooks

This second Nashville story takes place in 1996 and finds me in a hurry to get to the Bluebird Café at Hillsboro Pike, a nice suburb of Nashville. I was late and a little anxious and thereby not as alert and focused as I usually am when I'm on my own away from home.

I was driving a nice, new, rented white Oldsmobile in an area I had never been in before and I was lost. I pulled over to the side of the road to ask a man if I was heading in the right direction to get to Hillsboro Pike and told him I was going to the Bluebird Café and was late and lost. Before I knew it, he had his arm in the car through the passenger side window. Immediately, I thought of powering up the window but then wondered what I would do with this man running beside the car with his arm jammed in the window. I didn't want that and I thought he would be seriously hurt or killed so I watched as he unlocked the door and hopped inside. Once he was in he said, "Go straight."

"Do you know where the Bluebird Café is?" I asked.

"Yes," he said. "Now turn here." I did a series of turns and came to a stop sign. "Which way?" I asked, and he told me to keep straight.

Two things immediately happened. Time seemed to stand still right then. I was able to take in and see everything for what it was: I was in an old, run-down industrial area, heading into a dead end surrounded by a car wrecking yard, a transmission shop, and an old garage. About six men looking like ideal candidates for the FBI's "Most Wanted" posters were coming from between parked vehicles toward my oncoming car. They were mean-looking—snarling, big, tattooed galoots. Quickly, I spun the wheel and said, "No *way* I'm going straight, man, and I gassed it. God had given me calm nerves and the skill and ability to quickly see and size up what was about to go down. Through a series of turns, I ended up near where I had originally picked up this man. The guy was nervous now; and no wonder.

He knew I had realized what he had just tried to do. What he didn't expect was the God Factor. He blurted out, "Let me out here, man!"

I pulled over. "Wait!" I practically shouted as he was about to leave, and I put my hand into my inside vest pocket. A look of terror came over his face as he probably figured I was about to bring out a gun and shoot him. He froze. I pulled out one of my dad's personally designed gospel tracts, which said, "Do you know where you are going when you die?" and had pictures of angels on one side and devils on the other. The man looked so relieved that he smiled sheepishly and took the tract. "God bless," I said. I thought I even detected a look of shame as he got out of the car.

I ended up finding my way to the Bluebird Café by going to a gas station for directions. I made it to the Bluebird with about five minutes to spare somehow and, although it's not ideal for any performer to feel rushed, I managed to have a decent showcase.

Now you would think this is where this story ends but it doesn't. Because of my nerves and anxiety about making it to the Bluebird, I hadn't had much time to think about what had taken place with the near carjacking. After a performance your nerves are jacked up as well and you can have what is called "eustress," which is a form of excitement and stress: in this case, post-stress, of course. You're too busy wondering how the music folks you invited liked the show, and if the show will bring you closer to a deal, to think about anything else.

I drove back to my hotel and called Debi and told her about the showcase. It didn't even enter my mind to tell her about the confrontation. The next morning I was in "long drive home" mode and I had the trip plans filling my mind. Once I started driving I was in the zone; song thoughts, Bible verses, the scenery—that's all I was thinking. I love the wide-open road.

I made it home in fifteen hours. Debi made me a coffee and I sat down gratefully to enjoy it, picking up the *Toronto Star* and leafing through the sections. An article in the "Wheels" section caught my eye with a picture of an Oldsmobile like the one I had rented. I read about the Oldsmobile being the number-one car in North America for car thieves, not because of its value but because it was the car with the most interchangeable parts, meaning they could be easily used in other cars. *Then* I did some thinking about what had really happened that day before I got to the Bluebird, what might have become the last day of my life.

The guy who'd invited himself into my car had been a spotter and had noticed the Olds, knowing the facts that I had just read. He had also noticed the plates were from out of town and that I was alone. This was a route he had taken before and someone in the operation, a lookout, had alerted the others that an Olds was coming, a routine for them. They had been too eager, though; perhaps they had wanted to get it done and over with quickly since it was the end of the day. Maybe they had been tired. Whatever the case, had they waited a little longer I might have been trapped and they probably would have nabbed me. I also had two expensive guitars with me and other costly gear: the cords, microphones, and my harmonicas. After reading that article a little chill went down my spine and I looked up. "Thank You, Lord!" I whispered. They wouldn't have stolen the car and let me walk.

I told Debi about my close call. Part of me wished I hadn't as she was very upset with me and gave me a good scolding! Now, whenever I go out on a trip she sternly warns me to never pick up hitchhikers.

MEMPHIS MIRACLE

> *By the time I hit the Shelby County line, sun was sinking low.*
> *Radio tuned to that sweet soul music, I pushed the pedal to the floor, and the song on*
> *the radio reminded me of Mama, saying "Son you're going to make it if you try."*
> *So many years of hanging tough, now this boy's dream is on the line.*

> | From "Hang Tough" by Danny Brooks

Through some of the contacts I had made doing showcases at the Bluebird Café in Nashville, I met David Nicar. He was a friend of Tom Jackson's, a music motivator and instructor in Nashville, to whom I had been introduced earlier through Michelle Sim of Northern Praise Ministries. As I mentioned earlier, in Michelle's outreach to Canadian artists, one of her mandates is to help artists with whatever they need. She will bring in experts in their respective field to assist artists in preparing and promoting their music to the music industry.

David and I hit it off. Not long after, he took me to Memphis to do a showcase at the famed Joyce Cobb's club on Beale Street for the Memphis Crossroads Festival. It was a great club, across the road from the Rum Boogie and just down the road from B.B. King's club. He turned me onto an agent who booked me for four paying gigs in the area around the festival. However, once Debi and I and Caitlin, who was two years old, got down there and had a room rented for a week, I discovered the agent actually had only one gig for me. This was a shock to Debi and me and we wondered what we were going to do. We didn't have a lot of money and we had counted on the money earned to pay for our living expenses while we were there.

I performed the next day at Joyce Cobb's and shared our misfortune with David. He felt terrible for us, but also assured me that God would somehow provide. I was worried but I believed what he said.

We sold several CDs at this showcase, through which I met Eddie and Betty Willbanks. We ended up speaking and, again, I shared our dilemma. They offered to try and set something up at their church, where I could perform for a "Love Offering." The Willbanks were friends of David, and they attended the same church. Between them they arranged for us to perform at the Crossway Baptist Church in Memphis and the Love Offering and CD sales were far more than we would have ever made performing at the club dates that had fallen through. It wasn't the last time I played there.

To add to this incredible divine intervention, Eddie Willbanks was a friend of the legendary Jim Dickinson, who, apart from local notoriety, had produced a Rolling Stones record and was part of the Atlantic Records rhythm section. He also had a hand in the recordings of many soul greats including Aretha Franklin and Wilson Pickett.

I met Jim and did some mixes with him, at 315 Beale Street, a studio owned by Skip McGwinn, who used to drum for Dr. Hook & The Medicine Showband. I learned a lot from this very soulful, humble, and insightful man. He once said, "I hear the conflict and the resolution in your music, Danny." He also advised me not to take the frustrations of the business personally; it showed no favorites but eventually dumped on everybody equally. Jim was as much a historian as he was producer and shared many things about Memphis with me.

He told me to go to the bluffs one day and look at the Mississippi and let it speak to me. I did this and felt such a powerful presence that I wrote about it in a song called "Soulsville" many years later, recorded on my *Soulsville Souled Out 'n Sanctified* CD:

I wasn't born in Memphis, but Memphis lives in my soul.
No, I wasn't born down in Memphis, but Memphis lives in my soul.
Haven't been to Brother Al's church, but it already feels like home.

I took my dreams down to Beale Street, Lord you helped me watch
*   them grow.*
Stepped into Skip McGwinn's place, felt something burn in my soul.
Felt the Mississippi River, won't be the same no more.

Lord take me back to Soulsville one more time before I die.
Get the hallelujah boogie and the soul shivers down my spine....

One day Jim and I were sitting in one of the booths of the restaurant section in the Sun Records Studio on Union Street. Jim was sharing stories of Memphis. Rufus Thomas, Memphis blues, gospel, and funk legend, was holding court at the other end of the restaurant with the sightseers about to take the tour of the famed studio. Rufus was considered the "other King" in these parts, next to Elvis, and Stax Records became the force in the industry because of its early success with Rufus and his daughter Carla.

"Look at the table, Danny," Jim suddenly said. I looked and saw carvings made with a knife on the wooden tabletop. On closer scrutiny I saw the names: Jerry Lee Lewis, Elvis Presley, Carl Perkins, Johnny Cash, Rufus, and many others who'd been in the studio. Jim explained that this was how they signed their contract with Sam Phillips and Sun Records. Situations like this in my travels have made an impact on the music I write today, and I am indebted to the folks I have met along the way who have exposed me to them. [9]

Recently Jim worked on the music soundtrack for *Black Snake Moan* starring Samuel L. Jackson.

THE FLAGSTAFF MIRACLE

I was driving out of Soulsville, heading for the California coast.
Singing every song that ever touched my soul.

From "Jumpin' Jim Jericho" by Danny Brooks

In mid-October of '95, I left a sunny, warm Memphis behind (it was my fourth trip to Memphis) going through beautiful weather in north Texas and traveling west on the I 40, parallel to the famed old highway Route 66. Just before Flagstaff, I ran into a heavy snowstorm. I couldn't believe the sudden change in the weather. Judging by the amount of vehicles in the ditches and a large jackknifed truck, it had caught others off guard as well. I wasn't even properly attired for the sudden climatic change.

I made it to Flagstaff, where I got off at one of the exits to go to a restaurant and change into warmer clothes. I had something to eat and, doing some quick arithmetic, I realized I had better not rent a room for the night as I had to make my money last. I was on a month-long trip and I had to be very careful. I had already done another showcase in Nashville and another gig in Memphis at the Crossway Church and now I was driving out to Los Angeles to see my old friend and former bandmate, Steve Dudek, who was going to help shop my material and find some gigs. We were also going to write and record in his home studio (one of our collaborations, "Never Get Over You," was recorded on my *It's A Southern Thing* CD).

I figured I could sleep in the Glory Wagon (I was driving Dad's old truck with the stenciled Bible verses all over the whole vehicle) but then I thought I might freeze so I decided to head down the mountain in the snowstorm.

When you do a lot of driving you get tired and sometimes your thinking is way off. On this night that's how it was. I was guessing that the Mojave Desert wasn't too far away. Soon I discovered that I was the only one on the highway, leaving Flagstaff behind, and I heard on the radio that they had closed the road. It was dark and snowing and I was going down a mountain highway I had never traveled before. Suddenly, I hit ice. The truck spun and in that second I saw in my mind me going over the guardrail, tumbling down the mountain, turning into a giant snowball, not being found until spring thaw. I would never again see Debi and Caitlin and other family members. I cried out, "Oh God, please save me!"

The next thing I knew (and luckily no one else was on the highway or it would have turned out differently) I was going in the right direction. I was still shaking and I slowly drove to the next rest area where I pulled in and tried to relax. I managed to sleep on and off until the crack of daylight. I would discover I had quite a way to go before I hit the desert, but the first store I came to I bought a coffee and a cross pin that came with a little booklet on the power of the cross. I felt compelled to buy it and wear it and share this story with whomever I could.

THE QUEBEC MIRACLE

Danny, I want you to call everybody and tell them what I showed you.

| God

Around 1999, we had a band gig up in Noranda, Quebec, and we drove up in the Glory Wagon with the band gear. On the way up we noticed they had had some heavy winter weather the night before and that night it was slushy and dirty. It was a quiet night in the club and I was sure the inclement weather had something to do with it. We couldn't blame it on Michael Jackson being in town!

The next day, driving home, I was traveling at seventy miles per hour on an elevated two-lane highway. The sun was shining, although there was a bitter wind. Suddenly I hit black ice and the truck swung out sideways. Everyone gasped, frightened, and I gripped the wheel and tried to maintain control. Like a pendulum, the truck fishtailed, spinning out in the other direction. I was petrified but remained quiet. I saw the pristine countryside, the elevated highway, and that if the truck spun out we were going to roll down the side of the embankment, heavy band equipment and all (we had a Hammond and Leslie in the back—heavy, bone-crushing gear). We'd slide forever on the fields of sheer ice.

When the truck swung back the third time, I realized that the gaining momentum was going to take us into a complete spin and that was going to be it. I cried out loud, just as I had done in Flagstaff, "Oh God, please help us!"

The next thing I knew, the truck had stabilized and we were going in a straight line down the highway. I was able now to lightly apply the brakes, but we were still traveling at a good speed.

No one said a word. Then our keyboardist Peter Nunn said quietly, lightly patting my shoulder, "That was great driving, Danny."

"That wasn't my driving," I said. "When I yelled out it was because I was losing the truck and could feel it. That was God's doing."

That night I lay in bed, feeling the relaxation of sleep settling in, when all of a sudden I heard in my mind, "Danny, do you remember when the truck started to spin out?" I knew it was God speaking to me. "Yes," I responded. "Tell Me what happened," he said. I went through it all, the wider swings built out of the momentum we had been gaining, and that we would have spun out had we gone for another swing. God asked (and this was the million-dollar question), "Danny, when you cried out and the truck straightened, how do you think that happened? Were you still on ice or were you on dry pavement?"

I had been driving at seventy miles an hour, and I'd lifted my foot off the gas as soon as we hit the ice. We wouldn't have slowed down much in the next few seconds. We had been swinging because we were still on ice and then, suddenly, we were going straight. Had we been on ice or had we suddenly hit dry pavement? I said to God, as the light came on in my mind, "Your hand made us go straight, God; we were still on ice. If we had hit dry ground coming out from such a swing and gaining momentum, at that kind of speed the truck would have shuddered so hard it would have flipped over." God said, "I want you to call everybody tomorrow and ask each one the same question I asked you."

The next day I did just that and everyone realized that the truck would have flipped on dry pavement; that we still had to have been on ice. Only one was skeptical but at the same time he had to admit I had a point—that something had to have made the truck go straight because we would have flipped on dry pavement. That "something" was God's hand, I said, and He wanted everybody to know, which was why He had me call everybody. His arm is not too short to reach down to help, nor his ear too heavy to hear. Amen!

chapter twenty-six

The Loblaws Miracles

When least expected, Fate tumbles in.

| Percy Sledge

IN 1999 WE LIVED in a very crowded townhouse development where the park was no longer a safe place to bring your children. There were broken beer bottles in the children's area and we even found a syringe one day. We had been praying for a nice house on a farm since I had got out of rehab. We prayed for thirteen years. Here's how it all came about.

One day Debi gave me a local Milton newspaper and she told me that the Loblaws store was advertising for singers and musicians. I told her that I didn't sing in supermarkets; I was a professional. In short, it was beneath my standards of professional pride. She left for work and I thought about it and something told me that it was, after all, an opportunity and that I should give them a call. I had nothing to lose. I called the store in Milton and spoke with the store manager, Brian, who wanted me to come down for an audition. An audition for a grocery store manager! Not likely! I'd worked hard to get where I was and I was miffed that I had stooped to this nonsense in the first place. With all the willpower I possessed I tried to remain calm and politely told the manager that I didn't do auditions but if it was all right by him I would at least drop off my latest CD. He was surprised that I had a CD and we got to talking about my musical endeavors. I shared with him that I had been a Juno nominee, which basically sealed my fate and fortune as a "supermarket singer" for the next seven years. I still did my clubs, festivals, and church gigs but this was an added bonus as it paid well and eventually became consistently ten to twelve gigs a month in the daytime. Not hard to take.

After seeing the store manager, I worked for a year at his store and then at another store and then at a third, until there were seven stores at which I regularly played. This supplemented our income nicely, and then Debi got a new job in Burlington. This is how we came upon our beautiful farm in the Escarpment area, which, because of our increased income, we were now able to afford. Debi's new job turned out to be not far down the road from our farmhouse. The Milton Loblaws store was only seven miles away. Talk about things lining up! When we went to look at the farmhouse there was a lineup of people vying for residency because of the beautiful property and incredible view of the craggy escarpment across the road from us. How we were picked over all the other folks came down to this, and solidifies that you can't out-give God: I volunteered in the prison system and had recently received a ten-year certificate. Kelly, the woman who lived across the road from the farm, now our neighbor, was the head of prison volunteers and I was under her direction. Our new landlord selected us as tenants due to her personal recommendation. You reap what you sow! Our beautiful property has been a constant source of inspiration in my songwriting, and led to the *Righteous: Live at the Southside Shuffle* CD. We also recorded *Soulsville* here, and it is where I spent the many hours writing this book.

My work for Loblaws also qualified me as an employee and I was thus able to secure financing for my music. It is not a common thing to walk into a bank and say you are a musician and you need funds to do a recording. It can happen in Nashville but not up here in Canada. Yet, now I had three such loans from the Royal Bank and one from President's Choice (and to think I had balked when I first heard about singing at Loblaws).

With the secured financing we did the *Righteous* CD, but we ended up going over budget by $1,200. Debi and I wondered what we were going to do. We didn't have the money and our credit cards were maxed out. Out of the blue we got a call from Ian and Michelle Sim of Northern Praise Ministries. They wanted to bless us, which they did, paying the excess amount on the studio bill! AMEN!

Then, one day while performing in the Milton Loblaws store, I met a man named Bill when he came upstairs where I was performing and made a comment about all my harmonicas. He asked if I was selling them. I told him no, but that I was selling my music. He bought a couple of CDs from me and encouraged me by saying how much he enjoyed my music. A few months later I got a call from Bill. He wanted to hire me to do a gig at a retirement home where his mother was staying.

During this time I was on my knees one night asking God for a miracle. We were in financial trouble and I didn't know how we were going to cope. I said, "Lord, I don't know what You're going to do; I just have to believe that You can do it, and I do."

I did the gig at the retirement home and afterwards got to talking with Bill and his wife. Somehow we got on the topic of finances. I asked Bill the best way to deal with banks regarding consolidation and he asked why I wanted to go to a bank. I told him that they had already given me four loans thus far for my music. Bill said he could give me a much better deal than the bank and asked me how much I needed. To me it was a substantial amount, but to Bill it wasn't as substantial. "We'll consolidate your debts," he said. I was floored and told him I would speak to Debi and that we would pray about it. In speaking with Bill and Barb, his wife, I learned that they had retired early from the computer and software business they had founded.

When I got home and told Debi, we both agreed it was the answer to my cry to God for a miracle. Stuff like this doesn't happen every day! Debi and I still get a kick out of how I hadn't wanted to sing in a grocery store and we often share this story. If I hadn't called and got that job, we may never have moved to this beautiful farm, my income would not have increased the way it did, I wouldn't have obtained the loan to do *Righteous* and I may never have met Bill.

Later, Bill also offered to finance another CD recording. This turned out to be *The Soulsville Trilogy*, hence the recording of *Soulsville Souled Out 'n Sanctified*, which has received international critical acclaim and did very well on the Beach Music Radio Charts. The song "Other Side of the Cloud" from the *Soulsville* CD was named the number one song of 2005 by the National Association of Rhythm & Blues DJ's and the number 6 song for 2006. It also charted in the top ten best songs of the year on the Beach Music/Shag Top 50 charts for 2005–06. Also, the song was included on Southern Soul label One20inc, who promoted the song and my career in these parts, for which I am very thankful. I did a promotional trip and showcase at Judy's House of Oldies and Fat Harold's and I was able to lay groundwork for future touring with my new record *No Easy Way Out*. The recording was also recognized by the W.C. Handy Awards (now called the Blues Music Awards) and the pre-balloting committee contacted me to make a "by invitation only" submission. As well, my songs have been recognized by the International Songwriting Competition.

Summing up the experience, which all started with a small newspaper advertisement Debi had thankfully seen, I can't help but marvel at the turn of events, and how God connects all of us in ways that bring about these miracles. I had reluctantly called a supermarket to sing in a Loblaws store, whereby I started increasing my earning power to secure financing to start our own record label (His House Records) and do our first independent release. I then met a man—at this same supermarket-in-which-I-hadn't-wanted-to-sing—who bought my CDs, gave me encouragement, consolidated our debts, and then went on to finance His House Records!

How God brings things and people together is amazing, and my life is certainly testimony to that. Over the years I have been exposed to at least a million people in the Greater Toronto Area, which will one day translate into much better CD sales as more dots are connected in my career.

chapter twenty-seven

UCB Radio and Richard Wright

Son, you will never go wrong doing what's right.

| Dad

A FEW YEARS AGO, I heard from a gentleman named Gary Hooglivet from UCB Radio (United Christian Broadcasting) and he made some encouraging remarks about our 2002 *Saved! The Northern Blues Gospel All-Stars* CD. We traded a few e-mails and, as the saying goes, "from the little acorn grew the mighty oak." We have established quite a relationship since then.

A few years ago I went to Belleville, Ontario, and performed on the UCB Canada Radiothon to promote the new Christian station. There I met Gary Quinn, current station manager in Belleville. In talking, he handed me the card of a lawyer named Richard Wright, who acted for several established musicians in the entertainment business. Gary told me Mr. Wright was interested in getting behind promising musicians and helping them with their careers. Richard and I spoke several times over that year and he promoted my latest CD, *Soulsville*, to his contacts.

In the fall of 2004 I went to Belleville to do another radiothon. Gary Hooglivet and I had spoken about doing a radio show to promote my music and tell about my life. We ended up meeting in a busy coffee shop and he, having brought a tape recorder with him, recorded me right there in the midst of the hubbub. I chuckle now as I recall that at one point, he went over and asked the staff to turn down their house system because we were recording. I thought he was off his rocker to expect this to happen, but it did and I chalked it up to the incredible enthusiasm he exudes. I also wondered what kind of recording he was going to get but I was game and gave it my best.

Later, we recorded over twenty of my songs, which now, with our conversations, comprise a radio spot called "Behind the Blues with Danny Brooks," during which we talk about a message that is reinforced by one of my songs. The program is produced, of course, by Gary Hooglivet.

In early December when Gary had me come up to do the taping of the songs, he also had a prelaunch party for the new radio program. It was during this show that Richard Wright approached me and asked if I would be interested in writing my life story. He told me his brother Peter had commented that I had a story to tell and that I should write a book. He also went on to tell me that he had contacts in the publishing field, which would help as I went through the book process. And that is how this book came about. I had already had the idea and written the first 500 words in 2002, but quickly became overwhelmed by the task. On December 9, 2004, I came to the conclusion that, like a thousand-mile journey beginning with the first step, a book can be done one page at a time, and after a year I would have my book. It's easier to accomplish things when you look at a task that way. In a month, I had written about 92,000 words.

I am grateful for the experience and for the encouragement from everyone, especially Richard, and Stephanie, who did the early editing of this book and who have been a great encouragement to me and a big help in working with me to shape my thoughts and get the story out. Memories have poured out of me, and reliving my life has been not only a type of therapy and reconciling but also a wondrous affirmation of how God has kept me close.

chapter twenty-eight

"Bama Bound Miracle"
/Johnny Sandlin

The mighty Tennessee is rolling by,
I can see her now in my mind's eye,
The fields of cotton and the honeysuckle vine,
sweet soul music makes me feel so fine.

| From "'Bama Bound" by Danny Brooks

YEARS AGO I RECEIVED a call from independent review-
er Mitch Lopate, from New Jersey, who was publishing articles in
the *Gritz Southern Culture Magazine*. He really loved the *Saved! The
Northern Blues Gospel All-Stars* CD that was out in 2002. He reviewed
my later releases, *Soulsville Souled Out 'n Sanctified* and *Rock This House*,
and mentioned that I should contact Johnny Sandlin, famed Capricorn Records producer. Some of the folks Johnny produced were
the Allman Brothers, Bonnie Bramlett, Widespread Panic, Delbert
McClinton, Elvin Bishop, Marshall Tucker, Wet Willie, Dan Penn
and Eddie Hinton and many more. Mitch went on to tell me that my
music would go over great in the Muscle Shoals area and that Johnny
would not only love it, but would make a great record for me.

It sounded nice to hear this, but I felt it was a bit like picking up
the phone and calling George Martin, producer of the Beatles. You
don't just get a hold of these kinds of people and pique their interest
unless you have an inside connection. I didn't call Johnny. Mitch came
to a show that I did with Dennis, my bassist, in 2003 at the Sellersville
Theater just outside Philadelphia. He loved what he heard and saw,
and two years later printed his review of *Soulsville* in his first book,
Rock 'n Blues Stew. I was the only "no name" in this book and it was
kind of nice being mentioned between his reviews of George Harri-
son and Derek and the Dominos. Mitch sent the book to the folks he

interviewed, reviewed and did essays on and one of them was Johnny Sandlin.[10]).

Mitch became good friends with Johnny and Ann Sandlin through the writing and research for the book and, after sending a copy, he spoke with Johnny about me, and said that he had been telling me for some time to contact him. Johnny told him to contact me and that I was to give him a call at his studio, and in the latter part of 2005 I did just that. I certainly didn't need my arm twisted. I was very excited! Johnny was a real gentleman and we hit it off pretty well on the first telephone call. He would tell me later that when he first heard me speak, he figured I had to have a great singing voice, as I had such a gravelly sound. I was really impressed with Johnny's easygoing manner and would discover this is why he is such a great producer. Nothing seems to faze him. I agreed to send him my latest two CDs and he would contact me after listening to them. About a month went by and I figured perhaps he wasn't impressed and figured I would let it ride.

One night after a gig, I noticed the message light flashing in my little office and to my delight Johnny's voice was on it: "Danny, sorry for getting back a little late, but I love your voice and songwriting and would like for you to contact me." I was thrilled, called him the next day and he shared his thoughts about my music and songwriting and that I reminded him of Eddie Hinton. Johnny and Eddie had a band called The 5 Minutes when they were first starting to perform in Alabama. We spoke several times before our first meeting in early April of 2006. I met Johnny at his Ducktape Studio in Decatur, Alabama, which is about two hours due south of Nashville on I 65.

When I first arrived at the studio I immediately felt the history, warmth and special vibe that filled this wonderfully unique studio. You could sense the presence of Greg and Duane Allman, Eddie Hinton (their pictures were on the walls) and all the great Capricorn artists and Muscle Shoals players that shaped a genre and era of incredible music. We spent some time speaking and getting acquainted, which was as easy as sitting in your favorite old easy-back chair. I played him some new material and he liked what he heard and mentioned that he would like to record me at some point in the future. I had heard a little of Eddie Hinton before and when Johnny brought his lovely wife, Ann, into the studio to hear me sing, she mentioned that I reminded them of their good friend Eddie. Greg Martin and Chris Darrow had mentioned this to me as well. Eddie passed on in 1995 and was a great session guitarist and singer songwriter. Jerry Wexler and Ahmet Ertegun of Atlantic Records thought of Eddie as the "White Otis Redding," so it certainly did not offend me to be compared with him.

We met again in late September and by the time I arrived at Eddie's Attic in Atlanta, Georgia, where I was to perform, I had a message on my cell phone asking me how soon I could get back to Decatur and record. I've been around the block many times and have learned to be careful not to get overly excited as sometimes things just don't pan out. That's just the way it goes sometimes, but does it ever feel good to just let it go and be excited like a kid getting his favorite gift at Christmastime! I had a smile as wide as a Sumo wrestler's waistline. It felt like coming home after a long journey. I called and we agreed that I would come back down in November to lay down the bed tracks (drums, bass, guitar, some keys and scratch vocals).

I called Debi back home from Eddie's Attic and she was as happy with the good news. We've been through a lot together over the years and this was great news for both of us! Winston Churchill once said, "Never, never, never, never, never, give up!" After all the years of struggle and dashed hopes, this felt like something very special was shaping up, and still does over a year later with a multi-year deal with Johnny and Carl Weaver at Rockin' Camel Records.

I must say there was a haunting line from a great Bruce Springsteen song that was starting to bear down on my soul prior to this "dream coming true." It was from his song "Badlands," where he says, "You spend your life waiting for a moment, that just don't come." Man did that line speak to me! At times of doubt and frustration, I would say, "I'm going to do it, I won't quit, I can do all things through Christ, Who strengthens me; all things are possible." But still, that haunting line would pass through my mind and I would sometimes think that perhaps my dream had passed me by and left me standing in its wake; that I had blown it through the wasted years. When I got that call in Atlanta, I was released from thinking that life had passed me by; that my dreams were a thing of the past. Folks, it is never too late to dream and work on it. NEVER!

HEADING DOWN THE HIGHWAY
TO DECATUR, ALABAMA

> *I believe that dreams come alive and miracles for breakfast happen all the time.*
> *Yes I believe, I believe in miracles.*
>
> | From "Miracles for Breakfast" by Danny Brooks

I was about five hundred miles south of my home in Milton, Ontario, Canada, late at night and it was getting harder to keep my eyes open. I had performed the night before in Toronto, had three hours sleep and was now heading south on Interstate 71 in November 2006 to do the bed tracks on the new record at Johnny Sandlin's Ducktape Studios in Decatur, Alabama. As I had mentioned earlier, Mitch Lopate always thought I belonged down in the Muscle Shoals area and I was excited on the drive down thinking that I was going to the area where so many of my favorite artists and songs had come from. Here I am driving late at night, tired, excited and I should also mention that I was sick and taking penicillin, but nothing was going to stop me from going down to this dream come true session. God bless the American Dream!

Johnny arranged to have an incredible group of musicians at the session: David Hood who has performed with so many of the soul and rock giants; ditto for Spooner Oldham (Aretha Franklin, Bobby Blue Bland, The Staple Singers, Rod Stewart, Bob Seger, Paul Simon, Neil Young, Eddie Hinton to name but a few); and for Bill Stewart on drums (Wet Willie, the Allman Brothers, Alex Taylor), Scott Boyer, guitar from Cowboy (Capricorn Records) who had written songs for the Allman Brothers and Eric Clapton. When you are tired and sick and a little road weary, your thinking can go offside and the demons of doubt can really do a number on you and they were break dancin' all over me that night. I was starting to wonder what these guys, who have been a part of so many number-one and top-ten Billboard hits,

would think of my music. Then I asked myself if my songs could even
be considered album filler compared to some of these hit songs. If you
visit David Hood's or Spooner's web sites you get an idea of what I
was going through. I guess being alone, the new kid on the block and
in uncharted waters gave me a case of nerves. Add to that, I wasn't
feeling well and on some medication.

My cellphone rang, startling me in the dark confines of my truck.
It was Debi calling and she picked up right away on my condition. I
was about a hundred miles south of Cincinnati, near Louisville, and
she convinced me to pull over and rent a motel room and grab a good
night's sleep. I drove about another hundred miles and finally pulled
over at Cave City, not far from Greg Martin's (of The Kentucky Head-
hunters) place in Glasgow, Kentucky. I checked into the Comfort Inn
and almost immediately fell asleep. I got up seven hours later, read my
Bible, prayed, picked up my guitar and said, "God, I need Your help".

I went over the songs for the next hour and a half and I got inside
those songs like never before. I could feel it; I was in the zone and
encouraged. I put my guitars in the cases and said, "Thanks, God. I
think I'm going to be all right now." I even got a song idea out of it
all: "When We Sleep, Angels Speak." I headed on down south on
65 and four hours later I pulled into Decatur, Alabama. I'll tell you
something: all the years of doing the asphalt boogie, banging on doors
in Nashville (one time I even locked my keys in the car on music row
and it took me hours to get back in), doing showcases at the Bluebird
Café, it felt pretty darn good to be just whizzing through on my way
to do a record in Decatur with Johnny Sandlin and the Muscle Shoals
giants. I thought of rolling down the window as I passed the Nashville
exits and yelling, "Next time *y'all* will be callin' *me* and I'll probably be
too busy!" I didn't, but there was a feeling in my spirit to that effect.

I got to Johnny's studio the first day and Scott Boyer and I charted the songs. I played and he charted. (I look forward to doing some
writing with Scott, a great picker in the style of Steve Cropper and
Eddie Hinton.) When I walked into the studio the next day, which is
on Johnny's home property in a beautiful wooded area bordering the
Wheeler Wildlife Refuge in the Tennessee River Valley, the air was
full of electricity. I met all the players and although I had regained

some confidence, I was still a bit nervous. I guess it would be akin to a baseball player coming up from the farm system and having his first game in the majors. David Hood was a real gent (they all were) and broke the ice in a real cool way. Johnny was playing the song we were going to tackle first. Entitled "I Believe in Love Instantly," it's a song with a Percy Mayfield feel that I wrote for my daughter Caitlin, who had just turned fifteen and had met her first boyfriend earlier in the year. I wanted her to know that I understood what she may be going through.

David said in his laid-back southern drawl, "Well, Danny, y'all have come to the right place. Y'all could've been from down here.... Where'd you find this guy, Johnny?" Made me feel right fine, it did. We all worked at a comfortable rate with Johnny easing us in and out of songs, stories, and laughs and before the day was done we had five songs in the can. These guys played my songs like they already knew them and, in a way, I guess they did, as I had been drawing water from their well for years. The next day I met Spooner Oldham and that was special for me as I've always been a fan of his and Dan Penn's who wrote "Sweet Inspiration" for the Sweet Inspirations, "Cry Like a Baby" for the Box Tops, and "I'm Your Puppet" for James & Bobby Purify. Spooner also wrote "Out of Left Field" (Percy Sledge), and "A Woman Left Lonely" (Janis Joplin). This is interesting: four days earlier I was back home watching Neil Young's new DVD *Heart of Gold*, a performance at the Ryman Theater, that Debi had just bought and she points out Spooner Oldham. Now Spooner and I are sitting on this couch together listening to a track, "Keys To My Heart."

"Danny," he says, "I love your voice."

I say, "Thanks Spooner, but I know I'm a little rough in the throat."

"Don't matter," he says. "I like it just as it is."

This boy from Mt. Dennis is on cloud nine. A few times during the day, I had to hold back tears of joy and I still feel them well up as I write about it. It's difficult to express in words the joy of having recorded with Johnny and these players. I will always count it as a historical and musical highlight of my career. The song "Keys To My Heart" that Spooner commented on drew this response from Scott

Boyer: "Hey Spooner, you could've wrote this tune." That made me feel pretty good, and then they gave him the nod to do a beautiful Wurlitzer solo which added such a soulful dynamic to the song.

At the end of these bed track sessions, Johnny's wife, Ann, made up some great southern gumbo and we had ourselves a good feast and gabfest, which was a fitting conclusion to a soulful three days on the bed tracks.

On my December trip I finished doing my vocals (made changes, later, on some tunes), guitar and harmonica. Johnny also added Muscle Shoals guitarist Kelvin Holly, who plays with soulful fire. At one point I asked Johnny if he ever played with the Amazing Rhythm Aces, to which he replied, "As a matter of fact he plays with them and he's also Little Richard's guitarist." Johnny has amazing ears and can hear things that few people can and his laid-back folksy humor and outlook on things makes him a great person to be around.

Michael Pickett did a record with him years ago, with the Whiskey Howl band. He told me that Johnny was really something and he was right on! I look forward to doing future recordings in this studio, which is the most down-home, soulful place I've ever recorded in. Apart from the amazing old memorabilia such as old photos, posters, gold and platinum records on the walls in a rec-room setting, there was a framed daily planner page dated January first, 1969, with a stirring message that I wrote down word for word. It said:

This year I will be more thoughtful of my fellow man. Exert more effort in each of my endeavors, professionally as well as personally. Take love wherever I find it and offer it to everyone who will take it. In this coming year I will seek knowledge from those wiser than me and try to teach those who wish to learn from me. I love being alive and I will be the best man I possibly can.

— Duane Allman

Even now, as I finish typing this, I feel the electricity that ran through me as I first read it up on Johnny's wall that first meeting in April 2006. (No wonder it felt right when I got the call to do the record.) I felt the tears well up as I realized that Duane left this world shortly after writing these soulful and heartfelt words. He would have only two more Januarys after this before he passed over in a motorcycle accident on October 29, 1971. Tom T. Hall says in one of his songs about the passing of Clayton Delaney, and I believe it applies to Duane Allman: "I guess the good Lord loves a little guitar pickin' too."

I look back and see how fortunate I am to still be alive. In October of 1971, I was messed up from drugs and booze and was heading for the grave, like so many I knew, but the good Lord would give me a chance and put me in a prison first to see if He could get my attention. He did!

As I write this, Johnny had just finished mastering the new record *No Easy Way Out* at Masterfonics in Nashville, and, after two listenings, I am blown away by what he has done with this record. I am thrilled to have incredible soul singers Bonnie Bramlett, Carla Russell, Tina Swindell and Scott Boyer singing and to have the Muscle Shoals Horns on "Carry Me Jesus," which also features Roger Hawkins on drums. The Muscle Shoals Horns played on a couple of other songs and their history is as legendary as the Memphis Horns. James Pennebaker on pedal steel (Big & Rich/Delbert McClinton) added some amazing blues and country stylings on the record, as did Kelvin Holly who added some lap steel to his already hot guitar, featured on most tracks. He also played sitar on "Miracles for Breakfast," giving a unique sound to the tune.

The making of this record was an amazing experience and one I will never forget. There was not one moment of ego tripping, no harsh words or disagreements on parts, or complaints of any kind. There were absolutely no tense moments of any kind. That alone made the sessions truly remarkable; then factor in the players and their unforgettable performances. Man-oh-man! If there was such a thing as winning the Music Lottery, I won it, hands down! A great team needs to be coached by a great leader and I had that in producer Johnny Sandlin, who was helped by his righthand man, Jeremy Stephens, and assistant Jeff Coppage. This all took place in one of the warmest atmospheres I've ever been in. I spent whole nights in that studio, staying up and writing songs and sleeping on the couch so the spirit of the place would rub off on me.

As well as Johnny's involvement with the Allman Brothers, his work as Phil Walden's righthand man at Capricorn Records, the great artists he has worked with, he is one of the main architects of the southern rock music scene, a fact that's been acknowledged by his induction into the Alabama Music Hall of Fame. On top of all that, he is a warm, genuine human being who cares about others, and I am so looking forward to our next recording slated for the fall of 2008, back at his Duck Tape Music studio.

chapter twenty-nine

Divine Appointments

Call unto Me and I will answer you, and show you great and mighty things that you did not know.

| Jeremiah 33:3 (often referred to as God's Telephone Number)

EVER SINCE I DEDICATED my life to God and realized how I had affected everyone in my life before then, I have asked forgiveness and dedicated myself to having a positive influence on people through my actions and especially my music. I have not only experienced miracles but also amazing proof of God's mercy and grace. During the period I first got saved I cried out to God to be used, to be able to reach people and make a difference. This was very important to me as I was "souled" out for Him and wanted to share His love and grace. I had been part of the problem for so long; now I wanted to be part of the solution.

He answered my prayers and in sharing these next stories, I would like to show the incredible way that God works in people's lives.

THE REX HOTEL APPOINTMENT

We can run but we can never get away from God, and we may choose to not listen to Him, but if He has a specific plan for us to carry out, I believe we will eventually be brought in, to carry out His plans.

| Danny Brooks

I was setting up my equipment one evening for a solo performance in a fine old establishment, renowned for its jazz in downtown Toronto, and my senses picked up on a rather burly, rugged gentleman staring at me. At one point when our eyes made contact and I smiled at him, he called me over. He said, "Is your name Danny?" I replied yes. He said, "I remember you playing at one of our biker parties on a farm outside of London, and at a few other places." I remembered the London gig well. I had been stringing up lights on the barn where the metal roof was and suddenly heard pinging noises. A biker was shooting a shotgun at the roof to kill pigeons for a barbecue. I was lucky I didn't get hit!

We got to talking and he remarked that I looked well and fit and he asked me how I had got it all together, since he remembered me as not being in a good state. I shared my faith very simply, stating that if it weren't for God we likely wouldn't even be having this conversation. I told my story and how I came to my faith.

When I finished, he shook my hand and didn't let go for the next few minutes. It was a very firm handshake and I thought he might break my hand, but I said nothing. I now know, these years later, that it's what kept him holding back his tears although his eyes had been moist as he shared his story. He had been recently "retired" by his outlaw bike gang as the president of his chapter, which was part of a well-known international bike gang (from a different city), and he was sitting alone, drinking here in Toronto, coming to grips with what had happened and it was difficult for him. Turns out his wife had become a Christian and the pastor of her church would visit their home to minister. He related that when the preacher came he was usually working on his bike in the garage and he would just yell out to the preacher, "She's in the house." One day when this happened, the preacher replied, "I've come to see you today."

His eyes welled up as he recounted the rest of the story. He had asked the preacher what he wanted, to which the minister had answered, "I just want to tell you that I love you and care about you and I wish I had told you before, but I'm telling you now. God loves you so very much as well." As the biker's eyes watered and his hand gripped mine tightly he whispered, "Outside my wife, nobody ever told me that they loved me, that they cared." He also shared with me that part of him had wanted to hit the preacher but another part wanted to listen, so he listened. He admitted to me that he agreed with what the preacher talked about, that he had spent a life of crime and was not happy, and that he was wrestling with surrendering his life to Christ and being a better man for his wife, who dearly loved him.

I told the biker that I loved him too and that God had been the Power behind him being honorably let go as president of his gang chapter so he could have a godly relationship with his wife. He needed no convincing as I said it would have been impossible to just up and leave the gang, but God had provided the way. I told him that I had to get going to prepare for my gig but I asked if I could pray with him first and he said yes. I prayed that God would continue to work in his life and bring him to that place of peace through surrendering and asking for forgiveness. He thanked me and stayed for my first set and then left.

When I drove home that night, I tingled with Holy Ghost shivers. I thanked God for bringing the biker to the Rex that night and asked for His continued blessing on his life.

Many times I come home from club gigs and I wonder, "What am I doing, Lord?" and my spirit is downcast, but when these type of divine appointments take place I know exactly why I am where I am.

SHANGRI-LA BIKER RETREAT

When we are willing to share our faith, God will bring people to us at the most unusual places and times.

| Danny Brooks

Not long after my conversion, I was performing up north at a well-known outlaw biker gang's retreat on a two-hundred-acre farm. I didn't want to go but Danny K. said he was stuck and needed me to be part of the Woodstock Revisited show and I guess I caved in because I really needed the coin. Also, little did I know that God had planned another divine appointment.

After my portion of the show, Debi and I were walking around and listening to the other performers when a familiar face said, "Hello,

Danny." After sharing pleasantries he asked me about my stay at the Donwood, what it was like, how long it was, and if it had really helped. He also made mention of my newfound faith. As he broached these topics with me, at first he seemed hesitant and was looking around to make sure no one heard our conversation. I respected his position and concerns. I told him about my Donwood stay, and he admitted he needed help; that things were getting a little out of hand. He also asked me to keep what he was telling me to myself as he did not want anyone knowing about it. I shared my faith with him and he was very attentive to what I was saying. He said he knew that I was doing right and that he needed to do the same thing, but it was obvious that he was in a bind and didn't know how to proceed.

It's one thing to share your newfound faith with friends and co-workers at your workplace, and that takes courage, but it is another thing when you're involved with an outlaw gang and you're not fully aware of what God is capable of doing. I really felt for him and asked if I could quickly and quietly pray for him. He wanted it but was hesitant, looking around. I said we could keep our eyes open and I would be quick and he agreed. I quickly asked God to watch over him and to continue what He had started in my acquaintance's life, and to protect him and bring him into the Kingdom. He thanked me and just as quickly left. I realized why I had taken the gig and thanked God for using me in this way.

JAIL REPRISE

> *…inasmuch as you did it to the least of these My brethren, you did it to Me.*

> | Matthew 25:40

I remember when I first started to volunteer and perform in the prison system, I would get so worked up about what to say and how to say it, what to study and how I should prepare for it, that I almost got sick. Thankfully, God said to me, "Danny, do not worry about anything, just show up and I will be with you. Say what comes to your mind." At first I thought I just couldn't go without laboring over it, but I realized that after prayer I could and was ready. If we are studying our Bible every day and praying every day, we are ready for anything; we just have to be willing. God took my willingness, gave me peace, and everything worked out great!

I performed a concert once a month in the Vanier Institute for Women, the Ontario Correctional Institute (OCI), and the Young Offenders (I could write a book on this alone), alternating each month and sometimes going to other youth facilities. Needless to say, I have met some people who really needed to hear that "all things are possible with God."

In November 1993, I received a letter from an inmate at the OCI, now defunct, having made way for the super jail, the Maplehurst Prison, in Milton, Ontario. The letter states how the men in their unit were moved by my story and that four of them surrendered their lives to Christ the night of one of my concerts. This is remarkable because I had considered stopping my performance there; these conversions may not have taken place had I stopped going. It was the only prison of its kind anywhere, combining sex offenders and criminals with drug and alcohol problems. It worked because the prisoners knew beforehand that it was an experimental program and they were given the choice whether or not to go. That's not to say it didn't have its problems. It did, but in other prisons there would have been murders among the inmates. They would not have been able to co-exist, but here they co-existed and it worked. What helped them in their decision was that under this particular program they knew they would "shake better time," have more conveniences for their co-operation in this new trial program.

It was a difficult decision to continue there but I am happy that Kelly, who headed the volunteer program, helped convince me to stay. One of the reasons it had been hard to keep performing there was that this was the prison in which one of the inmates, Joseph Fredericks, convicted for abduction and sexual assault while out on parole in Brampton, had taken a young boy named Christopher Stephenson from a shopping mall and sexually assaulted and murdered him.

Psalm 139:22 says, "I hate them with perfect hatred; I count them my enemies." The verse before it states, "Do I not hate them, O Lord, who hate You? And do I not loathe those who rise up against You?" I know we are to love the sinner and hate the sin, but if ever there was a crime that prompted you to easily hate the sinner and even think about killing him yourself, regardless of the fact that you never would, it would be a crime like this. I speak here as a father.

Every sex offender in this particular prison had been molested as a kid. I had read a book by Dr. Rebecca Brown, who is a doctor of oncology with a deliverance ministry through which she helps people leave satanic cults. In the book she states that children who are sexually violated are attacked by people who are either demonically possessed or demonically controlled. The process thereby passes to the child a demonic attachment, a residue, if you will. The child grows up with this demonic baggage and is affected by it and if this is not properly addressed in a godly, spiritual manner, he or she will be in serious trouble.

I had asked Kelly, who had run the volunteer program for over ten years (and she read every case history), if any of the child molesters had started late in life with a perversion for children or if they had all been molested as children. She emphatically told me that, in her tenure at the prison, everyone who had been taken in thus far as a sex offender had been assaulted or molested as a child. This fact made me do some soul searching, and, don't get me wrong, while I still hated the crime and its perpetrators, it gave me some understanding I didn't have before. Was it their fault they were molested as a kid? Definitely not! Nor was it their fault that they had grown up with demonic baggage. (I believe Dr. Rebecca Brown was correct in her assessment.) I had to view these prisoners with a different understanding, and, aided by my desire to help the drug addicts, I decided to stay. I also decided to stay because one of the guards, a former Pentecostal preacher and now a "spirit guide," was involved with some strange "spiritual" group. He wanted me to go up north and worship or celebrate Fall Solstice. I figured a little spiritual balance was needed in the prison and I would stay and plead the Blood of Christ over the place and the inmates who needed it. They were in not only a physical prison but also a spiritual one, with the demonic residue of their childhood horrors and with this particular guard involved.

I have met many people from these prisons at some of my club and festival gigs and I am always touched when they come up to me and tell me how much they enjoyed my coming in. We did a CD release for *It's a Southern Thing* in the Vanier Women's Prison in 1998 and were covered by local cable TV and as well the CBC. Over the years I have taken part in holiday celebrations in prisons and I have always been encouraged by the inmates to "keep on keeping on," and I believe God was teaching us all about His humility and love. In 1995 I was presented with the Solicitor General & Correctional Service & Community Services Award and, later, received a ten-year pin with a letter from the Queen, who honored volunteers with her Queen's Jubilee Celebrations in 2002. I count it an honor as I have received and learned a great deal from the inmates during this period in my life.

I have heard many heartbreaking stories from the men and women in the prison system; these have been very important to my songwriting as I try to reach out and touch folks with their backs to the wall. As well, I am reminded of a fact that I put into a song entitled "Wheels Keep Spinning":

> *Children run and play on their way to school*
> *Before they learn all the ways of this world*
> *Why do we get so uptight about what we read in the news*
> *Why it's our example, they only follow after me and you*

It is up to every one of us to do our part in making this world a better place; our example makes the world what it is today. I believe the biggest thing anyone can accomplish here on this earth is to be a shining example for others to see and from which they can benefit. Anyone can give money away to a charity, which is good, or lend their name or talents to a worthy cause, but continuously upholding a standard of what is righteous—*this*, my friend, is the ultimate, and what we all should strive for.

RADIO LEGEND JOHN DONABIE

I raise my hands to testify, tears of joy falling from my eyes,
I thank the good Lord that I'm still standing at all.

| From "Still Standing Tall" by Danny Brooks

People all around us are affected by what we do or say. I am continuously amazed by what God has shown me in my life and how He has worked through and with me after He turned my seemingly impossible life around. The choices we make, the connections we establish—with God, these things are not accidental; rather, they are everyday manifestations of His intentions for all of us in building His Kingdom.

This next divine appointment really touched me. I came home one night after a gig and noticed my message light flashing on my phone. It was a long, encouraging message from John Donabie, a well-known radio personality. He stated that he had just come through a very serious illness. When he had heard my song "Still Standing Tall," he felt inspired to carry on and get well; he credited the song's message as one of the reasons he got well. John and I have become good friends. He has been and is currently a help to me in my music career.

I had written "Still Standing Tall" to tell about my past and the fact that so many of my old friends are not around anymore, yet here I am, still standing, learning that man can't do anything on his own; he gets through only with the help from God above. I never knew that my song would affect John, or anyone, the way it did; I just wanted to write an account of why I believe I'm still standing. But we don't have to see the bigger picture—just be willing to be a good example and God will use that for incredible purposes. I do not believe there is anyone alive today who cannot be used by God in the simplest of things to accomplish great things. It all comes down to our willingness, not our station or education—to a humble spirit that wants to make a difference.

THE WALKING MAN

You walked fifteen miles to come these fifteen feet to the altar.

| Danny Brooks

I was going to perform at my brother Michael's church up in Smith's Falls and I was unloading my equipment at around nine-fifteen a.m. to be ready for the ten-thirty service. A man said hello to my brother Michael and told him he had just walked fifteen miles and thought he would pop in the church. I figured they were friends and thought nothing of it.

After my sound check, this fellow went up to Michael and commented on how happy he was to have come to the church that morning, as he loved blues music, and was looking forward to my performance. My brother shared this with me, and after my performance and testimony and his service, Michael gave an altar call. This gentleman came up for prayer. My brother asked if I would go and pray for him. I went over and asked if I could pray with him and we spoke for a bit and then prayed. The man told me he could relate to a lot of what I spoke about, and that he had walked fifteen miles that morning, not planning to go to church, but when he was walking by, he felt something telling him to come in. I told him that God had him walk the fifteen miles to take the fifteen steps up to the altar; he smiled. He had been to church before on occasion but was not a regular churchgoer. His eyes misted up as I shared with him that God had a plan for him and had directed his path this morning, wanting him to be part of the family of God. I explained the sinner's prayer of simply asking God's forgiveness of sins and accepting Him to come into his life as Lord and Savior. While the man was hesitant to make a commitment, he wanted prayer and so we prayed. I gave him my latest CD as I knew God would use it to speak to this man; I trust that he has said the sinner's prayer since.

SOUTHSIDE SHUFFLE JAZZ & BLUES FESTIVAL

I used to wake the mornings with trepidation and the blues not far behind.
Then one day I got wise and now I'm soul satisfied.

| From "Soul Satisfied" by Danny Brooks

It was a beautiful sunny afternoon and the band and I were perform-ing on the main stage. There was a beer tent behind the seating in front of the stage, under which a large number of people were try-ing to hide from the sun and perhaps rid themselves of their thirst. After our performance, people came over to speak with us and buy CDs from the CD tent, but it wasn't till I got home that I was really touched; I had received a moving phone message.

This message came from someone from whom I had least expect-ed to hear it, since he was sort of a bandit, a good guy but a little on the wild side. He said that he and his band had been sitting in the beer tent drinking and watching us perform and the song "Soul Satisfied" had moved him. He stated that he was soul searching and that the song gave him encouragement. He went on to tell me to keep up the good work, that people are out there listening and watching, and you never know who you are touching and how it is affecting them. People need to hear the message, he said. He told me he had been struggling with a cocaine addiction for the past twenty years. He had been to see a minister and was taking his children to church, and he had a loving and supportive wife. He knew the path of salvation but was caught up in this insidious addiction.

This was quite a phone message of encouragement to me, a testa-ment that sometimes the types of people you least expect are searching and crying out to God. We need to be there for them and we can only do that by keeping up our daily struggle to do what is right and setting the right example. This may sound a little over the top but I'm going to say it anyway: the world is in real serious trouble and it depends on us to do something about it and save it. God can use our weaknesses to do this and we are a lot better off admitting we are weak than to fool no one but ourselves in thinking we are strong.

When I think of how God changed my life, has touched me with His grace, I affirm wholeheartedly that I want to make a difference and I won't ever give up or quit, and when I stumble I will admit it and ask for His forgiveness and carry on in doing what is right in the best way I can. People are dying and crying out every day, in the offices, the factories, strip clubs, nightclubs, in the world of high finance, the entertainment and sports worlds, the governments, and even the gangs and organized crime groups. Let us not discriminate based on how they look or the fact that they do not share the same doctrine as us; let's try to look at them through the eyes of Jesus, as people, His children, in need, in desperate need of love and understanding. God is calling us; are we listening or are we too busy showing Him what we can do for Him?

chapter thirty

My Family Today

Your troubles become your wisdom, for whom you meet a troubled soul
For you can hold them through the storm, before they get back home

| From "All God's Children Have to Cry, Sometime" by Danny Brooks

ALL FAMILIES HAVE THEIR share of hardships and regrets. There is no perfect church and there is no perfect family and there is no perfect institution of any kind on this earthly plane. Where there are people, there are problems, simple as that. I do believe though, that hardships are minimized and families can handle situations better when there is the element of faith involved. Faith can move mountains and it can overcome any hardships. It isn't always easy, but faith will always prevail.

I am so thankful that I was raised in a God-fearing household which enables me today to teach and show our children the power of love and prayer. Love covers a multitude of sin and prayer moves the Hand of God. Even the medical profession says that those who bring prayer into the operating room have the highest success rates in recovery. We saw this in Richard Bell, our keyboardist who had overcome cancer that riddled his body and he is the first to say it was the power of Prayer and his conversations with his Maker. After a nine-month fight he recently performed with us at Hugh's Room and a concert hall up in Alliston, Ontario. Sadly, Richard passed over on June 15, 2007, after being given a year's extension on his life. He was so brave and upbeat, that I could only hope to emulate him under similar circumstances.

One time while under heavy medication and tubes seemingly running everywhere from his body, I lamented and said, "Oh Richard, I'm so sorry…." to which he replied in a strained voice: "Don't worry Danny, I ain't leaving yet, I owe too many people too much money." Broke me right up. He was declared cancer-free before succumbing to the cancer that took him home. He once told me that he had made his peace with God and said he was ready, but if it was okay with God to give him a little extra time to do a few more things. He got about a year. I will never forget Richard's charm and ability to make you feel like you were important, a person of value. I will also never forget the lessons learned and what he did for me on a personal and professional level.

My mother always taught us the "God factor" in everything while my seven brothers and sisters and I were growing up. So did my dad, but it was Mom who daily had the opportunity to plant seeds in our daily lives. She was adamant about the golden rule "do unto others as you would have them do unto you," and always be kind, considerate and honest with others. She was, and still is, a very compassionate lady and I know that my ability to get down and soulful with a song comes from her. We had our share of troubles in our family, but faith, hope and love made all the difference in the world. Mom lives in her home in Etobicoke, Ontario, along with Peter, the youngest of the family. Peter can fix anything, and after a lifetime of taking everything he could in the house apart, driving my parents crazy at times, he developed a talent to fix engines, clocks, bikes. You name it; he can fix it. Peter has three beautiful daughters that live with their mom. Since I've started with the youngest, I'll proceed from there. Karla and I took similar paths, and fortunately for her, she left the party lifestyle long before I would and married a great guy and they have four beautiful daughters whose names all begin with "K." Doug has a business called Deco Labels & Tags.

Same with Kristin; she knew the wild side and then met a good man from Newfoundland or as we affectionately call them north of the Mason-Dixon line, "Newfies." Kristin is very talented, with an entrepreneurial spirit. They have three very gifted children and have their own MEDIchair business in Oakville. David, her husband, used to ride with the Christian Riders Motorcycle Club and was the president for a few years. They once were in a film, *God Rides a Harley*, about which David once remarked to me, "Jesus never would've rode a Harley if He was here. He would've ridden on a moped." Considering that Jesus came into Jerusalem on a donkey and not a stallion, I believe he's right.

Next is my brother Michael who once road-managed me in the seventies before entering Bible College. At that time he was no stranger to the goings-on of the world and the experience has seasoned him with a capacity to understand his fellow man. Michael went on to become a pastor and missionary and was in Liberia with his family during the civil war in the nineties. He and his family were fortunate to escape this war-torn area with their lives. Many of their neighbors and fellow Liberians were not as fortunate as there were some terrible atrocities. Shortly after they left Liberia, there was an explosion at a destroyed the airport and had they not left when they did, they may not have been so fortunate. Years later Michael and his family came back to Liberia for a time, and then back to Canada to pastor at a church in Smith's Falls. Michael and Sheila, his wife, and the two youngest of five children (twins) are about to embark on a new journey to Kenya where he will serve as the academic dean of the Bible College and will leave to go to Kenya in early 2008. (Anyone wishing to help Michael and his ministry can donate to the Pentecostal Assemblies of Canada marked "The Middlebrook Family" or through Northern Praise Ministries.)

Sister Shannon is next and, as mentioned earlier, we were a "team" growing up, reciting Bible verses and stories at the churches our dad would bring us to. Shannon is a registered nurse and is one of the strongest and most sensible people I know. Shannon and Leonard have two sons that they are proud of. I probably speak with Shannon the most of all my siblings and even at that, it is not all the time, however we enjoy those moments when we connect. We are close even in our absence. Shannon, Kristin and Karla keep Mom busy since Dad went to Heaven in '94 and I couldn't ask for better sisters.

Next is older brother Greg who lives out west in Calgary with Jo-Anne and Mark, their son. Greg and I were very close growing up and, as hippies, went on many adventures and trips together.

Unfortunately for Greg while growing up, part of his punishment when he got into any kind of trouble was to have me tag along. I loved it, but Greg didn't and what older brother wants his kid brother tagging along anyway. We have kind of drifted apart over the years but every now and then have a chat over the phone and catch up a bit on how things are going. I always looked up to my brother Greg and still do. He once made a comment that I'll never forget. It has helped me weather the difficult times in the music business: "When your back is to the wall that's the time you can make headlines."

I've written some songs about my oldest brother, Bill, who has been a major influence on my life. He always took time to instill confidence and self-worth in me while I was growing up. Bill went to Emmanuel Bible College in North Carolina and ended up feeling God led him to drive his own rig/truck and spread the Word that way, and he did all over North America. He also started his moving company, A. Bills' Express. I wrote "Brother Bill" on my *It's a Southern Thing* CD and "Carolina Shine" (the name of his truck) on my *Rough Raw & Simple* CD. Bill was a painter and drew great country scenes and odd-looking trees. He also wrote a self-help book under the name of Harold Ben-Judah. Bill had four children with Willie Mae, whom he met at Bible College. During my dark days Bill always impressed on me that God would listen to anything I had to say to Him and although I had no use for faith in those days, he always made Christianity sound like a cool thing and something worth looking into. Sadly, Bill was recently hospitalized, and is in long-term care.

I owe a great debt of gratitude to all my family members who prayed and helped me get back on my feet again. Thank you all so very, very much!

chapter thirty-one

How I Came to Be Published

When least expected, Fate tumbles in.

| Percy Sledge

I FEEL IT ONLY PROPER to finish this book with an account of how it got its start with world class publisher John Wiley & Sons. I had finished the book back in June of 2005 with the help of Stephanie VanderMuelen of Word By Word. Much like a record producer preparing good demos to shop to the major record labels, she prepared the story to shop the book to various publishers. I had sent the manuscript around and much like my experience in the music industry, I started to receive the rejections: "This isn't what we're looking for," or "We are already committed for the next few years," and so forth.

In my travels, I had met a gentleman in Nashville who knew some folks at Lifeway and Thomas Nelson Publishers. He was hopeful that he would be able to interest these publishers in the book. Around mid-September, 2006, I came home one day to see my phone message light flashing and was elated at the message. "Hello Danny, my name is Don Loney, and I am an editor with John Wiley & Sons. We are intrigued with your story, and would you please contact me at this number to discuss this further." Needless to say I was excited. My first thought was that perhaps someone who had turned the book down passed it to someone else in the business. Then I figured my Nashville connection had come through and found a publisher.

After playing phone tag for a bit, Don and I finally connected and, after opening pleasantries, we got down to business. Don said he was interested in my story. Would I consider writing about my life for his company? I replied that I had already written a book, and he asked what was the title and if it was published. I told him the title and said that I was shopping it. I asked him if he had heard about it. When he said no, "but I love the title," I was somewhat taken aback and said "Well, how did you hear about me, Don?"

I love this part.

He said, "I read a small article about you in the Toronto Blues Society's *Maple Blues* magazine, and I enjoyed the article and went to your web site and discovered more. I figured you had a story to tell."

A quick thought went through my mind: that it's the little things that count sometimes, and when least expected, fate tumbles in. [11]

Don asked me if I could give him a quick anecdote that would substantiate his interest in the book. I told him about the time my dad and pastor came to pray for me at my apartment when I was dealing speed, and about how, coming out of rehab fifteen years later, I was the only one still alive from that night. Don was moved by it and asked me to send the manuscript. As they say, the rest is history. We worked on the book for the next year and a half and I am indebted to Don and the team at John Wiley & Sons for their belief in me and the wealth of experience I have gained in the process. Always remember, little things mean a lot!

Epilogue

I am a firm believer in luck; the harder I work the more luck I get.

| "The Blue Collar Prophet" / Dad (a.k.a. Bible Bill, as his knowledge and Bible verse memorization rivalled that of Jack Van Impe)

LIFE IS HELD IN a delicate balance where the simple and little things mean a lot. Do not overlook them; do not dismiss them. The Good Book says there is profit in all labor: "Big things happen when little things are taken care of" (Proverbs 14:23).

It is my sincere hope that this book has been an inspiration and an encouragement and if it has been so to only one, even one person, then I have succeeded immensely, for who can put a value on one person's life?

I am learning more every day about God's grace, and about the power of example and its effect on those around us. I believe that what we do privately or publicly unleashes spiritual forces that will affect others' lives. I also believe what we do privately affects our public life. I am living proof of that; my story tells of the people I negatively influenced or hurt or even abandoned—but it also tells of God's love and amazing mercy and forgiveness. It relates how nothing is impossible when God has a plan. It tells of how we can be brought from the very depths of despair to enduring hope. It speaks of miracles even in the mundane, the affirmation of God's constant presence. The power of God's grace allowed me to touch so many lives in positive ways, not only through my commitment to Him and my example, but also through my music, which, thanks to His help, has reached thousands of people.

Many of us today are standing at a crossroads where there is everything to gain and everything to lose and it all depends on how we choose. This is it, no more wiggle room. What are you going to do?

I am going to work out my salvation with fear and trembling, knowing that I serve an almighty God, an all-knowing and all-loving God, who can give to me or take away from me, who can appoint me an eternity with Him or an agonizing eternity without Him. He wants to bless us all, but we must be prepared. We must choose to follow Him, and that is a lifetime commitment, a lifetime work-in-progress.

Thank you, God, for your provision and loving me in spite of myself. Thank you for teaching me what I needed to know to at least get started on this righteous path. I have a long way to go, I know, but so does everybody. I may not be what I want to be but, thanks to You, Lord, I am not what I used to be. Help me each day to approach that place where you want me to be.

End Notes

CHAPTER 2

1. I credit my dad to this day for teaching me hard lessons in life and the art of hustling. You could drop me in any city with ten bucks in my pocket and I would figure out a way to survive.

   I couldn't have had a better upbringing from Mom and Dad, as they taught us the real golden rule, about love, justice, and the Word of God. The Good Book says, "Train up a child in the way he should go, and when he is old he will not depart from it" (Proverbs 22:6), and I am living proof of that. Years later when, like in old Hank's song, "I Saw the Light," my dad would refer to me as "The Miracle Man." Today, that's just how I feel, too.

CHAPTER 5

2. In doing some research about Charles Manson on www.charliemanson. com and a few other sites, I made a startling discovery thirty-six years later that made me shiver. I found that the gibberish about "what it is" we had been hearing was in fact excerpts from a book entitled *As It Is* written by Robert de Grimston, a Satanic leader of the Process Church of Christ. I believe these many years later it was him reading that night. They held "worship" services at midnight, and upon reading this I pictured us back in this club thirty-six years ago. It was three weeks before the Sharon Tate murders. This de Grimston man and his wife influenced Charles Manson, who attended their meetings. They were at one time

involved in Scientology. They were considered too intelligent and willful to stay with Hubbard, but the communal residence philosophy was adapted by the de Grimstons and by Manson and his followers.

CHAPTER 13

3. My latest record, *No Easy Way Out*, features Kelvin Holly, guitarist for Little Richard.

4. Since that time (except for the period just before going into rehab, when I was really losing it, and the period afterward, when I was convalescing) I have been in music full time. Living in Canada, this is a success in itself. Ask anyone.

CHAPTER 14

5. Hunter S. Thompson, *Generation of Swine: Tales of Shame and Degradation in the '80s*, Summit Books, 1988. p. 43.

6. I am thinking of writing a book called *Miracles on the Road*, and this card game story would make a great movie scene. I still can't believe I survived that night.

CHAPTER 15

7. Sadly, Domenic succumbed to cancer in 2005 and, though he performed with many big names such as the James Gang, Bush, and the Guess Who, he will always be remembered for his fiery and absolutely stunning guitar heroics in the red-hot exciting Toronto band The Mandala.

CHAPTER 17

8. Later I wrote a song based on that conversation with God entitled "All I Want is Someone to Love," a rock/reggae tune that I would go on to perform live.

CHAPTER 25

9. Recently I got back from Muscle Shoals, and I was so moved that I wrote a song, "Baptized in the Fire of Soul." I will share this later in the

book, as it is part of an amazing story that involves my latest CD that was recorded in Decatur, Alabama with legendary Capricorn Records producer Johnny Sandlin.

CHAPTER 28

10. Others included in the book were Bobby Whitlock, Bonnie Bramlett (who sings on my new CD), and Levon Helm from The Band.

CHAPTER 31

11. Gary Tate, a local freelance music writer, had written a piece on me that I still use in my promo package and can be found on my web site's promo page.

Acknowledgments

THERE HAVE BEEN SO many people who have touched my journey through life in a positive way, especially during my most desperate times of need, whether for a job, food, a warm place to stay, kinship, or encouragement and support. Not one benevolent act was better or more important than another; they were all so vital to how I lived my life and got me to where I am today.

I know that God led us to each other, and for that and your kind, understanding, and generous hearts, I am utterly grateful.

Discography

Praise for **No Easy Way Out**

"Brooks is akin to the Phoenix who rose from the ashes of his youth spent battling his personal demons. He now spends his time playing for prisoners and church functions, spreading the word that, through faith, anything is possible. Give a listen to *No Easy Way Out* to see what we mean!"

— Sheryl and Don Crow, Music City Blues Society, Nashville, TN

Title: **No Easy Way Out** (2007)
Label: Rockin' Camel Records
Tracks: Ain't That the Truth; All God's Children; No Easy Way Out; Keys to My Heart; 'Bama Bound; Miracles for Breakfast; Lonesome Road; Where Sinners and Saints Collide*; Memphis, Tennessee; I Believe In Love; Carry Me Jesus**

All songs written by Danny Brooks (SOCAN)
*Co-written with Dean McTaggart
**Written by Ann Sandlin/ Johnny Sandlin/Carla Russell

Production Credits:
Produced by Johnny Sandlin
Recorded and mixed by Johnny Sandlin and Jeremy Stephens
Additional engineering by Jeff Coppage
Recorded and mixed at Duck Tape Music Studio, Decatur, AL
Mastered by Jonathan Russell at Masterfonics, Nashville, TN
Photos by Debra Middlebrook

Personnel: Danny Brooks: lead vocals/acoustic guitar/dobro/harmonica; David Hood: bass; Bill Stewart: drums; Spooner Oldham: Wurlitzer/ B3; Kelvin Holly: electric/acoustic guitars/lapsteel; Scott Boyer: electric guitar/vocals; James Pennebaker: pedal steel guitar; Kevin McKendree: piano/B3; Bonnie Bramlett: vocals; Tina Swindell: vocals; Charles Rose: trombone; Harvey Thompson: tenor and baritone sax; Vinnie Cieleski, Ken Watters: trumpet; Johnny Sandlin, Ann Sandlin, Jeff Coppage: handclaps/ tambourine/percussion.

Title: **Soulsville: Rock this House** (2005)
Label: His House Records
Tracks: Can't Keep a Good Man Down for Long; Hold On; Stand Up*; Yonder Cloud; Rock this House; You'll Find a Way; Good Love Is Hard to Find; Walks on Water; Never Go Wrong Doing Right; Down on My Knees; Unseen Hands; Tears from Heaven; Takes a Little Time

All songs written by Danny Brooks (SOCAN)
*Co-written with Richard Bell

Production Credits:
Produced by Richard Bell
Mixed by Doug Romanow at Fire Escape Studios

Personnel: Danny Brooks: lead vocals/acoustic guitar/harmonica; Richard Bell: Hammond B3/piano/Wurlitzer; Papa John King: guitar; Teddy Leonard: guitar; Dennis Pinhorn: bass; Bucky Berger: drums; Ed Zankowski: sax; Paul Cousee: tenor and baritone sax; Joe Allen: trumpet; John Mays, Hiram Joseph, Steve Ambrose, Amoy Levy, Julia Churchill: backup vocals; Doug Romanow: neuron synthesizer, accordion.

Title: **Soulsville: Souled Out 'n Sanctified** (2003)
Label: His House Records
Tracks: Soulsville; Soul Satisfied; Standing on the Rock; Lift Me Up; Comforter of My Soul; Nobody Knows You Like the Lord; Walk that Walk; You Won't Show; Fence Me In; Have Mercy; Glory Hallelujah; Souled Out 'n Sanctified; Other Side of the Cloud

All songs written by Danny Brooks (SOCAN)

Production Credits:
Produced by Richard Bell
Mixed by Doug Romanow at Fire Escape Studios, Toronto, ON

Personnel: The Rockin' Revelators are Danny Brooks: lead vocals/acoustic and electric guitar/harmonica; Amoy Levy: vocals; Ciceal Levy: vocals; Hiram Joseph: vocals; Bucky Berger: drums; Richard Bell: organ/piano/Wurlitzer/accordion; Mitch Lewis: acoustic and electric guitars/mandolin; Dennis Pinhorn: fretless and electric bass; Michael Fonfara: organ/piano/Wurlitzer

Special guests: Esther Kessler: vocals (Lift Me Up); Colin Linden: mandolin/ dobro

---

Title: **Saved! Northernblues Gospel Allstars** (2002)
Label: NorthernBlues
Tracks: Down by the Riverside; Still Standing Tall*; Place Called Hope; 24/7/365*; The Promise; Righteous Highway*; People Get Ready; Higher Ground; A Change Is Gonna Come; Saved!; Down by the Riverside (reprise); We Shall Overcome

*Written by Danny Brooks (SOCAN)

Production Credits:
Produced by Michael Fonfara and Frazier Mohawk at Pucks Farm, ON
Engineered by Walter Sobczac
Mixed by Keith Mariash
Mastered by Michael Jack at Phase One Recording

Personnel: Greg Cooper and Mark Mariash: drums; Tim Drummond: bass; Bob Yeomans and Danny Brooks: guitar; Michael Fonfara: piano/ Hammond B3; Vocals: The Northernblues Gospel Allstars: Danny Brooks; Amoy Levy; Ceceal Levy; Hiram Joseph; John Finley.

Title: **Righteous: Live at the Southside Shuffle** (2000)
Label: His House Records
Tracks: MP3/ Nothing Like the Name of the Lord*; MP3/Jesus Satisfies; MP3/Power In the Blood; He's All I Need*; I Saw John the Holy Number; I Know Jesus*; MP3/Hold Your Head Up*; MP3/Waiting for Your Ship*; Jesus Changed Me; Mother's Advice; MP3/Ain't That Good News*; Oh, Happy Day; Goin' Away and Leave You
* Written by Danny Brooks (SOCAN)

Production Credits:
Recorded live at The Southside Shuffle, Port Credit, Ontario, September 2000
Produced and mixed by Doug Romanow at Fire Escape Studios, Toronto

Personnel: The Rockin' Revelators are: Danny Brooks: vocals/guitar; Amoy Levy: vocals; Cecil Levy: vocals; Dennis Pinhorn: bass; Bucky Berger: drums; Terry Blersh: guitar; Vic D'arsie: organ; Pat Carey and Colleen

Allen: saxophones; Michael Fonfara: piano; Ken Whiteley: lap steel
Choir: Michelle Sim, Christine Bennett, Deana Malcolm, John Scarfo, Laura
Chadwick, Cathy Hartnett, Jim Leeks, Ian Sims.

Title: **It's a Southern Thing** (1998)
Label: His House Records
Tracks: Southern Thing; Show Up and Sing; Georgia Bound; Candito;
Brother Bill; More than This; Just a Little Faith; Prisoners of Hope**; The
Way it Goes; Wheels Keep Spinning; Never Get Over You*; Shutting Me
Down; Only Love Can Satisfy

All songs by Danny Brooks (SOCAN)
*Co-written with Steve Dudek
**Co-written with Debra Middlebrook

Production Credits:
Dave Gray: producer, tracks 6, 7, 13
Michael Fonfara: producer, tracks 5, 9
Danny Brooks and Peter Lee: producer, tracks 1, 2, 3, 4
Danny Brooks: producer, tracks 8, 10, 11, 12
Metal Works: producer tracks 8, 10, 11, 12
Mixed by Jim Dickinson at 315 Beale St., Memphis, TN

Personnel: Danny Brooks: lead vocals/guitar/harmonica; Dennis Pinhorn:
bass; Greg Anselic: drums; Al Cross: drums; Jim Cassons: drums; Memo
Acevedo: percussion; Vic D'arsie: piano; Peter Nunn: piano; Oliver
Schrorer: violin.

Backup Vocals: Johanna Vanderclay, Michelle Francis, Liz Tilden, Dutch
Robinson, Sharon Lee Williams

Title: **Rough Raw & Simple** (1993)
Label: Duke St/MCA

Title: **After the Storm** (1990)
Label: Duke St/MCA

CONTACT INFORMATION FOR DANNY BROOKS

Canada/Booking

HISHouse Records
www.dannybrooksmusic.com

Jane Harbury Publicity
1290 Dundas Street East
Toronto ON
M4M 1S6
Tel: 416-960-1568

USA

Rockin Camel Music
118 Chestnut Street
Gadsden, Alabama 35901
1-877-368-7428
info@rockincamel.com
www.rockincamel.com

Mark Pucci Media
5000 Oak Bluff Court
Atlanta, GA 30350
Tel: (770) 804-9555
Fax: (770) 804-0027
mpmedia@bellsouth.net
http://www.markpuccimedia.com